Advanced programming in Perl
for beginners.
With examples for geoscientists.

Dorian Oria San Martin

Order this book online at:

http://www.autoreseditores.com/

http://www.amazon.com/

ISBN-13: 978-1533018731

ISBN-10: 1533018731

Index

A friend of mine told me once that, in every thing he has done, he is the coauthor, because really the author is God.

I only hope to have been a good coauthor.

Preface

Despite the raising of Python as a scientific language, Perl continues being a great language to manipulate different types of formats, like LAS, SEGY, SEGD, different types of velocity model files, among others. Even though the last chapters of the book are oriented to geoscientists, everybody can learn the rudiments of Perl programming with this book. This book is targeted in those people who want to learn some advanced Perl skills, but do not want to buy basic, medium and advanced books. In this book you can learn advanced concepts, explained for beginners. All in one book.

Please, visit http://www.geoscience4all.com/, where you could find new Perl scripts with different purposes. Feel free to contribute with your own scripts.

I dream with having a place where we can contribute with the knowledge in geoscience, in particular in programming, with all the resources free.

If you want to participate in the project or contribute with your ideas, feel free to contact me, emailing me to: dorian@geoscience4all.com.

Take it easy, Perl is still a great language and it is still alive and useful. Anyway, I want not to limit the contribution only to Perl. I wrote another book, but in Spanish: Programación avanzada en VBA-Excel para principiantes (Advanced programming in VBA-Excel for beginners, available in Amazon) where I show examples for geoscientists as well. The point is that you can feel free to contribute with programs in any language.

I hope you to enjoy the book.

Chapter 1.

Introduction.

1.1 A brief history of Perl.

Perl is a script language created by Larry Wall, who released the first version in 1987 to the comp.sources.misc newsgroup. The language expanded rapidly over the next few years.

The reason for its creation was that Wall was unhappy by the functionality that sed, C, awk and the Bourne Shell offered him. He looked for a language that will combine all of their best features, while having as few disadvantages of its own.

The last version of Perl was released in 1994. This version was a complete re-write of the Perl interpreter, and introduced such things as hard references, modules, objects and lexical scoping. Several minor versions of Perl have appeared since then, and the most up-to-date stable version (as of October 2005) is 5.14.x.

1.2 Why Perl?

Perl is the abbreviation of **P**ractical **E**xtraction and **R**eport **L**anguage. Perl was originally named 'Pearl', after the Parable of the Pearl from the Gospel of Matthew. Larry Wall wanted to give the language a short name with positive connotations; he claims that he considered (and rejected) every word with three and four letters in the dictionary. He also considered naming it after his wife Gloria.

1.3 Overview.

Perl is a general-purpose programming language originally developed for text manipulation and now used for a wide range of tasks including system administration, web development, network programming, GUI development, and more.

The language is intended to be practical (easy to use, efficient and complete) rather than beautiful (tiny, elegant and minimal). Its major features include the support for multiple programming paradigms (procedural, object-oriented, and functional styles), reference counting memory management (without a cycle detecting garbage collector), built-in support for text processing, and a large collection of third-party modules.

1.4 Features.

The overall structure of Perl derives broadly from C. Perl is procedural in nature,

Advanced programming in Perl for Beginners.

with variables, expressions, assignment statements, brace-delimited code blocks, control structures, and subroutines.

Perl also takes features from shell programming. All variables are marked with leading sigils, which unambiguously identifies the data type (scalar, array, hash, etc.) of the variable in context. Importantly, sigils allow variables to be interpolated directly into strings. Perl has many built-in functions, which provide tools often used in shell programming (though many of these tools are implemented by programs external to the shell) like sorting, and calling on system facilities.

Other important features are:

- ✓ Perl takes the best features from other languages, such as C, awk, sed, sh, and BASIC, among others.
- ✓ Perl's database integration interface (DBI) supports third-party databases including Oracle, Sybase, Postgres, MySQL and others.
- ✓ Perl works with HTML, XML, and other mark-up languages.
- ✓ Perl supports Unicode.
- ✓ Perl is Y2K compliant.
- ✓ Perl supports both procedural and object-oriented programming.
- ✓ Perl interfaces with external C/C++ libraries through XS or SWIG.
- ✓ Perl is extensible. There are over 500 third party modules available from the Comprehensive Perl Archive Network (CPAN).
- ✓ The Perl interpreter can be embedded into other systems.

1.5 Resources.

It is possible to find several Perl binary distributions, ready to be used, in several operative systems, including Linux, Mac OS X and Windows. Some of them are available in:

- http://strawberryperl.com/ (for Windows)
- http://www.activestate.com/ (Windows, Linux, Mac OS X)
- http://dwimperl.com/ (Windows, Linux)
- http://www.citrusperl.com/ (Windows, Linux, Mac OS X)

However, many Linux distributions and the last Mac OS X versions come with Perl installed.

Windows does not come with Perl installed.

In ActiveState is possible to find binary modules, ready to be used.

The project CPAN (Comprehensive Perl Archive Network), at the time of writing, has 124,342 modules available. In chapter 6 it is explained how to install modules from CPAN.

I used to work with the Perl version available in http://www.activestate.com/. On this web site it is possible to find binary versions for Windows, Solaris, Mac, Linux. They have a lot of binary modules as well, ready to be used.

However, I installed the Perl version available for Windows from http://strawberryperl.com/ for testing the scripts, and I liked it!

I wrote this book using a MacBook Air computer. To run the scripts, I used the Perl version 5.16.0. The most recent version and the instructions to install it can be found at http://learn.perl.org/installing/

1.6 Installing Perl Tk.

Before, I mentioned the sites where it is possible to find Perl installer. Some of them are full versions, which means that they include compiled versions of the component Perl-Tk (i.e. the ActiveState distribution.) In the case of the distribution available in ActiveState, now Perl-Tk changed to Perl-Tkx. All the scripts shown and explained in chapter 7, are related to GUI (Graphical User Interfaces) and were written using Perl-Tk. However, all of them have a similar version in Perl-Tkx, available in the distribution of this book.

To reproduce the exercises shown here, I will explain how to install Perl-Tk in the most common OS: Linux, Windows and Mac OS X.

PCs with Linux and Mac OS X come with Perl installed, except Perl-Tk. In the case of Windows, I suggest to install the Perl interpreter available at http://strawberryperl.com/. Next, I will explain how to install Perl-Tk in these OSs.

In a terminal window (Command Prompt in Windows) write the following instructions (in Mac and Linux, you must do this as super user):

Advanced programming in Perl for Beginners.

perl -MCPAN -e shell

After this, you will see the cpan prompt (figure 1.1, enclosed in a rectangle)

```
● ○ ○                        ⌂ dorian — perl5.16 — 93×24
cpan[1]> install Bundle::CPAN
Fetching with LWP:
http://mirror.ucu.ac.ug/cpan/authors/id/A/AN/ANDK/Bundle-CPAN-1.861.tar.gz
Fetching with LWP:
http://mirror.ucu.ac.ug/cpan/authors/id/A/AN/ANDK/CHECKSUMS
Checksum for /var/root/.cpan/sources/authors/id/A/AN/ANDK/Bundle-CPAN-1.861.tar.gz ok
ExtUtils::MakeMaker is up to date (6.82).
Running install for module 'Test::Harness'
Running make for L/LE/LEONT/Test-Harness-3.30.tar.gz
Fetching with LWP:
http://mirror.ucu.ac.ug/cpan/authors/id/L/LE/LEONT/Test-Harness-3.30.tar.gz
Fetching with LWP:
http://mirror.ucu.ac.ug/cpan/authors/id/L/LE/LEONT/CHECKSUMS
Checksum for /var/root/.cpan/sources/authors/id/L/LE/LEONT/Test-Harness-3.30.tar.gz ok

  CPAN.pm: Building L/LE/LEONT/Test-Harness-3.30.tar.gz

Checking if your kit is complete...
Looks good
Writing Makefile for Test::Harness
Writing MYMETA.yml and MYMETA.json
cp lib/TAP/Parser/Result/Pragma.pm blib/lib/TAP/Parser/Result/Pragma.pm
cp lib/App/Prove/State/Result.pm blib/lib/App/Prove/State/Result.pm
cp lib/TAP/Parser/Iterator/Array.pm blib/lib/TAP/Parser/Iterator/Array.pm
```

Figure 1.1. Installing Perl-Tk.

In the cpan prompt, write the following instructions:

cpan> install Bundle::CPAN

cpan> reload cpan

cpan> install Tk

In case the installation fails, use the instruction:

cpan> force install Tk

1.7 IDE's for PERL.

Perl is an interpreted language. With this, you can make scripts. So, you can write them using a text editor, such as notepad, gedit or WordPad. However, it is possible to find several IDEs which make it easy to write Perl scripts. Some of them are free of charge and others are not. Some free options are below.

1.7.1   Open Perl IDE.

This is one of the best free Perl IDEs avaliable. It can be downloaded from: http://open-perl-ide.sourceforge.net/. In the link it is possible to find all the training material needed.

1.7.2   Perl Express.

Another interesting Perl IDE is Perl Express. This can be downloaded from: http://www.perl-express.com/. On its web site, it is possible to find all the necessary information to work with it.

1.7.3   Notepad++

This is the editor I prefer to use. It can be downloaded from http://notepad-plus-plus.org/.

1.7.4   gedit.

This editor comes with many Linux distributions. It is able to recognize the instructions of Perl scripts, so this is very useful to check syntax.

1.7.5   Komodo IDE.

I use this IDE in making the script in Mac OS X. It is available for free and available for Windows and Linux, as well. It can be downloaded from: http://www.activestate.com/komodo-ide. Figure 1.2 below shows how the IDE looks.

1.7.6   Padre.

This is an integrated development environment or, in other words, a text editor that is simple to use for new Perl programmers but also supports large multi-lingual and multi-technology projects. It can be downloaded from: http://padre.perlide.org/. Figure 1.3 shows how the IDE looks.

Advanced programming in Perl for Beginners.

Figure 1.2. Komodo IDE.

Figure 1.3. Padre IDE.

1.8 How to run a script.

It can be run directly from Perl IDEs or from the command line (in case of Windows) or from a shell (in case of Linux, Mac OSX or Unix). Figure 1.4 shows how to run a script from the command line (Windows).

1.9 Links of interest.

http://www.perl.org/
http://en.wikipedia.org/wiki/Perl
http://www.perl.com/
http://www.tkdocs.com
http://www.activestate.com/activeperl
http://www.cpan.org/

Figure 1.4. Running a Perl script from command prompt.

All the scripts explained in this book can be downloaded from: http://www.geoscience4all.com/index.php/descarga

In addition, in the web site http://www.geoscience4all.com you could find new perl scripts that could be interesting to you and useful for your job. Visit us regularly.

Chapter 2.

Variable Types & Operators.

2.1 Introduction.

Even though this book assumes that you have some knowledge about Perl, I will give you a brief explanation about the most important issues you have to know to do simple and great applications.

2.2 Variable Types.

2.2.1 Scalars.

A scalar represents a single value that can be a string, an integer or a floating-point number. Unlike other languages like C, in Perl it is not necessary to pre-declare the type of variable. It does not matter if we are talking about integer, double, real, boolean, etc., Perl will automatically convert between them as required.

Examples of scalars:

$a=25;

$text1='This is an example of a string";

$text2='This is another example of a string';

Something that is really important to remember is that the name of variables must start with the sign $.

2.2.1.1 Strings.

A string is a sequence of characters put together as one unit. Strings can be of any length and can contain any characters, numbers, punctuation, special characters (like '!', '#', and '%'), and even characters in natural languages besides English. In addition, a string can contain special ASCII formatting characters like newline (\n) and tab (\t). In Perl, strings must be quoted by a couple of single quotes (') or a couple of double quotes ("). For example, the string: hello everybody, should be quoted as 'hello everybody' or "hello everybody". Look at the following example:

Script 2.1

```
1   $a='hello everybody';
2   $b="hello everybody";
3   print "$a\n$b\n";
```

In this example, the output will be as shown in Figure 2.1.

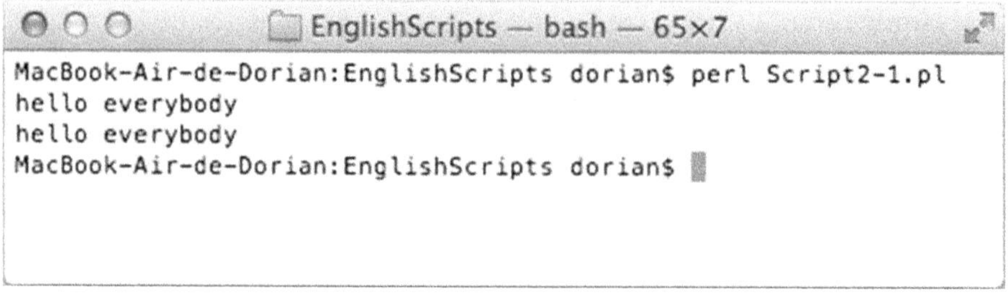

Advanced programming in Perl for Beginners.

Figure 2.1. Output of Script 2.1.

As you can see, the output in both cases is the same. But now, let's do some changes into every string, in order to see the differences between single and double quotes. Imagine we are interested in writing the expression: hello 'everybody':

Script 2.2

```
1  $a='hello \'everybody\'';
2  $b="hello 'everybody'";
3  print "$a\n$b\n";
```

In this case, we will get the results shown in Figure 2.2.

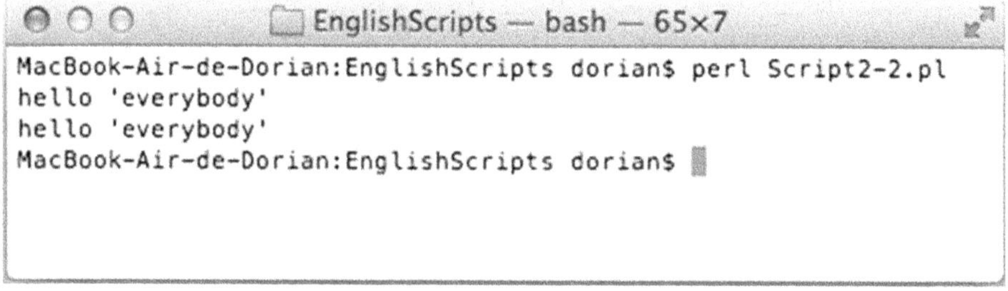

Figure 2.2. Output of the Script 2.2.

To be able to introduce single quotes into the first string, the character "\" must be included. But, in the second case, we did not need it.

Now, imagine we want to write the expression: hello "everybody". Look at the changes:

Script 2.3

```
1  $a='hello "everybody"';
2  $b="hello \"everybody\"";
```

```
3  print "$a\n$b\n";
```

And the output will be:

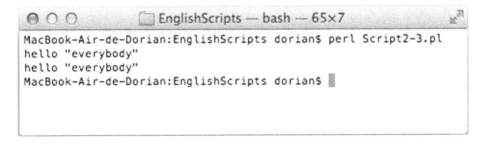

```
MacBook-Air-de-Dorian:EnglishScripts dorian$ perl Script2-3.pl
hello "everybody"
hello "everybody"
MacBook-Air-de-Dorian:EnglishScripts dorian$
```

Figure 2.3. Output of the Script 2.3.

Because in Perl there are several 'escape' characters such as: tabs, enters, spaces, etc., it is necessary to be careful when handling it.

For example, in interpolated double-quoted strings, various sequences preceded by a '\' character act differently. The following table shows the most common of these:

Table 2.1. Some common interpolated double-quoted strings.

String	Interpolates as:
"\\"	An actual, single backslash character
"\$"	A single $ character
"\@"	A single @ character
"\t"	Tab
"\n"	Newline
"\a"	Alarm (bell)
"\r"	Hard return
"\f"	Form feed
"\b"	Backspace
"\e"	Escape

Let's see the following Script:

Script 2.4

```
1  print "A backslash: \\\n";
2  print "Tab follows:\tover here\n";
3  print "Ring! \a\n";
```

Advanced programming in Perl for Beginners.

4 print "My email is dorian\\@geoscience4all.com\n";

Figure 2.4 shows the output of the script. Now, an interesting exercise would be to run the same script, but without one slash ("\") on line 1 (Figure 2.5)

Script 2.5

1 print "A backslash: \\\n";
2 print "Tab follows:\tover here\n";
3 print "Ring! \a\n";
4 print "My email is dorian\\@geoscience4all.com\n";

```
MacBook-Air-de-Dorian:EnglishScripts dorian$ perl Script2-4.pl
A backslash: \
Tab follows:     over here
Ring!
My email is dorian@geoscience4all.com
MacBook-Air-de-Dorian:EnglishScripts dorian$
```

Figure 2.4. Output of the Script 2.4.

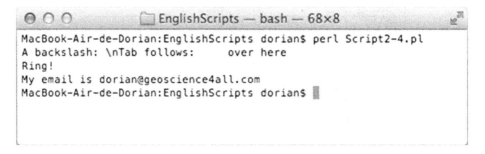

```
MacBook-Air-de-Dorian:EnglishScripts dorian$ perl Script2-4.pl
A backslash: \nTab follows:     over here
Ring!
My email is dorian@geoscience4all.com
MacBook-Air-de-Dorian:EnglishScripts dorian$
```

Figure 2.5. Output of the Script 2.5.

Can you see the differences?

Another interesting issue, that we can see when working with strings, is that any scalar variable, when included in a double-quoted string, interpolates.

Interpolation allows inserting the value of a scalar variable right into a double-quoted string. In addition, since Perl largely makes all data conversion necessary, we can often use variables that have integer and float values and interpolate them right into strings without a problem. In most cases, Perl will do the right thing.

Consider the following script:

Script 2.6

```
1   print "When were you born (year)?\n";
2   $year=<STDIN>;
3   ($sec,$min,$hour,$mday,$mon,$Cyear,$wday,$yday,$isdst) = localtime time;
4   $currentYear=1900+$Cyear;
5   $age=$currentYear-$year;
6   $a="Hi";
7   $friend="my dear reader";
8   print "$a $friend. You are approximately $age years old\n";
```

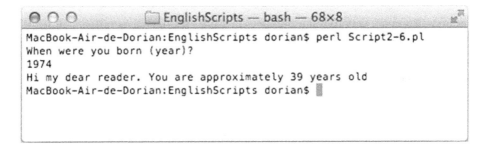

Figure 2.6. Output of Script 2.6.

I could make the calculus in the same line where the instruction '**print**' is. Let's see the following script:

Script 2.7

```
1   print "When were you born (year)?\n";
2   $year=<STDIN>;
3   ($sec,$min,$hour,$mday,$mon,$Cyear,$wday,$yday,$isdst) = localtime time;
4   $currentYear=1900+$Cyear;
5   $a="Hi";
6   $friend="my dear reader";
7   print "$a $friend. You are aproximately ".($currentYear-$year). " years
    old\n";
```

This script will produce the same output than the one shown in Figure 2.6. Look carefully at line 7. We made the calculus in the same line where the instruction **print**

Advanced programming in Perl for Beginners.

is. However, to get the age, we had to close the string previous to the calculus and the calculus had to be closed between parentheses. As a concatenation operator, Perl uses the symbol ".". Test yourself and see what would happen if you introduce the calculus into the same string, it means, changing the line 7 for something like:

print "$a $friend. You are approximately $currentYear-$year years old";

2.2.1.2 Numbers.

Perl has the ability to handle both floating point and integer numbers in reasonable ranges. There are three basic ways to express numbers in Perl. The simplest way is to write an integer value, without a decimal point, such as 35.

It is possible to write numbers with decimal point. It means numbers like 35.7.

The most complex way to write numbers is using exponential notation. These are numbers of the form $a*10^x$, where "a" is some decimal number, positive or negative, and "x" is some integer, positive or negative. In this way it is possible to express very large or very small numbers. For example $1.3x10^6$ could be written in Perl as 1.3E6, $3.56x10^{-5}$ could be 3.56E-5, etc.

Something interesting about Perl is that for best readability, very large numbers can be written such as the following:

235354729352 -> 235_35_47_29_352.

For example, look at the following script:

```
1  $a=235_35_47_29_352;
2  print "$a\n";
```

The symbol "_" makes more readable the number.

The output of this script can be seen in Figure 2.7.

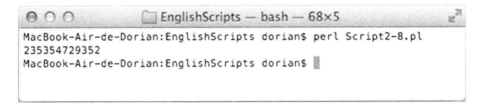

Figure 2.7. Output of Script 2.8.

2.3 Operators.

There is a variety of operators that work on scalar values and variables. These operators allow us to manipulate scalars in different ways. This section discusses the most common of these operators.

2.3.1 Numerical operators.

The basic numerical operators in Perl are like others that you may see in other high level languages. In fact, Perl's numeric operators were designed to mimic those in the C programming language. To better understand this, look at the following script:

Script 2.9

```
1   $a=3.5*3-1;
2   $b=5*$a/6;
3   $c=(5**2)**3;
4   $d=($c-sqrt(5))**2;
5   $e=$a%6;
6   print "a = $a\nb = $b\nc = $c\nd = $d\ne = $e\n";
```

The next table shows how the equations written in the script look:

Table 2.2. Math expressions and the equivalent expressions in Perl.

Math expression	Perl expression
$a = (3.5 * 3) - 1$	$a=3.5*3-1
$b = \dfrac{5 * a}{6}$	$b=5*$a/6
$c = (5^2)^3$	$c=(5**2)**3
$d = (c - \sqrt{5})^2$	$d=($c-sqrt(5))**2

Advanced programming in Perl for Beginners.

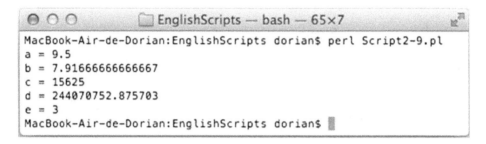

Figure 2.8 shows the output of Script 2.9.

```
MacBook-Air-de-Dorian:EnglishScripts dorian$ perl Script2-9.pl
a = 9.5
b = 7.91666666666667
c = 15625
d = 244070752.875703
e = 3
MacBook-Air-de-Dorian:EnglishScripts dorian$
```

Figure 2.8. Output of Script 2.9.

The operators work similar to the rules of algebra. When using the operators, there are two rules that you have to keep in mind: the rules of precedence and the rules of associability.

Precedence involves which operators will get evaluated first when the expression is ambiguous. For example, consider the first line of Script 2.9, which includes the expression 3.5*3-1. Since the multiplication operator "*" has precedence over the subtraction operator (-), the multiplication operation occurs first. Thus, the expression evaluates to 10.5 - 1 temporarily, and finally evaluates to 9.5. In other words, precedence dictates which operation occurs first.

In case of two operations having the same precedence, associability appears. Associability is either left or right. For example, in the expression in line 2 $b=5*$a/6, we have two operators with same level of precedence, * and /. Perl needs to make a choice about the order in which they get carried out. To do this, it uses the associability. Since multiplication and division are left associative, it works the expression from left to right, first evaluating to 47.5 / 6 (since $a was 9.5), and then finally evaluating to 7.9167.

You must be very careful with the level of precedence. For example, exponentiation is right associative. If you get the parenthesis out in line 3, the answer would be different. It means:

$c=(5**2)**3		$c=5**2**3
15625	→	390625

The output of the Script after changes will look like is shown in Figure 2.9.

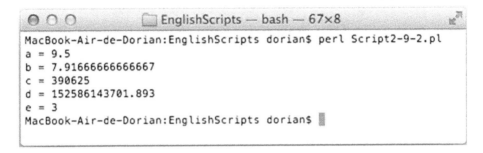

Figure 2.9. Output of Script 2.9 after elimination of parenthesis in line 3.

Perl first evaluates the expression 2**3 and after that 5**8. The next table shows the operators shown in Script 2.7.

Table 2.3. Operators and associability.

Operators	Associability	Description
**	Right	Exponentiation
*,/,%	Left	Multiplication, division, modulus
+,-	Left	Addition, subtraction

Another interesting issue that we can take advantage to mention is the way that the instruction **print** works with fractional numbers. As you can see in Figure 2.9, the value printed for $b has a lot of decimal values. The way to take control of the numbers of decimal to be printed is using the instruction **printf**. To show how this instruction works, we will make a little change in Script 2.9.

Script 2.10

```
1  $a=3.5*3-1;
2  $b=5*$a/6;
3  $c=(5**2)**3;
4  $d=($c-sqrt(5))**2;
5  $e=$a%6;
6  print "a = $a\nb = ";
7  printf "%.3f",$b;
```

Advanced programming in Perl for Beginners.

```
 8   print "\nc = $c\nd = ";
 9   printf "%.3f",$d;
10   print "\ne = $e";
```

Figure 2.10 shows the output after running the script.

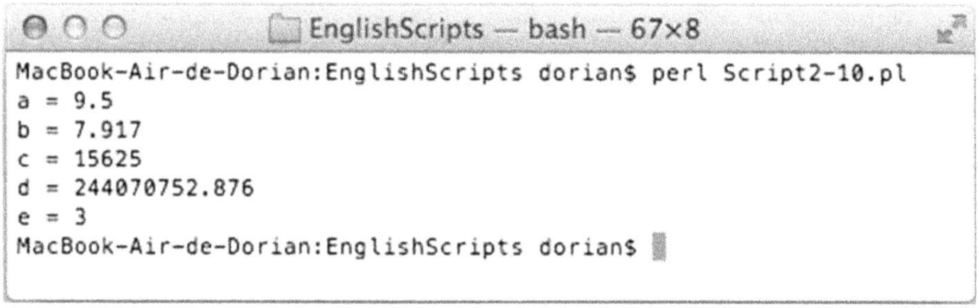

```
● ○ ○              EnglishScripts — bash — 67×8
MacBook-Air-de-Dorian:EnglishScripts dorian$ perl Script2-10.pl
a = 9.5
b = 7.917
c = 15625
d = 244070752.876
e = 3
MacBook-Air-de-Dorian:EnglishScripts dorian$ █
```

Figure 2.10. Output of Script 2.10.

2.3.2 Comparison operators.

Because Perl does automatic conversion between strings and numbers, it is not the same as numerically comparing two numbers, for example, than comparing the same numbers as ASCII string values.

2.3.2.1 Numeric comparison.

The operators shown in table 2.4 are used to compare two numbers. These operators are typically used in some type of conditional statement that executes a block of code or initiates a loop.

Table 2.4. Comparison operators.

Operator	Function
==	Equal to
!=	Not equal to
>	Greater tan
<	Less tan
>=	Greater than or equal to
<=	Less than or equal to

Consider the following script.

```
1   $a=1;
2   $b=2;
3   $c=$b-$a;
4   $equal=$a==$c;
5   $notEqual=$a!=$b;
6   $GreaterThan=$b>$a;
7   $LessThan=$c<$b;
8   $GreaterThanOrEqual=$c>=$a;
9   $LessThanOrEqual=$c<=$a;
10  print "Equal = $equal\nNot Equal = $notEqual\nGreater than =
    $GreaterThan\n".
11    "Less Than = $LessThan\nGreater Than Or Equal =
    $GreaterThanOrEqual\n".
12    "Less Than Or Equal = $LessThanOrEqual";
13  print "\n";
```

Perl allows storing the results of comparison in a variable. If the comparison is true, then the variable takes 1 as its value. Otherwise, the variable takes any value.

In Script 2.11, all the evaluated conditions are true. This can be seen in Figure 2.11.

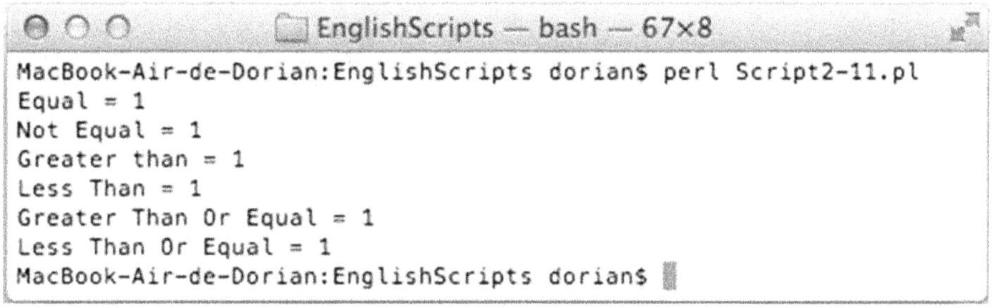

```
MacBook-Air-de-Dorian:EnglishScripts dorian$ perl Script2-11.pl
Equal = 1
Not Equal = 1
Greater than = 1
Less Than = 1
Greater Than Or Equal = 1
Less Than Or Equal = 1
MacBook-Air-de-Dorian:EnglishScripts dorian$
```

Figure 2.11. Output of Script 2.11.

2.3.2.2 String comparison.

This one is similar to the numerical comparison, but it works with strings. The next table shows these operators:

Table 2.5 Comparison operators.

Operator	Function
eq	Equal to
ne	Not equal to
gt	Greater tan
lt	Less tan
ge	Greater than or equal to
le	Less than or equal to

Strings are equal if they are exactly the same. So, "dorian" and "dorian" are equal, but "doria" and "dorian" are not.

You could try your own exercises with this. Later on, when we study the control structures, we will return to these topics (Chapter 3).

2.3.3 Assignment operators.

Assignment operators (Table 2.6) perform arithmetic operations and then assign the value to the existing variable. In Script 2.12, we set a variable ($a) equal to 8. Using assignment operators we will replace that value with a new number after performing some type of mathematical operation.

Table 2.6. Assignment operators.

Operator	Definition
+=	Addition
-=	Subtraction
*=	Multiplication
/=	Division
%=	Modulus
**=	Exponent

Script 2.12

```
1   $a=8;
2   print "The first value of a is $a\n";
3   $a+=7;
4   print "The new value of a is $a\n";
5   $a-=7;
6   print "The previous value of a was $a\n";
7   $a*=7;
```

```
8    print "The new value of a is $a\n";
9    $a/=7;
10   print "The previous value of a was $a\n";
11   $a%=7;
12   print "The new value of a is $a\n";
```

Figure 2.12 shows the output after running the script.

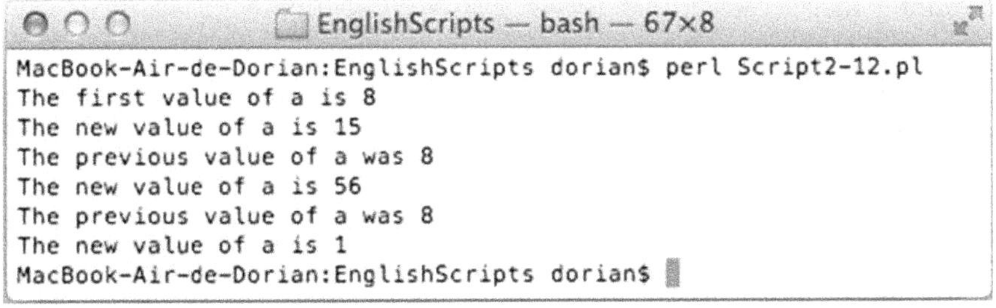

```
● ○ ○              EnglishScripts — bash — 67×8
MacBook-Air-de-Dorian:EnglishScripts dorian$ perl Script2-12.pl
The first value of a is 8
The new value of a is 15
The previous value of a was 8
The new value of a is 56
The previous value of a was 8
The new value of a is 1
MacBook-Air-de-Dorian:EnglishScripts dorian$ ▌
```

Figure 2.12. Output of Script 2.12.

2.3.4 Auto-Increment and decrement.

The auto-increment and auto-decrement operators in Perl work almost identically to the corresponding operators in C, C++, or Java. The following script shows how they work:

Script 2.13

```
1    $a=5;
2    $a++;        #This expression is the same than $a=$a+1;
3    print $a;
4    $b=7;
5    $b--;        #This expression is the same than $b=$b-1;
6    print "\n$b";
```

The next figure shows how the output of this script looks:

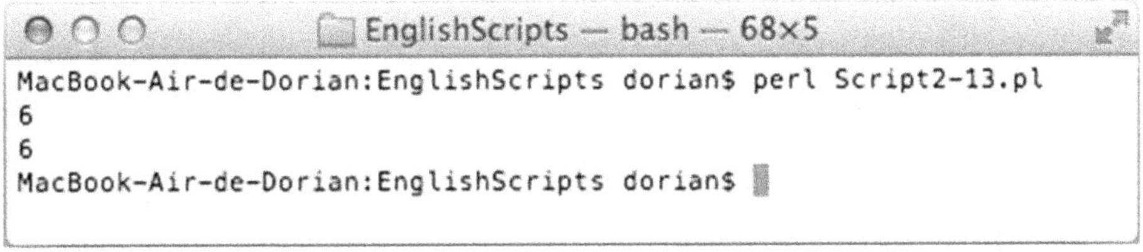

```
● ○ ○              EnglishScripts — bash — 68×5
MacBook-Air-de-Dorian:EnglishScripts dorian$ perl Script2-13.pl
6
6
MacBook-Air-de-Dorian:EnglishScripts dorian$ ▌
```

Figure 2.13. Output of Script 2.13.

Advanced programming in Perl for Beginners.

Let's make some changes to see one interesting feature about these operators.

```
1  $a=5;
2  $c=$a++ +4;
3  print "$a\t$c";
4  $b=7;
5  $b--;
6  print "\n$b";
```

Pay attention to line 2. What do you think will be the result after running this script? Look at Figure 2.14:

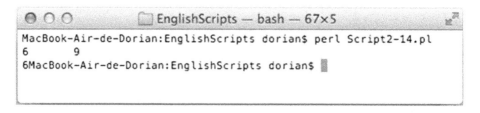

Figure 2.14. Output of Script 2.14.

Is it what you were expecting? Firstly, Perl calculates the value of $c, with the previous value of $a. However, after the line 2, $a will have a new value.

2.3.5 String operators.

The most common string operators you will see are the concatenation "." and duplication "x" operator. Look at the following script to see how they work:

```
1  $a="Hello ";
2  $b="my friend";
3  $c=$a x 3;
4  print $c.$b."\n";
```

Figure 2.15 shows the output after running the script.

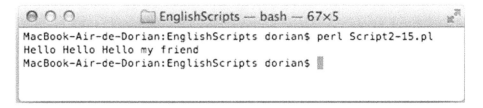

Figure 2.15. Output of Script 2.15.

In line 3, the operator "x" makes the string stored in $a be repeated 3 times. In line 4, we concatenate (using the symbol ".") the value of $c (Hello Hello Hello) with the string stored in $b.

Chapter 3.

Control Structures.

3.1 Introduction.

These structures are used to indicate to an algorithm what to do if a condition (or several) is (are) evaluated true or false. These conditions could be known, so it could be delimited in the times that a process must be repeated, or unknown, so it is necessary to wait until a condition is present to take action.

Let's see the different control structures available to understand them easier. You should use those with which you are comfortable.

3.2 If-Else.

In a flow, if a condition (or several) is (are) satisfied, then certain instructions are executed. For example, see the following script:

Script 3.1

```
1   $a=int(rand(10));
2   if ($a>3) {
3     print "$a is bigger than 3\n";
4   }
5   else {
6     print "$a is not bigger than 3\n";
7   }
```

After executing the script from the command prompt, the following picture can be seen:

```
MacBook-Air-de-Dorian:EnglishScripts dorian$ perl Script3-1.pl
1 is not bigger than 3
MacBook-Air-de-Dorian:EnglishScripts dorian$
```

Figure 3.1. Output of Script 3.1.

In the first line, an integer random value is assigned to $a. The number 10 indicates that the function **rand** will return a random fractional number greater than or equal to 0 and less than 10. The function **int** will return the integer part of that value. If $a is bigger than 3, then the following message is printed: $a is bigger than 3.

Advanced programming in Perl for Beginners.

Otherwise, if $a is not bigger than 3, print the message $a is not bigger than 3. The "\n" at the end of the message indicates to Perl to introduce a new line.

> **Important!**
> It is not necessary to have the "otherwise" condition (else) in this control structure. You can only use the sentence **if**. For example, Script 3.1 can be reduced to the first 4 lines, if there is no interest in doing something with a different condition.

3.3 If-Elsif-Else.

This control structure is used when there is more than one possible condition to be satisfied and possible instructions to follow. For example:

Script 3.2

```
1   $a=int(rand(10));
2   if ($a == 6) {
3       print "First condition satisfied";
4   }
5   elsif ($a == 4) {
6       print "Second condition satisfied";
7   }
8   elsif ($a == 5) {
9       print "Third condition satisfied";
10  }
11  else {
12   print "Any condition was satisfied";
13  }
14  print "\n$a\n";
```

In the script there are three conditions that are tested. The first one is activated when $a is equal to 6 (line 2). Something important to notice is that in the condition, two symbols "=" are used (see the table 2.4). This is necessary when two numbers are being compared.

The second option is evaluated in line 5 and the third one is evaluated in line 8.

The following picture shows the output after running the script three times.

> **Important!**
> The condition "**Else**" normally is used when we want to include all the universe of possibilities that are not restricted by the conditions (if or elsif).

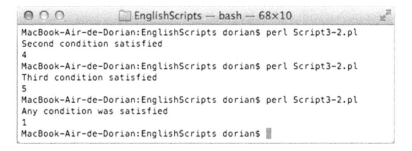

Figure 3.2. Output of Script 3.2.

3.4 Unless-Else.

This structure is the opposite of **If-Else**. It is the same as saying "If condition is not (!=)". In an **If-Else** structure, a true expression is validated, whereas in an **Unless-Else**, a false expression is validated. While the value is false, the expressions inside the block are executed. Let's try to get the same results we got with Script 3.1, but with this structure:

Script 3.3

```
1  $a=int(rand(10));
2  unless ($a>3) {
3    print "$a is not bigger than 3\n";
4  }
5  else {
6    print "$a is bigger than 3\n";
7  }
```

The following picture shows the output after running the previous script twice:

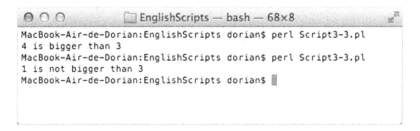

Figure 3.3. Output of Script 3.3.

Advanced programming in Perl for Beginners.

Can you see the differences? Another way to get the same results is with the following script, but with an If-Else structure.

Script 3.4

```
1  $a=int(rand(10));
2  if ($a<3) {
3    print "$a is not bigger than 3\n";
4  }
5  else {
6    print "$a is bigger than 3\n";
7  }
```

> **Important !**
> You should use the most comfortable structure for you.

3.5 While.

In Scripts 3.1, 3.3 or 3.4, if I want to get a number bigger than 3, then it is possible that I have to run the scripts several times until I get it. With "while" structure, we can get it with only one execution. For example:

Script 3.5

```
1  while ($a<3) {
2    $a=int(rand(10));
3    $i++;
4  }
5  print "The value $a was got in $i iterations\n";
```

Once the script is run, it will be shown as in Figure 3.4.

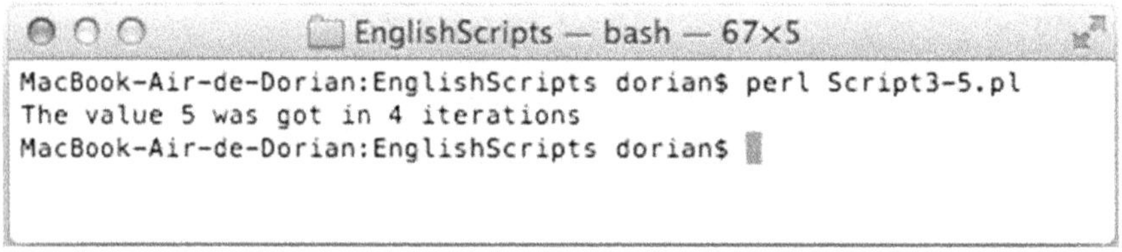

```
●○○              📁 EnglishScripts — bash — 67×5
MacBook-Air-de-Dorian:EnglishScripts dorian$ perl Script3-5.pl
The value 5 was got in 4 iterations
MacBook-Air-de-Dorian:EnglishScripts dorian$ ▌
```

Figure 3.4. Output of Script 3.5.

In this case, the condition $a>3 was satisfied after 2 iterations. Something interesting in this script is the concept of counter that has been introduced. In this case is the variable $i. Remember that the expression $i++ is equivalent to say $i=$i+1 (see 2.3.4). In this case, $i will be incremented by one, while condition $a>3 was not satisfied.

> **Important!**
> Notice that it was not necessary to initialize $i with the value 0. However, for a better readability, it is recommendable to do it.

3.6 Until.

This control structure is the opposite of "While". The block of instructions is executed while the conditional expression is false. Let's do some changes to Script 3.5 and it will look as follows:

Script 3.6

```
1  until ($a>3) {
2    $a=int(rand(10));
3    $i++;
4  }
5  print "The value $a was got in $i iterations\n";
```

The word **while** was changed by **until** and the character "<" was changed by ">".

The output of the script will look as shown in Figure 3.5.

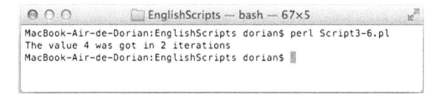

Figure 3.5. Output of Script 3.6.

3.7 Do-While-Until.

Unlike the control structures **while** and **until**, this control structure is executed at

Advanced programming in Perl for Beginners.

least once. The following example is a **Do-While** structure:

Script 3.7

```
1  do {
2    print "2x2 is: ";
3    $answer=<STDIN>;
4  } while ($answer!=4);
5  print "That's right\n";
```

After running, the output of the script it is shown in Figure 3.6.

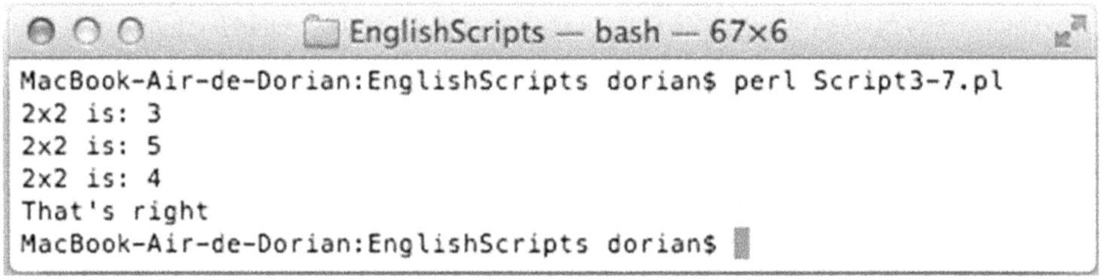

```
⊖ ○ ○                    EnglishScripts — bash — 67×6
MacBook-Air-de-Dorian:EnglishScripts dorian$ perl Script3-7.pl
2x2 is: 3
2x2 is: 5
2x2 is: 4
That's right
MacBook-Air-de-Dorian:EnglishScripts dorian$ ▊
```

Figure 3.6. Output of Script 3.7.

On purpose, we did not introduce the right answer in order to see the behaviour of the script. Because the first answer was not right, it asks again. According to the way it was programmed, it will be asking for the answer indefinitely until the right answer is introduced. You can make some changes in the script to avoid this, for example, using counters. A less elegant way to abort it, is using Ctrl+c. Figure 3.7 shows what happens after the program is aborted:

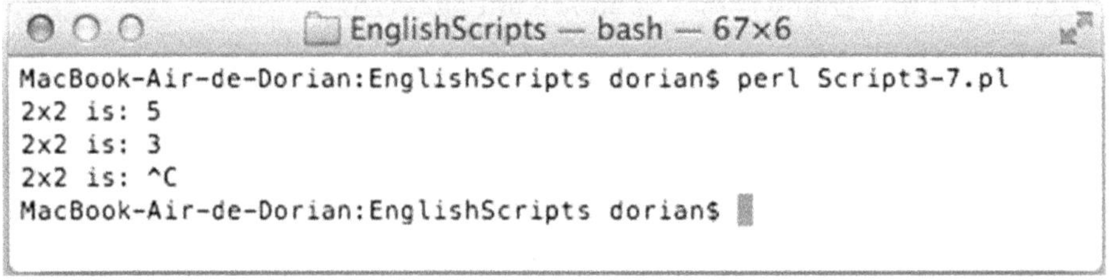

```
⊖ ○ ○                    EnglishScripts — bash — 67×6
MacBook-Air-de-Dorian:EnglishScripts dorian$ perl Script3-7.pl
2x2 is: 5
2x2 is: 3
2x2 is: ^C
MacBook-Air-de-Dorian:EnglishScripts dorian$ ▊
```

Figure 3.7. Stopping the execution of a script.

The following script does the same as Script 3.7, but using the control structure do-until.

```
1  do {
2    print "2x2 is: ";
3    $answer=<STDIN>;
4  } until ($answer==4);
5    print "That's right\n";
```

3.8 For-Next.

This control structure is normally used when the times that a process must be repeated are known.

For example, imagine that we want to calculate the area under the curve shown in figure 3.8, between $x_0 = 1$ until $x_n = 29$. The equation of the curve is

$$f(x) = x^2 + 3$$

To do this, we will use the following equation (rectangle rule)

$$area = \frac{(x_n - x_0)}{n} \sum_{k=1}^{n} f(x_k)$$

This rule is based on the fact that we are using many rectangles with base:

$$width\ of\ base = \frac{(x_n - x_0)}{n}$$

It means that the smaller the width of the base is, the better the approximation to the solution. The height of every rectangle is given by $f(x_k)$.

For a better understanding of the script, we named the variables such as they are in the equations. Line 1 contains the variable that stores the value of the bottom limit ($x0). The second line contains the variable for the upper limit ($Xn). The third line is the amount of rectangles we want to use to estimate the area under the curve (it means, the number of times we want the cycle for-next to be repeated). $sum in line 4 is a variable that allows calculating:

$$sum = \sum_{k=1}^{n} f(x_k)$$

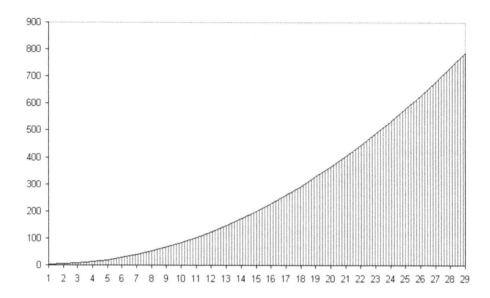

Figure 3.8. f(x)=x²+3.

Script 3.9

```
1   $x0=1;      # Bottom Limit
2   $Xn=29;     # Upper Limit
3   $n=300000;
4   $sum=0;
5   $x=$x0;
6   $widthOfBase=($Xn - $x0)/$n;
7   for ($t=0;$t<$n;$t++) {
8     $x=$widthOfBase + $x;
9     $sum=$sum+($x**2+3);
10  }
11  $area=$sum*$widthOfBase;
12  print "Area = ";
13  printf "%.5f",$area;
14  print "\n";
```

We have initialized $sum to zero. In line 5 it is initialized the variable $x, which value will be changing and feeding the equation of the curve. In line 6 the width of every rectangle is calculated. The control structure starts in line 7. In Perl, unlike Visual Basic for example, this structure does not use as final condition $t=$n. It is like in C or C++, it uses the condition $t<$n as final condition. This is because the first value of $t is zero. Later, when we see arrays, we will see that arrays are indexed from zero and not from 1 such as Visual Basic, for example.

According to the equation, the first value to be introduced in the equation must be x_1. This is because the variable $x was initialized with $x0 in line 5. Every value of x_k is generated in line 8 and the sum is calculated in line 9.

Finally, the area will be the product of $sum and $widthOfBase. Repeat the exercise with values of $n less than 300,000 (1,000 for example). If you remember infinitesimal calculus, the smaller the rectangle is, the more precise the calculus of the area will be ($n \rightarrow \infty$, $\Delta x \rightarrow 0$).

The following picture shows the output of the script:

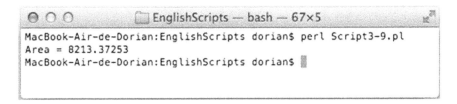

Figure 3.9. Output of Script 3.9.

Important!
Another interesting issue introduced in this script is the comments. These can be added preceded by the sign **#**. All that Perl sees after this symbol is taken as comment. A good script should be commented as much as possible. We usually have the knowledge fresh during programming, but after a long time, if we want to use it (or part of it), it could be not so easy, because it is necessary to remember what it does. Otherwise, if the script is commented, then the reuse of it will be easier.

3.9 Foreach.

This control structure is very interesting, because in this case it is not necessary to know the size of an array to access its content.

Script 3.10

```
1  @a=(1,2,3,4,5);
2  foreach $item (@a) {
```

Advanced programming in Perl for Beginners.

```
3   print "$item ";
4   }
5   print "\n";
```

The output of this script is shown in Figure 3.10.

```
● ○ ○              EnglishScripts — bash — 67×5
MacBook-Air-de-Dorian:EnglishScripts dorian$ perl Script3-10.pl
1 2 3 4 5
MacBook-Air-de-Dorian:EnglishScripts dorian$ ▌
```

Figure 3.10. Output of Script 3.10.

In this example, we have an array named @a. This array can be any array of information, and it could have hundreds, even thousands of elements. $item is a variable that works as temporal value of every element into the array.

With the same purpose, the script can be written as follows:

Script 3.11

```
1   @a=(1,2,3,4,5);
2   foreach (@a) {
3     print "$a[$i] ";
4     $i++;
5   }
```

> **Important!**
> A very interesting exercise would be trying to reproduce the same processes with the other control structures.

> **Important!**
> In this script we have introduced a new kind of variable: array. It is @a. We will work with this variable in detail in chapter 4.

3.10 Control instructions.

3.10.1 Next.

In some cases, during the execution of a block of instructions, if one expression is not desired to be evaluated, the instruction **next** is used to skip it and continue with the next iteration. Imagine we want to calculate a table of values for the function cotangent (a) (**cos(a)/sin(a)**), with the variable "a" varying between -5 and 5 (figure 3.11)

As you possibly know, **sin(a)** is zero when **a** is -2π, -π, zero, π, 2 π, so the value of the expression will not be possible to be calculated in those points. In this case, we want to skip the calculations when **a** is zero. Let's see how the script will look:

```
1  print "X Values\tY Values\n";
2  for ($i=-5;$i<6;$i++) {
3    next if ($i==0);
4    $value=cos($i)/sin($i);
5    $value=sprintf("%.3f",$value);
6    print "$i\t$value\n";
7  }
```

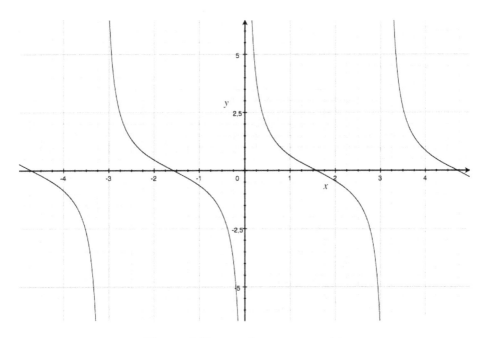

Figure 3.11. Function cotangent (a).

The output of Script 3.12 is shown in the following figure.

Advanced programming in Perl for Beginners.

```
● ○ ○                    EnglishScripts — bash — 67×13
MacBook-Air-de-Dorian:EnglishScripts dorian$ perl Script3-12.pl
X Values          Y Values
 -5        0.296
 -4       -0.864
 -3        7.015
 -2        0.458
 -1       -0.642
  1        0.642
  2       -0.458
  3       -7.015
  4        0.864
  5       -0.296
MacBook-Air-de-Dorian:EnglishScripts dorian$ ▊
```

Figure 3.12. Output of Script 3.12.

As it can be seen in the previous figure, the calculus was omitted when the value of "a" ($i into the script) is zero. This is done in line 3. With the instruction **next** we are telling the script: "Do not do the calculation when $i is zero. Evaluate the next $i value".

3.10.2 Last.

This instruction is similar to the instruction **next**, but the processes are not skipped, but are finished.

Let's change the instruction **next** into the previous script and let's see the differences:

Script 3.13

```
1   print "X Values\tY Values\n";
2   for ($i=-5;$i<6;$i++) {
3     last if ($i==0);
4     $value=cos($i)/sin($i);
5     $value=sprintf("%.3f",$value);
6     print "$i\t$value\n";
7   }
```

The output of this script is shown in Figure 3.13. Unlike the previous one made with **next**, this ends when the variable $i takes the value of zero.

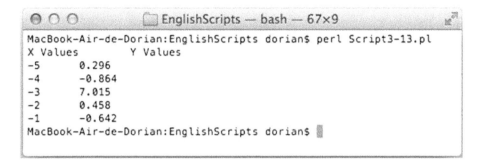

```
MacBook-Air-de-Dorian:EnglishScripts dorian$ perl Script3-13.pl
X Values          Y Values
-5        0.296
-4       -0.864
-3        7.015
-2        0.458
-1       -0.642
MacBook-Air-de-Dorian:EnglishScripts dorian$
```

Figure 3.13. Output of Script 3.13.

3.11 Basic math functions.

The following table is a summary of some basic math functions:

Table 3.1. Some basic math functions and expressions.

Math expression	Perl expression
$a = 5^2$	$a=5**2
$b = \sqrt{a}$	$b=sqrt($a)
$b = \sqrt[n]{a}$	$b=$a**(1/$n)
$c = \sin(a) + \cos(b)$	$c=sin($a)+cos($b)
$b = \ln(a)$	$b=log($a);
$b = \tan(a)$	$b=tan($a) or $b=sin($a)/cos($a)
$b = e^a$	$b=exp($a)
$b = \|a\|$	$b=abs($a)
$b = int(a)$	$b=int($a)

The previous table is only a summary of the main math functions available in Perl. Perl has a lot of functions that can be consulted in the available help that comes with it.

Chapter 4.

Arrays and hashes.

4.1 Arrays.

A Perl array is always a list of scalars. An array can contain strings, numbers and both of them simultaneously. Following there is an example of an array that shows how to access every element on it:

Script 4.1

```
1  @array=(1,2,4,8.25,3,sin(3));
2  foreach $element (@array) {
3    print "$element\n";
4  }
```

In this example, the array @array contains numbers.

Important!
Notice the use of symbol @ to name arrays.

Important!
Look at that there is something interesting in the way to express numbers: as a function (*sinus* in this case)

Important!
An interesting issue about arrays in Perl is that the index numbering starts at zero. It means that the first element of @array is $array[0]

If you try to assign an array to a scalar value, you will get the size of the array. So, if you want to get the last value of an array, this will be $array[length of array-1]. Taking as example the previous array:

Script 4.2

```
1  @array=(1,2,4,8.25,3,sin(3));
2  $a=@array;          # $a is the length of array @array
3  print "The array contains $a elements\n";
4  print "The first element of the array is $array[0]\n";
5  print "The last element of the array is $array[$a-1]\n";
```

Figure 4.1 shows the output of Script 4.2.

Because there is a way to know the length of an array, every element in it can be accessed with a for/next control structure.

Advanced programming in Perl for Beginners.

```
1  @array=(1,2,4,8.25,3,sin(3));
2  $a=@array;
3  for ($i=0;$i<$a;$i++) {
4    print "The element number ".($i+1)." of the array is $array[$i]\n";
5  }
```

```
● ○ ○              EnglishScripts — bash — 67×7
MacBook-Air-de-Dorian:EnglishScripts dorian$ perl Script4-2.pl
The array contains 6 elements
The first element of the array is 1
The last element of the array is 0.141120008059867
MacBook-Air-de-Dorian:EnglishScripts dorian$
```

Figure 4.1. Output of Script 4.2.

Figure 4.2 shows the output of Script 4.3.

```
● ○ ○              EnglishScripts — bash — 67×8
MacBook-Air-de-Dorian:EnglishScripts dorian$ perl Script4-3.pl
The element number 1 of the array is 1
The element number 2 of the array is 2
The element number 3 of the array is 4
The element number 4 of the array is 8.25
The element number 5 of the array is 3
The element number 6 of the array is 0.141120008059867
MacBook-Air-de-Dorian:EnglishScripts dorian$
```

Figure 4.2. Output of the Script 4.3.

Script 4.4 shows an array that contains strings and numbers simultaneously.

```
1  @array=("hello ","every ","body","\nThis is our ",4,"th example of
   arrays\n");
2  foreach $word (@array) {
3    print "$word";
4  }
```

Figure 4.3 shows the output of this script.

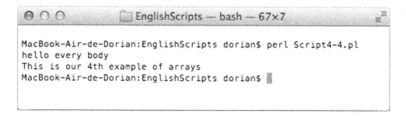

Figure 4.3. Output of Script 4.4.

You do not need to use a control structure to print elements of an array. See the following script:

Script 4.5

```
1  @array=("hello"," every ","body","\nThis is our ",4,"th example of
   arrays\n");
2  print @array;
```

As you will see, the output is the same as the one shown in Figure 4.3.

A shortcut to eliminate the quotes in a list area is **qw**. The above example would have the array line changed to:

Script 4.6

```
1  @array=qw(hello every body. This is our 4th example of arrays);
2  foreach $word (@array) {
3   print "$word ";
4  }
5  print "\n";
```

This method only works when you are dealing with one-word selections though. **qw** symbolizes a quoted comma delimitated list.

If you want to assign the first value of an array into a scalar, the instruction would be:

($firstElement)=@array;

Since a scalar variable can only hold one piece of data, it will take the first element of the array automatically. This does not change the array values at all.

Advanced programming in Perl for Beginners.

> **Important!**
> If you do not use parenthesis to enclose the variable, you will get the size of the array.

To assign the first two elements of an array into scalar values:

($firstElement,$secondElement)=@array;

To copy an array to a new (second) array:

@array2=@array;

To add a new value to the beginning of an array, the UNSHIFT command is used:

unshift(@array,*newelement*)

You can get the same effect without **unshift**:

@array=(*newelement*,@array);

To add a new value to the end of an array:

@array=(@array,*newelement*);

To remove the first value of an array the SHIFT command is used:

shift(@array);

You can store the removed value into a scalar at the same time too:

$result=**shift**(@array);

To remove the last element of an array:

pop(@array);

To remove the last element of an array and store it in a scalar:

$result=**pop**(@array);

To replace a specific element in an array:

$array[number]=$newelement;

Let's see an example to resume all of this:

```
1   @array=qw/2 3 4 13 6 7 8/;
2   $length=@array;
3   ($firstElement,$secondElement)=@array;
4   print "Elements in \@array are: @array\nThe length has $length
    elements.\n";
5   print "The first element of the array is: $firstElement\n";
6   print "The second element of the array is: $secondElement\n";
7   @array2=@array;
8   print "The array \@array2 is a copy of the array \@array\n";
9   unshift(@array,9);
10  print "These are the components of \@array after insert the number 9:
    @array at the beginning of the array\n";
11  @array=(@array,1);
12  print "These are the components of \@array after insert the number 1:
    @array at the end of the array\n";
13  $array[4]=5;
14  print "These are the components of \@array after change number 13 for
    the number 5: @array\n";
15  print "The elements of \@array2 are: @array2\n";
16  $FirstElement=shift(@array2);
17  $LastElement=pop(@array2);
18  print "The elements of \@array2 after extract $FirstElement and
    $LastElement are: @array2"."\n";
```

The output of this script can be seen in Figure 4.4.

```
⊙ ○ ○                    EnglishScripts — bash — 112×14
MacBook-Air-de-Dorian:EnglishScripts dorian$ perl Script4-7.pl
Elements in @array are: 2 3 4 13 6 7 8
The length has 7 elements.
The first element of the array is: 2
The second element of the array is: 3
The array @array2 is a copy of the array @array
These are the components of @array after insert the number 9: 9 2 3 4 13 6 7 8 at the beginning of the array
These are the components of @array after insert the number 1: 9 2 3 4 13 6 7 8 1 at the end of the array
These are the components of @array after change number 13 for the number 5: 9 2 3 4 5 6 7 8 1
The elements of @array2 are: 2 3 4 13 6 7 8
The elements of @array2 after extract 2 and 8 are: 3 4 13 6 7
MacBook-Air-de-Dorian:EnglishScripts dorian$
```

Figure 4.4. Output of Script 4.7.

To sort an array, use the instruction **sort**. There are different ways to use it. Let's see some of them.

Advanced programming in Perl for Beginners.

To sort an array in ASCII (alphabetical) order:

sort(@array);

Example:

1	@array=("dorian","anama","paula","victor","surya");
2	@arraySorted=**sort**(@array);
3	print "The original array is: @array\n";
4	print "The sorted array is: @arraySorted"."\n";

The output of the script can be seen in Figure 4.5.

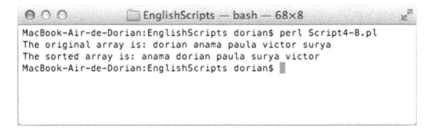

Figure 4.5. Output of Script 4.8.

To sort an array in reverse ASCII (alphabetical) order:

sort {$b cmp $a} (@array);

Example:

1	@array=("dorian","anama","paula","victor","surya");
2	@arraySorted=**sort**{$b cmp $a }(@array);
3	print "The original array is: @array\n";
4	print "The sorted array is: @arraySorted"."\n";

Figure 4.6 shows the output after running Script 4.9.

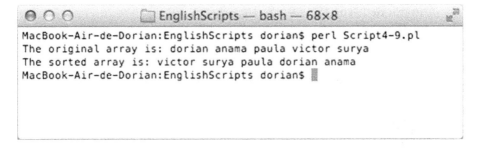

Figure 4.6. Output of Script 4.9.

To sort an array in numeric ascending order:

sort {$a <=> $b} (@array);

Example:

Script 4.10

```
1   @array=(4,5.6,1,-0.6,12,5);
2   @arraySorted=sort{$a <=> $b }(@array);
3   print "The original array is: @array\n";
4   print "The sorted array is: @arraySorted"."\n";
```

Figure 4.7 shows the output after running the previous script.

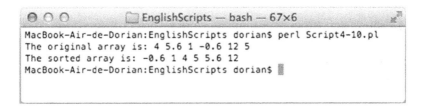

Figure 4.7 Output of Script 4.10

To sort an array in numeric descending order:

sort {$b <=> $a} (@array);

Example:

Script 4.11

```
1   @array=(4,5.6,1,-0.6,12,5);
```

Advanced programming in Perl for Beginners.

```
2  @arraySorted=sort{$b <=> $a }(@array);
3  print "The original array is: @array\n";
4  print "The sorted array is: @arraySorted"."\n";
```

Figure 4.8 shows the output after running Script 4.11.

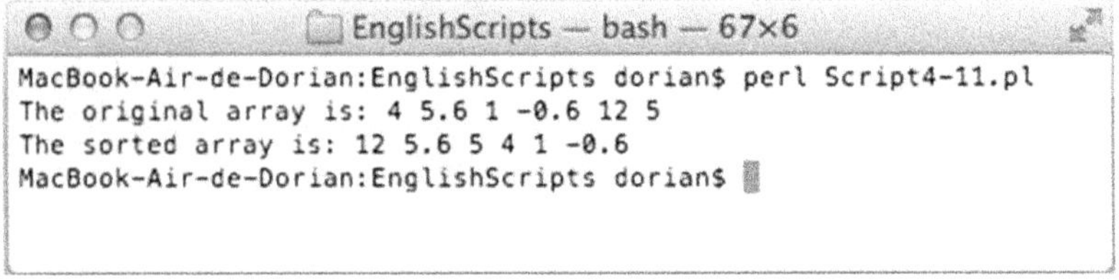

```
● ○ ○              EnglishScripts — bash — 67×6
MacBook-Air-de-Dorian:EnglishScripts dorian$ perl Script4-11.pl
The original array is: 4 5.6 1 -0.6 12 5
The sorted array is: 12 5.6 5 4 1 -0.6
MacBook-Air-de-Dorian:EnglishScripts dorian$ 
```

Figure 4.8 Output of Script 4.11

To reverse the value elements in an array:

reverse(@array);

Example:

Script 4.12

```
1  @array=(1,2,3,4,5,6,7,8,9);
2  @arrayReverse=reverse(@array);
3  print "The original array is: @array\n";
4  print "The sorted array is: @arrayReverse"."\n";
```

Figure 4.9 shows the output after running Script 4.12.

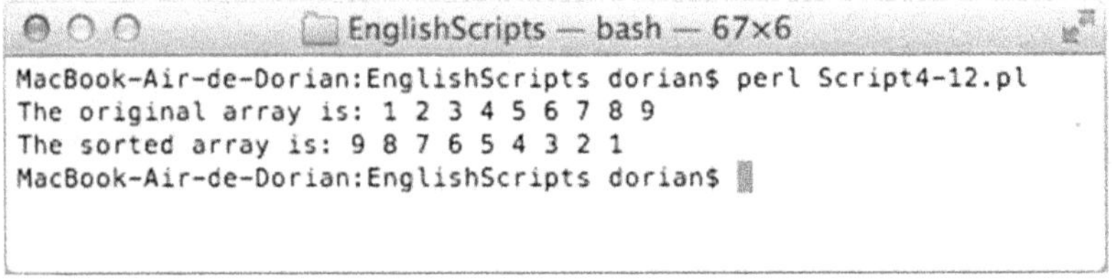

```
● ○ ○              EnglishScripts — bash — 67×6
MacBook-Air-de-Dorian:EnglishScripts dorian$ perl Script4-12.pl
The original array is: 1 2 3 4 5 6 7 8 9
The sorted array is: 9 8 7 6 5 4 3 2 1
MacBook-Air-de-Dorian:EnglishScripts dorian$ 
```

Figure 4.9. Output of Script 4.12.

4.2 Hashes.

A hash represents a set of key/value pairs. Every couple of values in a hash represents a key and its correspondent value. For example:

%hash=("dorian",39,"anama",29,"victor",9,"paula",6, "surya",1);

This hash represents the members of my family and their corresponding ages. If I want to access to the age of one of my children, let's say Victor, I must write:

$hash{"victor"}, where "victor" is the key.

Let's see the following example:

Script 4.13

```
1  %hash=("dorian",39,"anama",29,"victor",10,"valentina",7);
2  @keys=keys(%hash);
3  foreach $element (@keys) {
4    print "$element is $hash{$element} years old\n"
5  }
```

The output of Script 4.13 is shown in Figure 4.10.

```
MacBook-Air-de-Dorian:EnglishScripts dorian$ perl Script4-13.pl
valentina is 7 years old
dorian is 39 years old
victor is 10 years old
anama is 29 years old
MacBook-Air-de-Dorian:EnglishScripts dorian$
```

Figure 4.10. Output of Script 4.13.

One of the most important differences between hashes and arrays is that while in an array the "key" is the position of an element into the array, for accessing to an element into a hash it is more important to know its key.

As you can see in the previous script, it is possible to make an array of the keys with the instruction **keys** (line 2). The same can be done to get the values, with the instruction **values**. Let's see the following example:

Script 4.14

```
1  %hash=("dorian",39,"anama",29,"victor",10,"valentina",7);
2  $i=0;
3  @keys=keys(%hash);
4  @values=values(%hash);
5  foreach $element (@keys) {
6    print "$element is $values[$i] years old\n";
```

Advanced programming in Perl for Beginners.

```
7   $i++;
8  }
```

The output of the script is the same as the one shown in Figure 4.10.

If you want to change the value of an element in the hash array, you can use the following instruction:

$hash{dorian}=25;

If you want to add a new element to the hash array, you can use an expression similar to the previous one, but with a different key:

$hash{surya}=1;

The following example shows the behaviour of the script:

Script 4.15

```
1   %hash=("dorian",39,"anama",29,"victor",10,"valentina",7);
2   $hash{surya}=1;
3   $i=0;
4   @keys=keys(%hash);
5   @values=values(%hash);
6   foreach $element (@keys) {
7    print "$element is $values[$i] years old\n";
8    $i++;
9   }
10  print "\n";
11  $hash{dorian}=25;
12  print "Now, Dorian will be $hash{dorian} years old\n";
```

Figure 4.11 shows the output of Script 4.15.

Otherwise, if you want to delete an element of the hash array, the following instruction can be used:

delete $hash{dorian};

If you want to eliminate the entire hash, the following instruction can be used:

undef %hash;

If you want to empty the hash, without eliminating it, you can use the following instruction:

%hash=();

```
MacBook-Air-de-Dorian:EnglishScripts dorian$ perl Script4-15.pl
valentina is 7 years old
dorian is 39 years old
victor is 10 years old
surya is 1 years old
anama is 29 years old

Now, Dorian will be 25 years old
MacBook-Air-de-Dorian:EnglishScripts dorian$
```

Figure 4.11. Output of Script 4.15.

Chapter 5.

Handling text files.

5.1 Text files.

I think the best way to understand this is using an example. Firstly, let's create a text file using any text editor. Add the following lines:

This is the first line
This is the second line
This is the third line
This is the last line

After that, the file should look as shown in Figure 5.1:

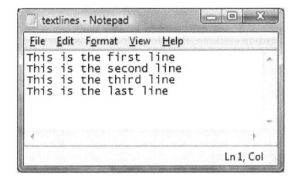

Figure 5.1. Text file.

5.2 Read only access.

Once the text file is done, use the following script to access it.

Script 5.1

```
1  open (IN,'textlines.txt');
2  $line=<IN>;
3  while ($line) {
4    print "$line";
5    $line=<IN>;
6  }
7  print "\n";
8  close IN;
```

In the first line the file **textlines.txt** is opened. As you can notice, the complete path to the file is not indicated. This is because it is located in the same directory as

Advanced programming in Perl for Beginners.

the script is. The word IN is a file handler. You can use any name, but capital letters are usually used.

Because the access of the text file is line by line, the second line indicates that every line read into textlines.txt is assigned to the variable $line.

The third line means something like this: while $line is other than empty, read the file.

All the instructions between "{" and "}" are considered part of the while control structure. So, while $line is not empty, print the value of $line and assign to $line the next value into the file ($line=<IN>).

The line 5 guarantees that Perl can read the entire file.

Finally, with the instruction **close**, the file is closed. We have had access to this file only for reading.

Figure 5.2 shows the output of the script.

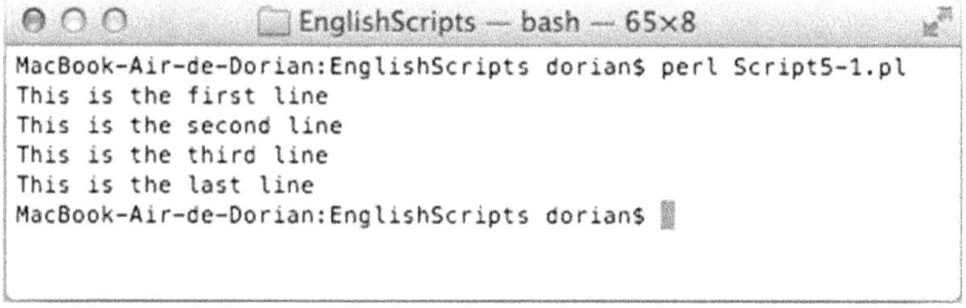

Figure 5.2. Output of Script 5.1.

The same script, but with fewer lines is:

Script 5.2

```
1   open (IN,'textlines.txt');
2   while ($line=<IN>) {
3     print "$line";
4   }
5   close IN;
```

The output will be as shown in Figure 5.2.

Because we use "enter" (represented by the invisible character "\n") after every line to make the file textlines.txt, it was not necessary to add the character "\n" in the third line of the script. However, let's see the previous one with some changes:

Script 5.3

```
1  open (IN,'textlines.txt');
2  while ($line=<IN>) {
3    chomp $line;
4    print "$line";
5  }
6  close IN;
```

The instruction **chomp** directs Perl interpreter to eliminate the character "\n" if it is found. After running this script, you will see:

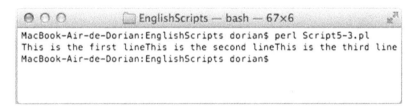

Figure 5.3. Output of Script 5.3.

Let's see a different example with almost the same result:

Script 5.4

```
1  open (IN,'textlines.txt');
2  while ($line=<IN>) {
3    chop $line;
4    print "$line";
5  }
6  close IN;
```

The instruction **chop** removes the last character of every line, independently of what the character is. In this example, because the last character of every line is an "enter", the result is almost the same than the one that was shown in Figure 5.3. See Figure 5.4.

When I created my text file, I intentionally did not use 'enter' at the end of the last line. So, look carefully at the end of the line printed in the previous figure and you will notice that the word line does not have the last letter. This is because the last character in this line was not the character "enter" but the letter "e".

Advanced programming in Perl for Beginners.

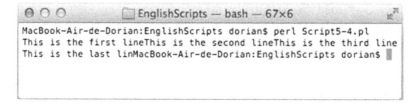

Figure 5.4. Output of Script 5.4.

Important!

I use to use the instruction **chomp** to be sure I eliminated this character at the end of every line I am reading. The advantage is that chomp does not work if the character "enter" (\n) is not present. So, it is innocuous. It does not happen the same with the instruction **chop**. This instruction always will eliminate one character at the end of the line.

Now, let's see how after removing 'enter' I can use it again. Let's see the following script:

Script 5.5

```
1   open (IN,'textlines.txt');
2   while ($line=<IN>) {
3     chomp $line;
4     print "$line\n";
5   }
6   close IN;
```

Simply adding \n to the line where the instruction **print** is written, I have added the character "enter" again. The output of this script is the same as the one shown in Figure 5.2.

It is common that a lot of data used by geoscientists comes in columns. For example, imagine that the information shown in Figure 5.5 represents depth and any measured variable.

To generate the values for the column "value", I have used the function RAND()*10 in OpenOffice Calc. I saved this data as text CSV, using tabs as separators. After every line, Calc adds the character "enter" (\n), so if you open the file and go to the end of the file, you will see an empty line. One of the applications of chomp is to avoid reading this empty line. Script 5.6 opens the file **data.csv** in read-only mode.

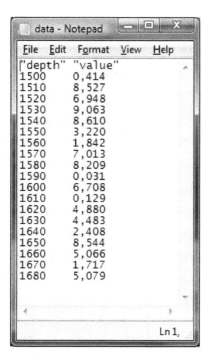

Figure 5.5. Example of dataset.

```
1    open (INPUT,'data.csv');        #open the file
2    $i=0;                           #initialize the counter $i to zero
3    while ($line=<INPUT>) {    #start the control structure to read the file
4     chomp $line;        #eliminate the "\n" character from every line
5     if ($i>0) {     #because the first line does not contain data, but the
6     #names of the columns, this condition is to skip them.
7       @arrayLine=split('\t',$line); #Every line into the text file is separated by
8     # one tab (\t)
9       $depth[$i-1]=$arrayLine[0];  #When the condition is satisfied, $i is
     equal to 1. Because
10    #Perl indexes its array from zero, we use the expression
11    #$i-1. Because we have two columns of data, the first
12    #element of @arrayLine will be always depth. The second
13     #one will be the measured value. The array @arrayLine
14    #will always be overwritten. depth and value are arrays of
15    #one dimension.
16     $value[$i-1]=$arrayLine[1];
17    }
18    $i++;                        #increment the value of the counter
```

```
19 }
20 $i--;                    #$i=$-1. At the end of the while, the array will have
   a
21                          #minor length, because the process started when
   $i=1
22 close INPUT;             #close the file
23 print "Depth Value\n";   #print a header
24 for ($j=0;$j<$i;$j++) {  #starts a for/next structure to access every
   element of
25                          #arrays depth and value.
26  print "$depth[$j] $value[$j]\n"; #print the values of depth and value
27 }
```

As you noticed, in this case we used comments into the script to explain how every line works. As it gets bigger, the use of comments is more necessary.

Something interesting in this script is the use of the instruction **split**. This instruction 'splits' a string into as many parts as they have separated by a character or group of them. The instruction has two parameters: the first one (before the first comma) is the character that separates values into the string and the second one is the string that we want to split. For example, in the string "hello every body", every word is separated by the space character, so, a way to split is using the instruction:

@array=split(" ", "hello every body")

This instruction generates an array, where every element is, in our example, a word of the string. So, the first element of the array $array[0] is "hello". The second one ($array[1]) is "every" and the last one ($array[2]) is "body". Now, let's go back to our script to read the information from the text file **data.csv**.

Figure 5.6 shows the output of Script 5.6.

5.3 Access to write.

There are two main ways to access files in write mode: overwriting or adding information to them. To do the first, it is necessary to add the character ">" at the beginning of the file we want to open. For example:

open (OUTPUT,'>data.csv);

To add information to an existing file, the characters ">>" must be added at the beginning of the name of the file. For example:

open (OUTPUT,'>>data.csv');

With this option, the new information will be added at the end of the file.

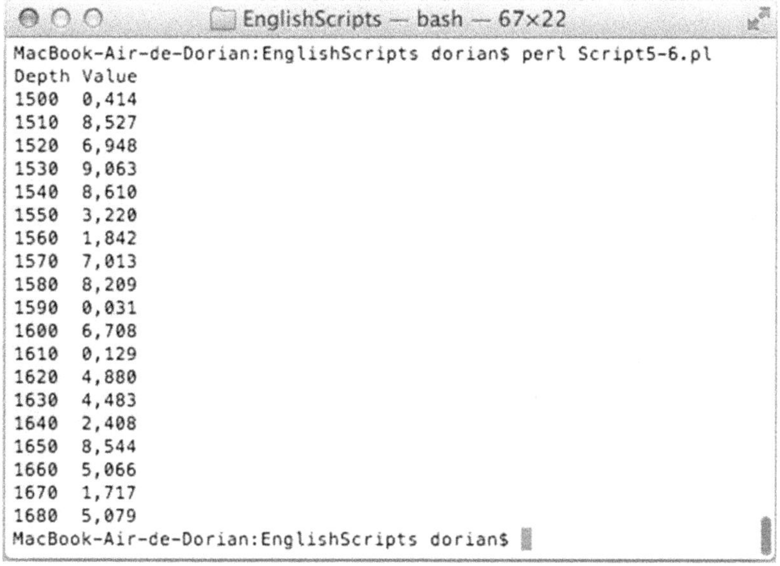

```
  ● ○ ○                    EnglishScripts — bash — 67×22
MacBook-Air-de-Dorian:EnglishScripts dorian$ perl Script5-6.pl
Depth Value
1500  0,414
1510  8,527
1520  6,948
1530  9,063
1540  8,610
1550  3,220
1560  1,842
1570  7,013
1580  8,209
1590  0,031
1600  6,708
1610  0,129
1620  4,880
1630  4,483
1640  2,408
1650  8,544
1660  5,066
1670  1,717
1680  5,079
MacBook-Air-de-Dorian:EnglishScripts dorian$
```

Figure 5.6 Output of Script 5.6.

Let's make some changes to Script 5.6, in order to show how the write access mode works.

Script 5.7

```
1    open (INPUT,'data.csv');
2    $i=0;
3    while ($line=<INPUT>) {
4     chomp $line;
5     if ($i>0) {
6      @arrayLine=split('\t',$line);
7      $depth[$i-1]=$arrayLine[0];
8      $value[$i-1]=$arrayLine[1];
9     }
10    $i++;
11   }
12   $i--;
13   close INPUT;
14   open (OUTPUT,'>SelectedData.txt');
15   print OUTPUT "Depth\tValue\n";
```

```
16   for ($j=0;$j<$i;$j++) {
17   if ($depth[$j]<=1600) {
18    print OUTPUT "$depth[$j]\t$value[$j]\n";
19   }
20   }
21   close OUTPUT;
```

This will not generate an output to command prompt. The result, after running it, is a new file called **SelectedData.txt**. According to the script, we are interested in extracting all the couples of values Depth-Value, where the value of depth is less than or equal to 1600 (line 17).

In the first line the file **data.txt** is opened in read-only mode. In line 2, the variable $i is initialized. This variable will be used to count the number of lines of the input file. In line 3 the control structure to read the input file starts. In line 4 the character "\n" is eliminated from the end of the line. In line 5, the conditional **if** tells Perl to avoid the first line of the input file (the line with headers). Because I know the file was created using tabs (\t) as separators, in line 6 I used this character as a separator in the instruction **split**. The condition to get into the control structure **if** is that $i is bigger than 0. It means the condition is satisfied when $i is 1. So, in lines 7 and 8 we are reading the values of depth and value and saving them in the arrays @depth and @value. Because the arrays in Perl are indexed from 0, we use as counter $i-1. This guarantees the first index will be 0.

Remember that the instruction **split** creates an array, whose elements will be those that were separated in the line ($line) by the character tab ("\t"). This new array is @arrayLine (line 6). The first element ($arrayLine[0]) was (and will always be assigned to) the variable $depth[$i-1]. The second element ($arrayLine[1]) was (and will always be assigned to) the variable $value[$i-1].

In line 10, the variable $i is being incremented as the file is read. Because this variable counts the line into the input data, we subtract one from its value (line 12) to use it as size of the new arrays (@depth and @value).
In line 13 we close the input file. In line 14 we open the output file in write-mode. In line 15 the headers of the columns are written. In line 16 the control structure **for** starts. We use this structure to read all the elements of the arrays @depth. Notice that the maximum index to be read is when $j<$i, it means, $j less than the size of the array. Remember that this must be this way, because the arrays are indexed to 0. In line 17 we are filtering the input data to those whose depth is less than or equal to 1,600. Those that comply with this condition are written in the output file in line 18. Finally, the output file is closed in line 21. Figure 5.7 shows the output file of this script.

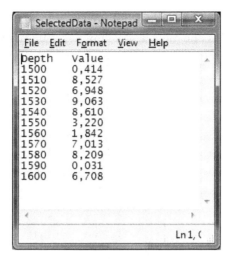

SelectedData - Notepad

File Edit Format View Help

```
Depth     value
1500      0,414
1510      8,527
1520      6,948
1530      9,063
1540      8,610
1550      3,220
1560      1,842
1570      7,013
1580      8,209
1590      0,031
1600      6,708
```

Ln 1, (

Figure 5.7. Output file of Script 5.7.

Let's make some changes, in order to add information to the file SelectedData.txt:

Script 5.8

```
1   open (INPUT,'data.csv');
2   $i=0;
3   while ($line=<INPUT>) {
4    chomp $line;
5    if ($i>0) {
6     @arrayLine=split('\t',$line);
7     $depth[$i-1]=$arrayLine[0];
8     $value[$i-1]=$arrayLine[1];
9    }
10   $i++;
11  }
12  $i--;
13  close INPUT;
14  open (OUTPUT,'>>SelectedData.txt');
15  for ($j=0;$j<$i;$j++) {
16   if ($depth[$j]>1600) {
17    print OUTPUT "$depth[$j]\t$value[$j]\n";
18   }
19  }
20  close OUTPUT;
```

Can you see the differences? Check lines 14 and 16 (compare line 16 with line 17

Advanced programming in Perl for Beginners.

in the previous script). The idea of it, is to show how to add information to a file. Finally, the output of this one must be the same as data.csv (see Figure 5.8):

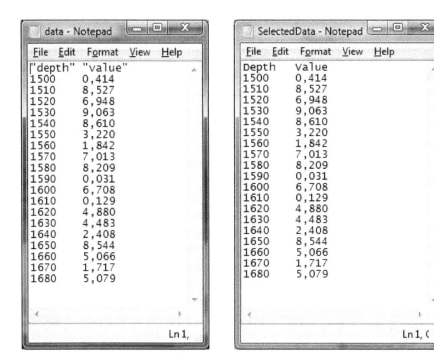

Figure 5.8. Comparing the file data.csv with the file SelectedData.txt.

5.4 Regular expressions.

Regular expressions allow pattern matching with text documents. In geosciences there are lots of programs that generate many different text files, with different types of format: velocity laws in GeoFrame™ and OpenWorks™, LAS files, instrumental tests of seismic recording systems like Sercel™, I/O™ systems and Box™. Perl has a lot of useful functions to handle text files and organize them in order to understand them better.

5.4.1 Understanding patterns.

To understand these concepts easier, let's see the following example. We have a file with a portion of a header of a LAS file.

The content of the file can be seen below:

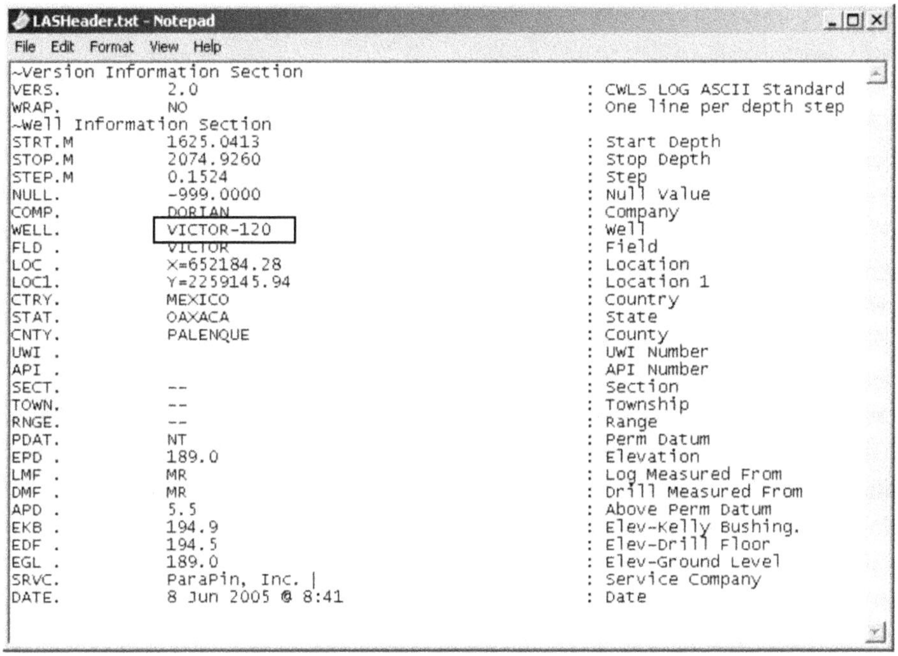

Figure 5.9. Example of a LAS file header.

The exercise consists of finding the name of the well (in this example, the name of the well is VICTOR-120). So, we can use a pattern to look for the word WELL. Remember that Perl is case sensitive, so there is a difference between WELL and the word well and Well and so on.

Let's see the following script:

Script 5.9

```
1  $string2Search='WELL';
2  open (IN,'LASHeader.txt');
3  $line=<IN>;
4  while ($line) {
5    chomp $line;
6    if ($result=$line=~/$string2Search/) {
7      @array=split(' ',$line);
8      $WellName=$array[1];
9    }
```

Advanced programming in Perl for Beginners.

```
10    $line=<IN>;
11    }
12    close IN;
13    print "Well name is $WellName\n";
```

In the first line the string that will be used as a pattern has been defined as the word "WELL". The variable that will take the value is $string2Search.

The file shown in Figure 5.9 is opened in the second line. The file is read from line 3 to line 11. The most important instruction in these lines is located in line 6. The variable $string2Search has been closed between /. With ~/$string2Search/ we are asking if the pattern "WELL" is located into the variable $line (not exactly, only contained). If the result is positive, the variable $result assumes 1 as true value. In our script, if the condition in line 6 is true, we build an array from variable $line. With the option single quotes ' ' (there is a space between them), the instruction **split** *splits* the variable $line in elements separated by one or more spaces (it does not matter if there is one or more spaces). According to Figure 5.9, the array will contain three elements. Because Perl index arrays from zero, the name of the well will be in the second element of the array, it means, in $array[1].

Figure 5.10 shows the output of Script 5.9.

```
⊖ ○ ○              EnglishScripts — bash — 67×5
MacBook-Air-de-Dorian:EnglishScripts dorian$ perl Script5-9.pl
Well name is VICTOR-120
MacBook-Air-de-Dorian:EnglishScripts dorian$ ▊
```

Figure 5.10. Output of Script 5.9.

A few changes in the last script will let us know the number of the line where the pattern matched.

Script 5.10

```
1    $string2Search='WELL';
2    $numberOfLine=0;
3    open (IN,'LASHeader.txt');
4    $line=<IN>;
5    while ($line) {
6      chomp $line;
7      $numberOfLine++;
```

```
8    if ($result=$line=~/$string2Search/) {
9     @array=split(' ',$line);
10    $WellName=$array[1];
11    $foundInLine=$numberOfLine;
12    }
13    $line=<IN>;
14   }
15   close IN;
16   print "Well name is $WellName and was found in line $foundInLine\n";
```

The output of the script is shown in Figure 5.11.

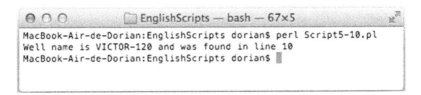

```
● ○ ○              EnglishScripts — bash — 67×5
MacBook-Air-de-Dorian:EnglishScripts dorian$ perl Script5-10.pl
Well name is VICTOR-120 and was found in line 10
MacBook-Air-de-Dorian:EnglishScripts dorian$
```

Figure 5.11. Output of Script 5.10.

Even though Perl has a lot of tools to handle regular expressions, we will see here the most important for our practical uses.

Let's see the following script:

Script 5.11

```
1    $string2Search='DATE. *';
2    $numberOfLine=0;
3    open (IN,'LASHeader.txt');
4    $line=<IN>;
5    while ($line) {
6     chomp $line;
7     $numberOfLine++;
8     if ($result=$line=~/$string2Search/) {
9      $lineTemp=$line;
10     $foundInLine=$numberOfLine;
11     }
12     $line=<IN>;
13    }
14    close IN;
15    print "The line where the expression was found contains the following
      information: \n$lineTemp\n";
16    print "This information was found in line $foundInLine\n";
```

The script is almost the same as the previous one. The main difference is what we are looking for with it. In this case, we are looking for the line that contains the string 'DATE', followed by any spaces. The character '*' located after the space in the expression means that any quantity of spaces will satisfy the pattern. Working with the same file shown in Figure 5.9, the output of the script will look like as shown in Figure 5.12:

```
MacBook-Air-de-Dorian:EnglishScripts dorian$ perl Script5-11.pl
The line where the expression was found contains the following info
rmation:
DATE.            8 Jun 2005 @ 8:41                        : Date
This information was found in line 31
MacBook-Air-de-Dorian:EnglishScripts dorian$
```

Figure 5.12. Output of Script 5.11.

Before to continue, it is necessary to note that the use of variable $string2Search can be omitted. Instead of that, the line 8 in the previous script can be changed by:

if ($result=$line=~/DATE. */) {

The option "+" is the opposite of the option "*". Let's see the following example:

Script 5.12

```
1   $string2Search='DATE.+ ';
2   $numberOfLine=0;
3   open (IN,'LASHeader.txt');
4   $line=<IN>;
5   while ($line) {
6     chomp $line;
7     $numberOfLine++;
8     if ($result=$line=~/$string2Search/) {
9       $lineTemp=$line;
10      $foundInLine=$numberOfLine;
11    }
12    $line=<IN>;
13  }
14  close IN;
15  print "The line where the expression was found contains the following
      information: \n$lineTemp\n";
```

16   print "This information was found in line $foundInLine\n";

Unlike the previous script, in this case the spaces are after the character "+". The following picture is the output of this one:

```
● ○ ○                    EnglishScripts — bash — 76×5
MacBook-Air-de-Dorian:EnglishScripts dorian$ perl Script5-12.pl
The line where the expression was found contains the following information:
DATE.         8 Jun 2005 @ 8:41                    : Date
This information was found in line 31
MacBook-Air-de-Dorian:EnglishScripts dorian$
```

Figure 5.13. Output of Script 5.12.

In both cases, it is possible to use characters after or before the character "+" or "*". For example, look at the following script:

Script 5.13

```
1    $string2Search='DATE.+ ';
2    $numberOfLine=0;
3    open (IN,'LASHeader.txt');
4    $line=<IN>;
5    while ($line) {
6      chomp $line;
7      $numberOfLine++;
8      if ($result=$line=~/$string2Search/) {
9        $lineTemp=$line;
10       $foundInLine=$numberOfLine;
11     }
12     $line=<IN>;
13   }
14   close IN;
15   print "The line where the expression was found contains the following
       information: \n$lineTemp\n";
16   print "This information was found in line $foundInLine\n";
```

In this case, we are looking for the name of country (CTRY into the file). So, we have changed the pattern for 'CTRY.+ M' (There is a space between + and M). The following picture shows the output after running the script:

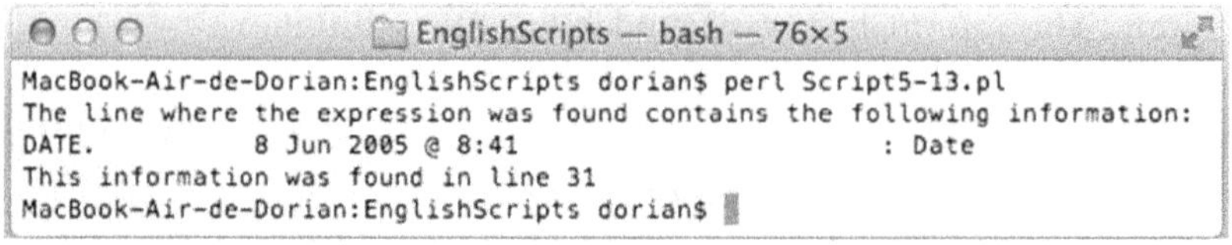

Advanced programming in Perl for Beginners.

Figure 5.14. Output of Script 5.13.

In this script, the pattern 'CTRY.+ M' will allow looking for a string where there will be one or more spaces between the character "." and the character "M". Do the test, changing the pattern by 'CTRY. *M' (there is a space between the character "." and the character "*").

The special character "?" allows that zero or one of the previous characters activate the matching. The following is an example of the use of this special character:

Script 5.14

```
1   $string2Search='STR?';
2   $numberOfLine=0;
3   open (IN,'LASHeader.txt');
4   $line=<IN>;
5   while ($line) {
6     chomp $line;
7     $numberOfLine++;
8     if ($result=$line=~/$string2Search/) {
9       $lineTemp=$line;
10      $foundInLine=$numberOfLine;
11      print "The line where the expression was found contains the following
        information: \n$lineTemp\n";
12      print "This information was found in line $foundInLine\n";
13    }
14    $line=<IN>;
15  }
16  close IN;
```

In this script, the string $string2Search has been changed by 'STR?'. Look at the following picture to see the output of the script and which lines matched with the pattern:

```
● ○ ○                    EnglishScripts — bash — 76×14
MacBook-Air-de-Dorian:EnglishScripts dorian$ perl Script5-14.pl
The line where the expression was found contains the following information:
STRT.M        1625.0413                         : Start Depth
This information was found in line 5
The line where the expression was found contains the following information:
STOP.M        2074.9260                         : Stop Depth
This information was found in line 6
The line where the expression was found contains the following information:
STEP.M        0.1524                            : Step
This information was found in line 7
The line where the expression was found contains the following information:
STAT.         OAXACA                            : State
This information was found in line 15
MacBook-Air-de-Dorian:EnglishScripts dorian$
```

Figure 5.15. Output of Script 5.14

If you wish to specify how many times a character must appear, the characters " {"
and "}" must be used. See the following example:

$string2Search='WEL{1,2}'

In this case, the only values that will match with the pattern are:

WEL

WELL

If the maximum times that a character must appear in a string are desired to be
specified, the following configuration can be used:

$string2Search='WEL{0,2}'

Otherwise, if it is desired the minimum times, the following configuration can be
used:

$string2Search='WEL{2,}'

If the exact number of times that the pattern must match is desired, use the
following configuration:

$string2Search='WEL{2}'

In this case, only the word WELL will satisfy the pattern.

Changing the value of $string2Search for 'WEL{2}' in the previous script, we will
observe the following output:

Advanced programming in Perl for Beginners.

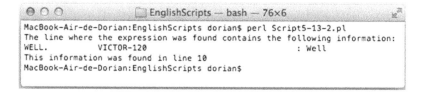

Figure 5.16. Output after having changed the value $string2Search for 'WEL{2}' in Script 5.14.

Now, let's see the special character ".". When this is used, any character different to the new line character (\n) will activate the match. See the following script:

Script 5.15

```
1   $string2Search='ST.P';
2   $numberOfLine=0;
3   open (IN,'LASHeader.txt');
4   $line=<IN>;
5   while ($line) {
6     chomp $line;
7     $numberOfLine++;
8     if ($result=$line=~/$string2Search/) {
9       $lineTemp=$line;
10      $foundInLine=$numberOfLine;
11      print "The line where the expression was found contains the following
        information: \n$lineTemp\n";
12      print "This information was found in line $foundInLine\n";
13    }
14    $line=<IN>;
15  }
16  close IN;
```

After running this script, you will be able to see the following output:

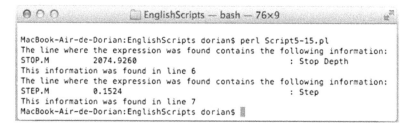

Figure 5.17. Output of Script 5.15.

In this case, the strings that matched with the pattern were:

STOP and STEP (the character "." worked like "O" or "E").

In the following, we will see the use of the special characters "[" and "]". These characters are used when there are several options looking for matching. Let's see the following examples:

```
1   $XCoord='X[:=]';
2   $YCoord='Y[:=]';
3   $numberOfLine=0;
4   open (IN,'LASHeader.txt');
5   $line=<IN>;
6   while ($line) {
7    chomp $line;
8    $numberOfLine++;
9    if ($result1=$line=~/$XCoord/) {
10    $lineTemp=$line;
11    $foundInLine=$numberOfLine;
12    print "East coordinate of the well can be found in $foundInLine\n";
13    print "The line is:\n $lineTemp\n";
14    print "So, the X coordinate is: $X\n";
15   }
16   if ($result2=$line=~/$YCoord/) {
17    $lineTemp=$line;
18    $foundInLine=$numberOfLine;
19    print "North coordinate of the well can be found in $foundInLine\n";
20    print "The line is:\n $lineTemp\n";
21   }
22   $line=<IN>;
23  }
24  close IN;
```

In this script we are looking for the coordinates of the well. In this case we are looking for X coordinates and Y coordinates. The variables $XCoord and $Ycoord contain the patterns to be used for searching. In both variables, the characters ":" and "=" between "[" and "]" mean that the expressions X: or X= and Y: or Y= will match with the patterns. The following picture shows the output of the script:

Advanced programming in Perl for Beginners.

```
000                    EnglishScripts — bash — 76×9
MacBook-Air-de-Dorian:EnglishScripts dorian$ perl Script5-16.pl
East coordinate of the well can be found in 12
The line is:
   LOC .          X=652184.28                        : Location
So, the X coordinate is:
North coordinate of the well can be found in 13
The line is:
   LOC1.          Y=2259145.94                       : Location 1
MacBook-Air-de-Dorian:EnglishScripts dorian$
```

Figure 5.18. Output of Script 5.16.

The most important issue with the use of square brackets is that they can be used with any combination of characters: numbers, symbols, etc.

There are some cases where we are not sure whether a word could have been written using capital or lower-case letters or a combination of both of them. Let's see the following script:

Script 5.17

```
1   $string2Search='well';
2   $numberOfLine=0;
3   open (IN,'LASHeader.txt');
4   $line=<IN>;
5   while ($line) {
6    chomp $line;
7    $numberOfLine++;
8    if ($result=$line=~/$string2Search/i) {
9     $lineTemp=$line;
10    $foundInLine=$numberOfLine;
11    print "The line where the expression was found contains the following
      information: \n$lineTemp\n";
12    print "This information was found in line $foundInLine\n";
13    }
14   $line=<IN>;
15  }
16  close IN;
```

In this case, we are using the word 'well' as a pattern. In line 8, we have added the letter i after the last "/". Now, let's see the output of the script:

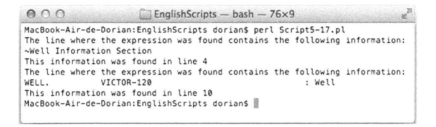

Figure 5.19. Output of Script 5.17.

As it can be seen in the previous picture, the match is activated with the words: Well and WELL.

Chapter 6.

Subroutines & Modules.

6.1 Subroutines.

In computer science, a subroutine (function, method, procedure, or subprogram) is a portion of code within a larger program, which performs a specific task and is relatively   independent   of   the   remaining   code   (taken   from http://en.wikipedia.org/wiki/Subroutine)

The structure of a subroutine in Perl is as follows:

sub NameOfTheSubroutine {

    instructions;

}

Let's see the following example:

Script 6.1

```
1   $a=5;
2   $b=5;
3   $d=sum($a,$b);
4   print "$a + $b = $d\n";
5
6   sub sum {
7   $c=$_[0]+$_[1];
8   }
```

This script computes the sum between two numbers, which variables are $a and $b. $d will content the value of the sum after the **sub sum** is invoked. Because $a and $b are the variables, these are put between parenthesis as part of parameters of the subroutine **sum**. When a subroutine is invoked, the Perl interpreter looks for the sub into the script. In Perl, there is a special variable (actually an array) that contains the last values of a list. This variable is @_ and its elements will be $_[0], $_[1], $_[2]... and as many parameters as have been passed to the subroutine. In our example, the parameters have been two: $a and $b. Into the sub is evaluated the expression $_[0] + $_[1]. Internally, $_[0] contains the value of $a and $_[1] contains the value of $b. The order is important when the parameters are invoked into the subroutine. Figure 6.1 shows the output of the script. Of course this is a very simple example, but later in the book we will see more complex exercises.

The subroutines return the last evaluated computation. In the previous one, the last

Advanced programming in Perl for Beginners.

value is $c.

A subroutine does not necessarily have to return a value. It can do its own outputs to the screen or to files. Moreover, a subroutine can be invoked into another subroutine.

Figure 6.1. Output of Script 6.1.

6.2 Packages and modules.

A package is something like a subroutine or a set of them, but they belong to a separate file. The packages are usually named with extension **.pm**.

A module is basically a package, but it has been created to be reused. Because Perl has grown around an immense community of programmers, it is possible to find a lot of modules made by others, ready to be used. Many of them can be found at www.cpan.org. However, we will see how we can do our own modules and how they can be used. Let's see the following example. Imagine we want to calculate some values from points shown in Figure 6.2: distance between points, sines and cosines of angle α, slope of the straight line. Every calculation will be made using a different subroutine but into one package.

To do this, we have made a main script, where the values of the variables are (coordinates of points) and the invocation to the subroutines that will make the calculations, belonging to a package named **trigonometrics**. This package has been saved as a file named with the same name and extension .pm: **trigonometrics.pm**, and it is located in the same directory where the main one is.

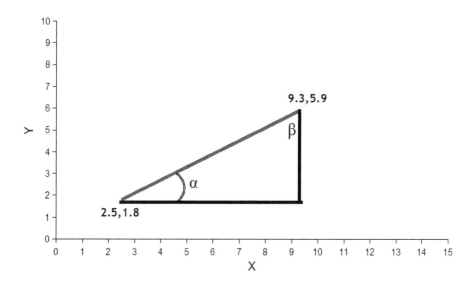

Figure 6.2. Straight line.

The next one corresponds to calculator.pl:

Script 6.2

```
1   use trigonometrics qw(dist sinus cosines $x2 $y2 $x1 $y1);
2   $x2=9.3;
3   $y2=5.9;
4   $x1=2.5;
5   $y1=1.8;
6   $d=dist;
7   $e=sines;
8   $f=cosines;
9   $slope=sprintf("%.4f",$e/$f);
10  print "Distance between points ($x2,$y2) - ($x1,$y1) is: $d\n";
11  print "The sine of the angle alfa is:      $e\n";
12  print "The cosine of the angle alfa is:      $f\n";
13  print "Slope if the straight line is:      $slope\n";
```

The following is the module trigonometrics.pm:

Script 6.3 (trigonometrics.pm)

```
1   package trigonometrics;
2   require Exporter;
3   @ISA=qw(Exporter);
```

Advanced programming in Perl for Beginners.

```
4   @EXPORT_OK=qw(dist sinus cosines $x2 $y2 $x1 $y1);
5
6   sub dist {
7   $e=sqrt(($x2-$x1)**2+($y2-$y1)**2);
8   sprintf("%.4f",$e);
9   }
10
11  sub sines {
12  my $f=($y2-$y1)/$e;
13  sprintf("%.4f",$f);
14  }
15
16  sub cosines {
17  my $g=($x2-$x1)/$e;
18  sprintf("%.4f",$g);
19  }
```

In the first line of the main script (Script 6.2) we find a Perl reserved word: **use**. This word is used to tell Perl interpreter that this package will be used in the execution of it (or could be used) It is important that the name of the file be the same as the package. After the name of the package comes the reserved word **qw**, followed by a parenthesis. The subroutines and the variables used within the subroutines, which are in the package, must be indicated by using parentheses and separated by blanks. Notice that the elements are sorted in the same way as they are in the package (line 4 into **trigonometrics.pm**). In the package, the first 4 lines are mandatory. In these lines are the instructions that allow the communication between the main script and the package.

The following picture shows the output after running Script 6.2.

```
MacBook-Air-de-Dorian:EnglishScripts dorian$ perl Script6-2.pl
Distance between points (9.3,5.9) - (2.5,1.8) is: 7.9404
The sine of the angle alfa is:                0.5163
The cosine of the angle alfa is:              0.8564
Slope if the straight line is:                0.6029
MacBook-Air-de-Dorian:EnglishScripts dorian$
```

Figure 6.3. Output of the Script 6.2.

6.3 Reusing modules.

As you could see in the help file of Perl, the numerical functions available in Perl are: **abs, atan2, cos, exp, hex, int, log, oct, rand, sin, sqrt** and **srand**. It is possible that with this you can generate other functions. However, it is possible that someone else has already made it. At least in my case, before I start to make a script, I search the web to check if someone has previously made something similar. For example let's take a module of trigonometric functions that can be found in www.cpan.org. The module is **Math-Complex-1.37** and can be downloaded from http://search.cpan.org/~jhi/Math-Complex-1.37/lib/Math/Trig.pm. In this address, we can see all the necessary help to use this module.

Many of the Perl modules are simply file with .pm extensions. If it is not necessary to compile code (this means, there is not C code into the zip file), then look at the following instructions:

1. Download the file (in this example is Math-Complex-1.37.tar.gz).
2. Decompress it.
3. Search the folder where the files with the extension .pm are. In this case, they are under the folder Math. Copy this folder to the path C:\Perl\lib. This is one of the folders where Perl always looks for the modules that are invoked from a script (in Windows).

Now, let's take the purpose of the previous one as example. Instead of use our own package, let's use the module Trig, located in the file Trig.pm. Because Perl looks for modules in C:\Perl\lib, it is necessary to give it the complete path where the module is. This is made using the instruction **use Math::Trig** (line 1 of the following script). This is the equivalent of telling Perl to look for module in C:\Perl\lib\Math\Trig.pm. Of course, this address will be different, depending on the operating system.

Script 6.4

```
1  use Math::Trig;
2  $x2=9.3;
3  $y2=5.9;
4  $x1=2.5;
5  $y1=1.8;
6  $d=dist($x2,$x1,$y2,$y1);
7  $AlfaAngleSines=sprintf("%.5f",asin(($y2-$y1)/$d));
```

```
8   $AlfaAngleCosines=sprintf("%.5f",acos(($x2-$x1)/$d));
9   $AlfaAngleTan=sprintf("%.5f",atan(($y2-$y1)/($x2-$x1)));
10  $BetaAngleSines=sprintf("%.5f",asin(($x2-$x1)/$d));
11  $BetaAngleCosines=sprintf("%.5f",acos(($y2-$y1)/$d));
12  $BetaAngleTan=sprintf("%.5f",atan(($x2-$x1)/($y2-$y1)));
13  $degreesAlfa=sprintf("%.5f",rad2deg($AlfaAngleSines));
14  $degreesBeta=sprintf("%.5f",rad2deg($BetaAngleSines));
15  $sum=sprintf("%.5f",$degreesAlfa+$degreesBeta);
16  print "Distance between points ($x2,$y2) - ($x1,$y1) is: $d\n";
17  print "Angle alfa, calculated using sine function is: $AlfaAngleSines
    radians\n";
18  print "Angle alfa, calculated using cosine function is: $AlfaAngleCosines
    radians\n";
19  print "Angle alfa, calculated using tan function is:  $AlfaAngleTan
    radians\n";
20  print "Angle Beta, calculated using sine function is:  $BetaAngleSines
    radians\n";
21  print "Angle Beta, calculated using cosine function is: $BetaAngleCosines
    radians\n";
22  print "Angle Beta, calculated using tan function is:  $BetaAngleTan
    radians\n";
23  print "Angle alfa, in degrees is: $degreesAlfa\n";
24  print "Angle Beta, in degrees is: $degreesBeta\n";
25  print "Because it is a right triangle, the sum of Alfa + Beta is: $sum\n";
26
27  sub dist {
28  sprintf("%.5f",sqrt(($_[0]-$_[1])**2+($_[2]-$_[3])**2));
29  }
```

All the trigonometric functions used from line 7 to 14 are not natively available in Perl, but available in the module Trig (Trig.pm). The following picture shows the output after running the script:

```
MacBook-Air-de-Dorian:EnglishScripts dorian$ perl Script6-4.pl
Distance between points (9.3,5.9) - (2.5,1.8) is: 7.94040
Angle alfa, calculated using sine function is:    0.54258 radians
Angle alfa, calculated using cosine function is: 0.54258 radians
Angle alfa, calculated using tan function is:     0.54258 radians
Angle Beta, calculated using sine function is:    1.02822 radians
Angle Beta, calculated using cosine function is: 1.02822 radians
Angle Beta, calculated using tan function is:     1.02822 radians
Angle alfa, in degrees is: 31.08754
Angle Beta, in degrees is: 58.91267
Because it is a right triangle, the sum of Alfa + Beta is: 90.00021
MacBook-Air-de-Dorian:EnglishScripts dorian$
```

Figure 6.4. Output of Script 6.4.

There are some cases when the Perl modules come with C code that must be compiled. In these cases, it is possible to use the following instructions (personally, I prefer this way, because the installer knows exactly where to put every file.) Open a terminal window (or shell or command prompt) and type:

- perl -MCPAN -e shell (Figure 6.5)
- After pressing "Enter", the shell windows will look like Figure 6.6.
- From the cpan command line, type: install Bundle::CPAN (Figure 6.7).
- Once the installation ends, type: reload cpan.
- It is possible you do not know the exact name of the module you want to install. To search in the repository, from the cpan command line type:

> i /trig/

This instruction returns a list of several modules that have the word "trig" as a part of its name. Figure 6.8 shows an extract of the window with the searching results. Enclosed in a rectangle, we have the name of the module we want to install.

- In the cpan command line, type: install Math::Trig.

In order to get help about any Perl module, exit from cpan command line (with the instruction **exit**) Once done, type:

perldoc Math::Trig

And you will see something similar to what it is shown in Figure 6.9.

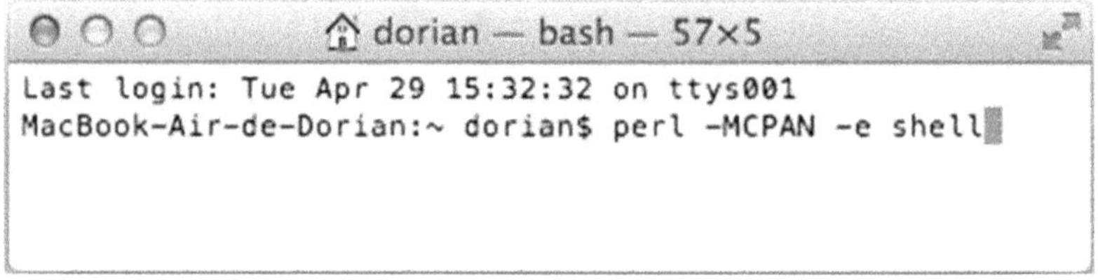

Advanced programming in Perl for Beginners.

Figure 6.5. Instruction to load cpan from shell.

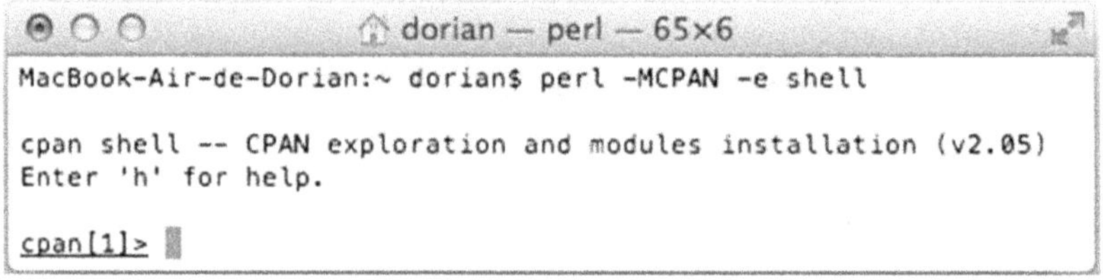

Figure 6.6. cpan after loaded.

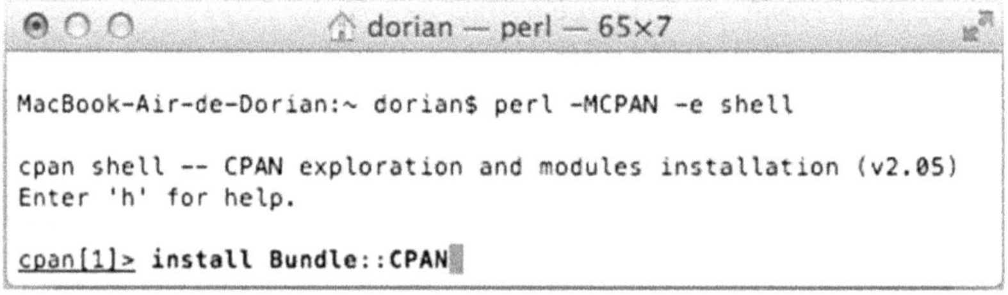

Figure 6.7. Instruction to upgrade the latest version of CPAN.pm.

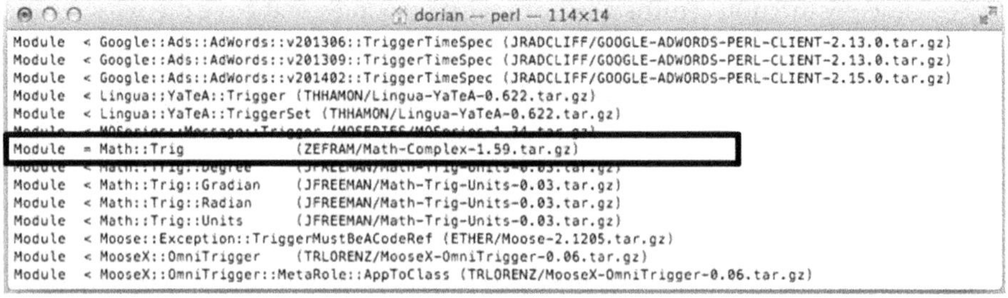

Figure 6.8. Instruction to upgrade the latest version of CPAN.pm.

```
●  ○  ○                          ⌂ dorian — less — 89×34
perlbrew::perls::perl-perlbrew::perls::perl-5.16.0::lib::5.16.0::Math::Trig(3)



NAME
       Math::Trig - trigonometric functions

SYNOPSIS
           use Math::Trig;

           $x = tan(0.9);
           $y = acos(3.7);
           $z = asin(2.4);

           $halfpi = pi/2;

           $rad = deg2rad(120);

           # Import constants pi2, pip2, pip4 (2*pi, pi/2, pi/4).
           use Math::Trig ':pi';

           # Import the conversions between cartesian/spherical/cylindrical.
           use Math::Trig ':radial';

              # Import the great circle formulas.
           use Math::Trig ':great_circle';

DESCRIPTION
       "Math::Trig" defines many trigonometric functions not defined by the
       core Perl which defines only the "sin()" and "cos()".  The constant pi
       is also defined as are a few convenience functions for angle
       conversions, and great circle formulas for spherical movement.

:▊
```

Figure 6.9. Help of the module Math::Trig.

Chapter 7.

The power of Perl Tk.

7.1 Introduction.

Perl Tk is a set of tools that allows Perl to be visual, like Visual Basic for instance. Without these kind of tools it is not possible to program visual applications with windows, buttons, text boxes (Entry widgets), etc. Each one of these objects are known as *widgets*. Following is an example code of a window with Perl Tk. Figure 7.1 shows the window.

Script 7.1

```
1  use Tk;
2  $mw = MainWindow->new;
3  MainLoop;
```

Windows   OS-X

Figure 7.1. Output of Script 7.1 on Windows and OS-X.

In the first line the instruction to invoke Perl Tk is declared. Only due to the inclusion of this line, it is possible to do a lot of things similar to another visual language. I do not know of a free version that easily allows drawing buttons such as Visual Basic or Visual C#. Instead of this, all my 'visual' scripts are 'hand made' (writing the drawing instruction). However, you will see that with time, it will become easier.

In the second line, the main window is built. The third line instructs the window be drawn.

Advanced programming in Perl for Beginners.

Following, we will begin to add more complexity to our applications.

7.2 Labels.

With labels you can add instructions, titles, comments, etc., to an application. Let's see the following example:

Script 7.2

```
1   use Tk;
2   $mw = MainWindow->new;
3   $label=$mw->Label(-text=>"Our first complex Perl/Tk Script");
4   $label->pack;
5   MainLoop;
```

We added two more lines to the previous script. In the third line, a label is built into the main window and stored in the variable $label. The reserved word to use labels is **Label**. Between parentheses, the parameters that will describe the label are written, including the string of characters that we want to show. Once an object is built, you can refer it only with the name of the variable you used. The Perl interpreter will always know that $label belongs to $mw (main window).

In the fourth line, the instruction pack allows you to fix the label in a default position inside the main window.

Figure 7.2 shows the output of the previous script:

Figure 7.2. Output of Script 7.2.

7.3 Buttons.

A button is commonly used, after having introduced parameters to the scripts, to execute a set of instructions. Let's see the following one:

```
1   use Tk;
2   $mw = MainWindow->new;
3   $label=$mw->Label(-text=>"Our first complex Perl/Tk Script");
4   $label->place(-x=>0,-y=>2);
5   $label2=$mw->Label(-textvariable=>\$string);
6   $label2->place(-x=>0,-y=>80);
7   $button=$mw->Button(-text=>'OK',-command=>\&task);
8   $button->place(-x=>0,-y=>20);
9   $cleanButton=$mw->Button(-text=>'Clean String',-
    command=>\&clean);
10  $cleanButton->place(-x=>60,-y=>20);
11  MainLoop;
12
13  sub task {
14  $string="You have pressed the OK button";
15  }
16
17  sub clean {
18  $string="";
19  }
```

Figure 7.3 shows the output of the script (left side). After pressing the button 'OK', a message appears under buttons (Figure 7.3, right side). After pressing the button 'Clean String', the window will look as it appears in the left side.

This is introducing new and slightly more complex instructions. In the fourth line we are using the reserved word **place**, instead of **pack**, in order to take control of the exact position of the widget. With this option it is possible to assign coordinates to the position and they are referred to the upper left corner of the window. The coordinates of the upper left corner are x=0, y=0 and they increase to the right and the bottom of the window.

In the fifth line, we have defined a label widget, but in this case we are using an option that allows that the parameter text can change and not to be fixed as in the case of $label (line 4). This option is **-textvariable** and its value can change if the variable $string changes.

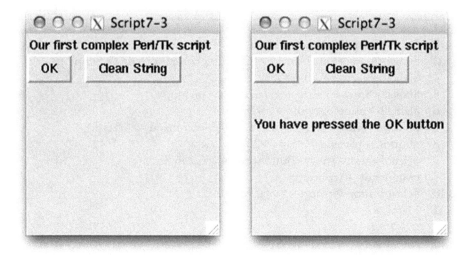

Figure 7.3. Output of Script 7.3.

In the seventh line, we have added another option to the button $button. The option is **-command** and it must be followed by the name of a subroutine that will be invoked after pressing the button. In this example, after pressing the button $button, the instructions of the subroutine **task** will be executed.

In the ninth line we have created another button, named $cleanButton. This button will clean to $label2. This will be done after executing the subroutine clean.

7.4 Radiobutton.

With this widget, we have the possibility to offer several options before the execution of a program, but only one can be selected at time. For example, gender (male or female), beverages (coffee, tea, water), energy sources (explosives, vibrators), seismic acquisition (land, marine), etc. The options can be more than two. Let's see the following example:

Script 7.4

```
1  use Tk;
2  use Tk::Radiobutton;
3
4  #This variables make that no radiobutton is selected
5  $onoffg=0;
```

```perl
6    $onoffb=0;
7
8    #Construction of the main window
9    my $top = new MainWindow(-title=>'Test RadioButton');
10   $top->configure(-width=>442);
11   $top->configure(-height=>200);
12   $top->resizable(0,0);
13
14   $labelTypeTest=$top->Label(-text=>'Type Test');
15   $labelTypeTest->place(-x=>6,-y=>15);
16
17   #Radiobuttons
18   $geo=$top->Radiobutton(-command=>sub{&check_geo},-
     selectcolor=>'lightgreen',-text=>'Geophones',-variable=>\$onoffg);
19   $geo->place(-x=>6,-y=>40);
20
21   $box=$top->Radiobutton(-command=>sub{&impbox},-
     selectcolor=>'lightgreen',-text=>'Boxes',-variable=>\$onoffb);
22   $box->place(-x=>6,-y=>65);
23   ##############################################
24
25   #Label to show a message
26   $LabelMessage=$top->Label(-textvariable=>\$message);
27   $LabelMessage->place(-x=>6,-y=>95);
28
29   #Button to exit
30   $exitbutton=$top->Button(-text=>'Exit',-command=>sub{exit});
31   $exitbutton->place(-x=>380,-y=>155,-width=>50);
32   ##############################################
33
34   #Message about the autor
35   $mensaje=$top->Label(-text=>'This software has been made by Dorian
     Oria');
36   $mensaje->place(-x=>2,-y=>125);
37
38   $email=$top->Label(-text=>'e-mail: dorian_oria@yahoo.com');
39   $email->place(-x=>63,-y=>140);
40
41   MainLoop;
42
43   #End of the construction of main window
44   ##############################################
45
```

Advanced programming in Perl for Beginners.

```
46   sub check_geo {
47   $onoffg="";
48   $onoffb=0;
49   $message="You have pressed the Geophone option";
50   }
51
52   sub impbox {
53   $onoffg=0;
54   $onoffb="";
55   $message="You have pressed the Box option";
56   }
```

When this script is executed, the following window comes up:

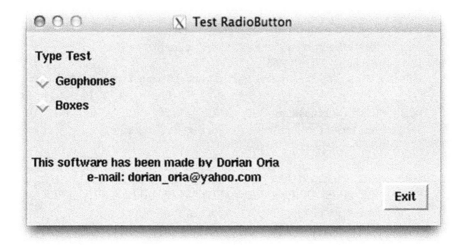

Figure 7.4. Output of Script 7.4.

Pressing the option 'Geophones', the window will be as follows:

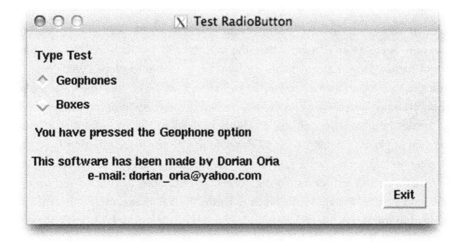

Figure 7.5. Output of Script 7.4, after selecting the option 'Geophones'.

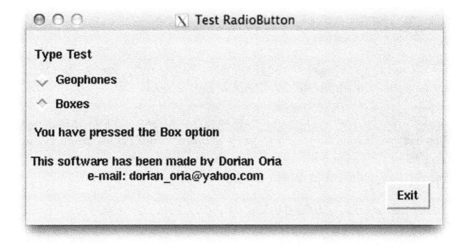

Figure 7.6. Output of Script 7.4, after selecting the option 'Boxes'.

In this one, we have tried to simulate a program that performs testing of geophones and boxes (equipment used in seismic data acquisition). The variables $onoffg (geophones) and $onoffb (boxes) (lines 5 and 6) allows controlling the appearance of the buttons when one of them is selected. At the beginning, because they are not selected, the value of their variables is equal to 0. This is shown in Figure 7.4.

Advanced programming in Perl for Beginners.

From lines 9 to 12, the main window is built. In lines 14 and 15 the label 'Type Test' is written. Radiobuttons are drawn from line 18 to 22. Remember that the expression $geo=$top-> means that the widget will be anchored to the main window named $top. Later we will see that it is possible to place a widget inside another, not necessarily anchored to the main window. To be able to use the widget Radiobutton it is necessary to previously invoke the corresponding module. This is done using the instruction in line 2. The behaviour of the expression '->' is the equivalent of point (.) in C# or Visual Basic. In line 18 the first Radiobutton is built. Between parentheses there are several options (there are more than these ones) that define methods and properties for the widget. For example, the option **-command** is the equivalent to a method. It indicates to the widget to execute the instructions contained in the subroutine 'check_geo'. The rest of the options are properties:

- **-selectcolor** gives the color to the widget (in this case light green).
- **-text** is the label next to the widget.
- **-variable** is the default value when the widget is launched. The value of this variable will allow changing the status of the Radiobutton from selected to unselected or vice versa.

You must not forget the use of the character '-' before the properties or method. Every property or method must be separated by a comma (,).

Once the widget is defined, it is necessary to give it a position in the main widget. Remember that this can be done with **pack** or **place**. I prefer to use **place**, because the control of the position is easier. If the location of the widget is omitted, Perl Tk will not be able to draw it in the main widget.

The other Radiobutton is defined in lines 21 and 22. In order to avoid complications in these first scripts, every time a Radiobutton be pressed, a message will appear into the main widget, indicating the option selected. The label that will contain this message is defined in lines 26 and 27. Notice that in this case, instead of using the property **-text**, we have used the property **-textvariable**. In this case, the message shown by the Label will change, depending on the value of the variable $message (this is an example, the name can be anyone).

A button to exit the application is defined in lines 30 and 31. This can be done by invoking the instruction 'exit' (it is invoked like a subroutine with the method - command.

Between lines 35 and 39, two messages are added. They are added using the widget Label.

When the first Radiobutton is selected, the subroutine **check_geo** is executed. In this subroutine the values of the variables $onoffg and $onoffb are changed, in order to create the effect that one of them have been selected. The fact to assign to $onoffg="" and 0 to the other one, makes the effect that the first one has been selected. The opposite is done in the case that Boxes is selected. In line 49, $message take the value of an expression, indicating in this case that the option 'Geophones' has been selected. Depending on the selected option, the value of $message will change.

7.5 Checkbutton.

Unlike Radiobutton, this widget allows selecting more than one option. For example, areas of interest for you: sports, travel, books, movies, etc. In text processor you have seen that it is possible to change the properties of a text font: italic, bold, color, underlined, etc. Taking into account the previous example, checking instruments in seismic data acquisition operation usually includes, in the case of geophones, the following tests: resistance, leakage, tilt and noise. We can choose to make all the tests on the fly or one at time (this is useful in the case only one test must be repeated). Let's see the following example:

Script 7.5

```
1    use Tk;
2    use Tk::Radiobutton;
3    use Tk::Checkbutton;
4
5    #This variables make that no radiobutton is selected
6    $onoffg=0;
7    $onoffb=0;
8
9    #Construction of the main window
10   my $top = new MainWindow(-title=>'Test RadioButton');
11   $top->configure(-width=>442);
12   $top->configure(-height=>200);
13   $top->resizable(0,0);
14
15   $labelTypeTest=$top->Label(-text=>'Type Test');
16   $labelTypeTest->place(-x=>6,-y=>15);
17
```

```
18  #Radiobuttons
19  $geo=$top->Radiobutton(-command=>sub{&check_geo},-
    selectcolor=>'lightgreen',-text=>'Geophones',-variable=>\$onoffg);#,-
    value=>0);
20  $geo->place(-x=>6,-y=>40);
21
22  $box=$top->Radiobutton(-command=>sub{&impbox},-
    selectcolor=>'lightgreen',-text=>'Boxes',-variable=>\$onoffb);
23  $box->place(-x=>6,-y=>65);
24  ###############################################
25
26  #Checkbuttons
27  $LabelTypeGeophoneTest=$top->Label(-text=>'Geophone Test');
28  $LabelTypeGeophoneTest->place(-x=>140,-y=>40);
29
30  $ResistanceCheckButton=$top->Checkbutton(-
    command=>sub{&Resistance},-text=>'Resistance',-variable =>
    \$valorR,-state => 'disable');
31  $ResistanceCheckButton->place(-x=>140,-y=>60);
32  $LabelRes=$top->Label(-textvariable=>\$SelMesR);
33  $LabelRes->place(-x=>280,-y=>60);
34
35
36  $LeakageCheckButton=$top->Checkbutton(-
    command=>sub{&Leakage},-text=>'Leakage',-variable => \$valorL,-
    state => 'disable');
37  $LeakageCheckButton->place(-x=>140,-y=>80);
38  $LabelRes=$top->Label(-textvariable=>\$SelMesL);
39  $LabelRes->place(-x=>280,-y=>80);
40
41  $TiltCheckButton=$top->Checkbutton(-command=>sub{&Tilt},-
    text=>'Tilt',-variable => \$valorT,-state => 'disable');
42  $TiltCheckButton->place(-x=>140,-y=>100);
43  $LabelRes=$top->Label(-textvariable=>\$SelMesT);
44  $LabelRes->place(-x=>280,-y=>100);
45
46  $NoiseCheckButton=$top->Checkbutton(-command=>sub{&Noise},-
    text=>'Noise',-variable => \$valorN,-state => 'disable');
47  $NoiseCheckButton->place(-x=>140,-y=>120);
48  $LabelRes=$top->Label(-textvariable=>\$SelMesN);
49  $LabelRes->place(-x=>280,-y=>120);
50  ###############################################
51
```

```perl
52   #Label to show a message
53   $LabelMessage=$top->Label(-textvariable=>\$message);
54   $LabelMessage->place(-x=>6,-y=>95);
55
56   #Button to exit
57   $exitbutton=$top->Button(-text=>'Exit',-command=>sub{exit});
58   $exitbutton->place(-x=>380,-y=>155,-width=>50);
59   ########################################
60
61   #Message about the autor
62   $mensaje=$top->Label(-text=>'This software has been made by Dorian
     Oria');
63   $mensaje->place(-x=>2,-y=>145);
64
65   $email=$top->Label(-text=>'e-mail: dorian_oria@yahoo.com');
66   $email->place(-x=>63,-y=>160);
67
68
69   MainLoop;
70
71   #End of the construction of main window
72   ########################################
73
74   sub check_geo {
75   $onoffg="";
76   $onoffb=0;
77   $ResistanceCheckButton->configure(-state => 'active');
78   $LeakageCheckButton->configure(-state => 'active');
79   $TiltCheckButton->configure(-state => 'active');
80   $NoiseCheckButton->configure(-state => 'active');
81   $message="You have pressed the\n Geophone option";
82
83   }
84
85   sub impbox {
86   $onoffg=0;
87   $onoffb="";
88   $ResistanceCheckButton->configure(-state => 'disable');
89   $LeakageCheckButton->configure(-state => 'disable');
90   $TiltCheckButton->configure(-state => 'disable');
91   $NoiseCheckButton->configure(-state => 'disable');
92   $message="You have pressed the\n Box option";
93   }
```

```perl
94
95   sub Resistance {
96   if ($valorR==1) {
97    $ResistanceCheckButton->configure(-fg=>'red');
98
99    $SelMesR="Selected Resistance";
100  }
101  if ($valorR==0) {
102   $ResistanceCheckButton->configure(-fg=>'black');
103   $SelMesR="Unselected Resistance";
104  }
105  }
106
107  sub Leakage {
108  if ($valorL==1) {
109   $LeakageCheckButton->configure(-fg=>'red');
110   $SelMesL="Selected Leakage";
111  }
112  if ($valorL==0) {
113  $LeakageCheckButton->configure(-fg=>'black');
114   $SelMesL="Unselected Leakage";
115  }
116  }
117
118  sub Tilt {
119  if ($valorT==1) {
120   $TiltCheckButton->configure(-fg=>'red');
121   $SelMesT="Selected Tilt";
122  }
123  if ($valorT==0) {
124   $TiltCheckButton->configure(-fg=>'black');
125   $SelMesT="Unselected Tilt";
126  }
127  }
128
129  sub Noise {
130  if ($valorN==1) {
131   $NoiseCheckButton->configure(-fg=>'red');
132   $SelMesN="Selected Noise";
133  }
134  if ($valorN==0) {
135   $NoiseCheckButton->configure(-fg=>'black');
136   $SelMesN="Unselected Noise";
```

137 }
138 }

We have taken Script 7.4 and we have added some lines in order to complicate it a little bit more. In this case, we want to add Checkbuttons. We will not explain the whole script, only those lines that are new for us.

When it is executed, you will see the following window shown in Figure 7.7.

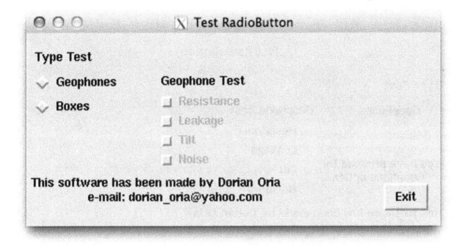

Figure 7.7. Output of Script 7.5.

Because we are adding another widget (in this case Checkbuttons) we have included line 3. We are telling to Perl Tk that it includes the necessary module to work with it. The idea in the design of it, is that the checkbuttons be activated when user selects 'Geophones' in the Type Test and be disabled when the option 'Boxes' is selected.

The corresponding checkbuttons for every test are added from line 27 to 49. Notice that programming checkbuttons is very similar to programming radiobuttons. We have added an extra property: **-state**. This property is intended to show the checkbuttons that are activated, only if the option 'Geophones' is selected. When the option 'Boxes' is activated, then the checkbuttons option is disabled. Another difference is that the option **-variable**. This variable will take the values 1 or 0, depending on whether the checkbutton is selected or not. After every checkbutton,

Advanced programming in Perl for Beginners.

a label is added, whose behavior will depend on whether the checkbutton is selected or not. It is added only as an example of how configurable and powerful these widgets can be. In this case, every time you select or deselect a checkbutton, a message will indicate if the widget is active or not. These messages will be changed when the checkbuttons are selected and this will occur in the corresponding subroutine.

When the 'Geophones' option is selected, then the checkbuttons are activated, as is shown in Figure 7.8. Notice the color of text of every checkbutton is changed to black.

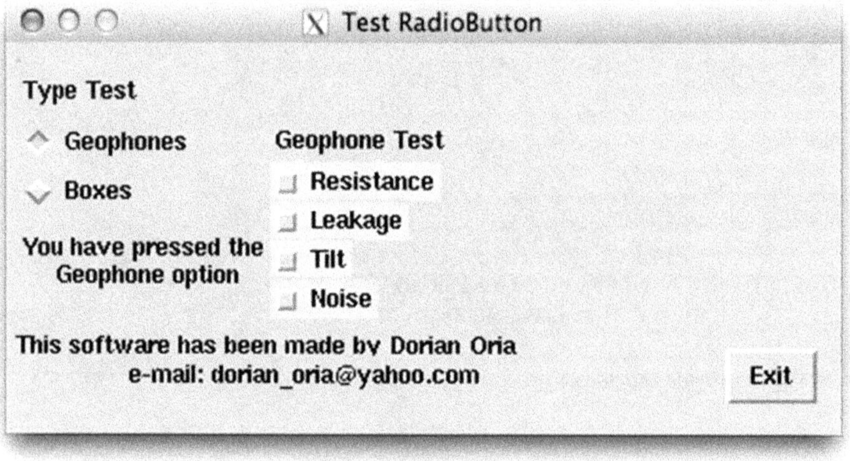

Figure 7.8. Output of Script 7.5, after having selected the option 'Geophones'.

Four subroutines were added, one for every geophone test. These are between lines 95 and 138. We will explain the first one (Resistance) and this explanation will be applicable for all of the subroutines.

If $ValorR=1 (this variable was defined for the Checkbutton $ResistanceCheckButton), then the font is colored with red. The value 1 indicates the checkbutton is selected. In addition, the label located beside the checkbutton changes its value, indicating that the widget has been selected (Figure 7.9). When $ValorR=0, it means the checkbutton is deselected, the font is colored with black and the message is changed (Figure 7.10).

It is possible to select 'Boxes' without deselect every geophone test. Figure 7.11

shows how the application looks after selecting 'Boxes', with checkbuttons selected for geophone tests.

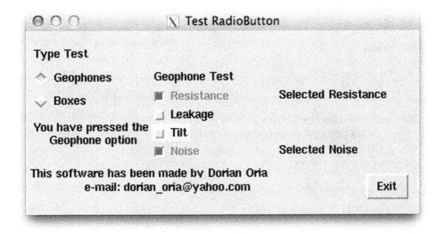

Figure 7.9. Output of Script 7.5, after having selected two tests of the option 'Geophones'.

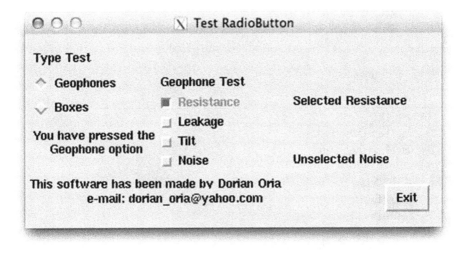

Figure 7.10. Output of Script 7.5 after unselect the option 'Noise'.

Advanced programming in Perl for Beginners.

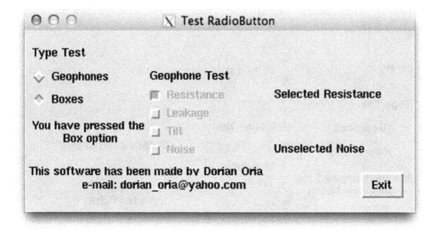

Figure 7.11. Output of Script 7.5, after select the option 'Boxes'.

7.6 Entry widget.

This widget allows the input of values of variables into the program. It is the equivalent of textboxes in Visual C# or Visual Basic. The values can be numbers or text strings. For example, strings can be path of files, names, addresses, etc. Continuing with our script, we will use entry widgets to add the cutoff parameters, used to know which tests are OK or not for the geophones. Let's see the following one:

Script 7.6

```
1   use Tk;
2   use Tk::Radiobutton;
3   use Tk::Checkbutton;
4
5   #This variables make that no radiobutton is selected
6   $onoffg=0;
7   $onoffb=0;
8
9   #Construction of the main window
10  my $top = new MainWindow(-title=>'Test Widgets');
11  $top->configure(-width=>600);
12  $top->configure(-height=>200);
13  $top->resizable(0,0);
14
15  $labelTypeTest=$top->Label(-text=>'Type Test');
```

```
16   $labelTypeTest->place(-x=>6,-y=>15);
17
18   #Radiobuttons
19   $geo=$top->Radiobutton(-command=>sub{&check_geo},-
     selectcolor=>'lightgreen',-text=>'Geophones',-variable=>\$onoffg);#,-
     value=>0);
20   $geo->place(-x=>6,-y=>40);
21
22   $box=$top->Radiobutton(-command=>sub{&impbox},-
     selectcolor=>'lightgreen',-text=>'Boxes',-variable=>\$onoffb);
23   $box->place(-x=>6,-y=>65);
24   ##########################################
25
26   #Checkbuttons
27   $LabelTypeGeophoneTest=$top->Label(-text=>'Geophone Test');
28   $LabelTypeGeophoneTest->place(-x=>140,-y=>40);
29
30   $ResistanceCheckButton=$top->Checkbutton(-
     command=>sub{&Resistance},-text=>'Resistance',-variable =>
     \$valorR,-state => 'disable');
31   $ResistanceCheckButton->place(-x=>140,-y=>60);
32   $LabelRes=$top->Label(-textvariable=>\$SelMesR);
33   $LabelRes->place(-x=>240,-y=>60);
34
35   $LeakageCheckButton=$top->Checkbutton(-
     command=>sub{&Leakage},-text=>'Leakage',-variable => \$valorL,-
     state => 'disable');
36   $LeakageCheckButton->place(-x=>140,-y=>80);
37   $LabelRes=$top->Label(-textvariable=>\$SelMesL);
38   $LabelRes->place(-x=>240,-y=>80);
39
40   $TiltCheckButton=$top->Checkbutton(-command=>sub{&Tilt},-
     text=>'Tilt',-variable => \$valorT,-state => 'disable');
41   $TiltCheckButton->place(-x=>140,-y=>100);
42   $LabelRes=$top->Label(-textvariable=>\$SelMesT);
43   $LabelRes->place(-x=>240,-y=>100);
44
45   $NoiseCheckButton=$top->Checkbutton(-command=>sub{&Noise},-
     text=>'Noise',-variable => \$valorN,-state => 'disable');
46   $NoiseCheckButton->place(-x=>140,-y=>120);
47   $LabelRes=$top->Label(-textvariable=>\$SelMesN);
48   $LabelRes->place(-x=>240,-y=>120);
49   ##########################################
```

```
50
51  #Text boxes with cut values for geophones
52  $res_text=$top->Label(-text=>'< Resistance <',-
    foreground=>'darkgreen');
53  $res_text->place(-x=>430,-y=>60);
54  $lim_inf = $top->Entry(-width => '6', -relief => 'sunken',-
    background=>'red');
55  $lim_inf->place(-x => 380,-y=>60);
56  $lim_sup=$top->Entry(-width => '6', -relief => 'sunken',-
    background=>'red');
57  $lim_sup->place(-x => 530,-y=>60);
58  $leak_tetxt=$top->Label(-text=>'Leakage >');
59  $leak_tetxt->place(-x=>380,-y=>80);
60  $lim_leak= $top->Entry(-width => '6', -relief => 'sunken',-
    background=>'lightgreen');
61  $lim_leak->place(-x => 450,-y=>80);
62  $tilt_text=$top->Label(-text=>'Tilt <');
63  $tilt_text->place(-x=>380,-y=>100);
64  $lim_tilt= $top->Entry(-width => '6', -relief => 'sunken',-
    background=>'yellow');
65  $lim_tilt->place(-x => 450,-y=>100);
66  $noise_text=$top->Label(-text=>'Noise <');
67  $noise_text->place(-x=>380,-y=>120);
68  $lim_noise= $top->Entry(-width => '6', -relief => 'sunken',-
    background=>'lightblue');
69  $lim_noise->place(-x => 450,-y=>120);
70
71  #Label to show a message
72  $LabelMessage=$top->Label(-textvariable=>\$message);
73  $LabelMessage->place(-x=>6,-y=>95);
74
75  #Button to exit
76  $exitbutton=$top->Button(-text=>'Exit',-command=>sub{exit});
77  $exitbutton->place(-x=>530,-y=>155,-width=>50);
78  #######################################
79
80  #Message about the autor
81  $mensaje=$top->Label(-text=>'This software has been made by Dorian
    Oria');
82  $mensaje->place(-x=>2,-y=>145);
83
84  $email=$top->Label(-text=>'e-mail: dorian_oria@yahoo.com');
85  $email->place(-x=>63,-y=>160);
```

```perl
86
87
88   MainLoop;
89
90   #End of the construction of main window
91   ############################################
92
93   sub check_geo {
94   $onoffg="";
95   $onoffb=0;
96   $ResistanceCheckButton->configure(-state => 'active');
97   $LeakageCheckButton->configure(-state => 'active');
98   $TiltCheckButton->configure(-state => 'active');
99   $NoiseCheckButton->configure(-state => 'active');
100  $message="You have pressed the\n Geophone option";
101  }
102
103  sub impbox {
104  $onoffg=0;
105  $onoffb="";
106  $ResistanceCheckButton->configure(-state => 'disable');
107  $LeakageCheckButton->configure(-state => 'disable');
108  $TiltCheckButton->configure(-state => 'disable');
109  $NoiseCheckButton->configure(-state => 'disable');
110  $message="You have pressed the\n Box option";
111  }
112
113  sub Resistance {
114  if ($valorR==1) {
115   $ResistanceCheckButton->configure(-fg=>'darkgreen');
116   $SelMesR="Selected Resistance";
117  }
118  if ($valorR==0) {
119   $ResistanceCheckButton->configure(-fg=>'black');
120   $SelMesR="Unselected Resistance";
121  }
122  }
123
124  sub Leakage {
125  if ($valorL==1) {
126   $LeakageCheckButton->configure(-fg=>'darkgreen');
127   $SelMesL="Selected Leakage";
128  }
```

Advanced programming in Perl for Beginners.

```
129   if ($valorL==0) {
130   $LeakageCheckButton->configure(-fg=>'black');
131     $SelMesL="Unselected Leakage";
132   }
133   }
134
135   sub Tilt {
136   if ($valorT==1) {
137     $TiltCheckButton->configure(-fg=>'darkgreen');
138     $SelMesT="Selected Tilt";
139   }
140   if ($valorT==0) {
141     $TiltCheckButton->configure(-fg=>'black');
142     $SelMesT="Unselected Tilt";
143   }
144   }
145
146   sub Noise {
147   if ($valorN==1) {
148     $NoiseCheckButton->configure(-fg=>'darkgreen');
149     $SelMesN="Selected Noise";
150   }
151   if ($valorN==0) {
152     $NoiseCheckButton->configure(-fg=>'black');
153     $SelMesN="Unselected Noise";
154   }
155   }
```

The next figure is the output of this script.

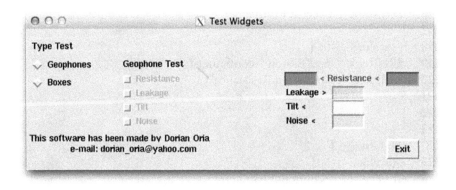

Figure 7.12. Output of Script 7.6.

The difference between this and the previous one is between lines 51 to 69, where every Entry widget is added. For every Entry, we have added a label, indicating what value it represents. These values can be introduced directly from the user or can be read from a file. In this case, the values will be introduced by the user.

Practically the construction of all the widgets is very similar. There are several exceptions, depending on the expected behaviour, but many of them have similar characteristics. As you can see, we have defined background color, width and relief. Remember that for more details you can consult the help that comes with Perl.

However, we will make a comment about Entry widgets. Let's take as an example the Entry of the variable leakage. The name of the Entry widget is $lim_leak (line 60) But as a value, this cannot be used in any calculus into the script. To make this possible there are two options:

- Use the instruction get, in order to extract the value from the widget
- When creating the widget, use the option -textvariable=>\$variable

Examples:

For the first case, to get the value from the widget we would use the following instruction:

$value_of_leakage_limit=$lim_leak->get;

For the second case, we would have to change line 60 for:

$lim_leak= $top->Entry(-width => '6', -relief => 'sunken',-background=>'lightgreen',-textvariable=>\$value_of_leakage_limit);

Later, when the script becomes more complicated, we will see how we can use the values introduced via Entry widgets.

7.7 Listbox.

This is a practical way to offer the user a lot of options to take into account in the script, in comparison with Checkbutton and Radiobutton widgets. For example, if you want to choose the model of a car you like, communities where you can be registered on the Internet, the range of salary, etc. This widget allows the possibility to choose one or more options at a glance (it can be designed in this way).

Advanced programming in Perl for Beginners.

In the next example, we will change the Checkbuttons for a Listbox.

```
1   use Tk;
2   use Tk::Radiobutton;
3   use Tk::Listbox;
4
5   #This variables make that no radiobutton is selected
6   $onoffg=0;
7   $onoffb=0;
8
9   #Construction of the main window
10  my $top = new MainWindow(-title=>'Test Widgets');
11  $top->configure(-width=>570);
12  $top->configure(-height=>300);
13  $top->resizable(0,0);
14
15  $labelTypeTest=$top->Label(-text=>'Type Test');
16  $labelTypeTest->place(-x=>6,-y=>15);
17
18  #Radiobuttons
19  $geo=$top->Radiobutton(-command=>sub{&check_geo},-
    selectcolor=>'lightgreen',-text=>'Geophones',-variable=>\$onoffg);#,-
    value=>0);
20  $geo->place(-x=>6,-y=>40);
21
22  $box=$top->Radiobutton(-command=>sub{&impbox},-
    selectcolor=>'lightgreen',-text=>'Boxes',-variable=>\$onoffb);
23  $box->place(-x=>6,-y=>65);
24  #####################################
25
26  #Listbox
27  $TestListbox=$top->Listbox(-selectmode =>'multiple',-height=>4,-
    bg=>'darkgreen',-fg=>'yellow');
28  $TestListbox->insert('end','Resistance',"Leakage","Tilt","Noise");
29  $TestListbox->configure(-state=>'disabled');
30  $TestListbox->place(-x=>170,-y=>40);
31
32  #####################################
33
34  #Text boxes with cut values for geophones
35  $res_text=$top->Label(-text=>'< Resistance <',-
    foreground=>'darkgreen');
```

```
36   $res_text->place(-x=>390,-y=>60);
37   $lim_inf = $top->Entry(-width => '6', -relief => 'sunken',-
     background=>'red');
38   $lim_inf->place(-x => 330,-y=>60);
39   $lim_sup=$top->Entry(-width => '6', -relief => 'sunken',-
     background=>'red');
40   $lim_sup->place(-x => 490,-y=>60);
41   $leak_tetxt=$top->Label(-text=>'Leakage >');
42   $leak_tetxt->place(-x=>330,-y=>80);
43   $lim_leak= $top->Entry(-width => '6', -relief => 'sunken',-
     background=>'lightgreen');
44   $lim_leak->place(-x => 400,-y=>80);
45   $tilt_text=$top->Label(-text=>'Tilt <');
46   $tilt_text->place(-x=>330,-y=>100);
47   $lim_tilt= $top->Entry(-width => '6', -relief => 'sunken',-
     background=>'yellow');
48   $lim_tilt->place(-x => 400,-y=>100);
49   $noise_text=$top->Label(-text=>'Noise <');
50   $noise_text->place(-x=>330,-y=>120);
51   $lim_noise= $top->Entry(-width => '6', -relief => 'sunken',-
     background=>'lightblue');
52   $lim_noise->place(-x => 400,-y=>120);
53
54   #Label to show a message
55   $LabelMessage=$top->Label(-textvariable=>\$message);
56   $LabelMessage->place(-x=>2,-y=>95);
57
58   #Label to show the selected test
59   $SelectedTestLabelMessage=$top->Label(-
     textvariable=>\$SelectedTestMessage,-justify=>'left');
60   $SelectedTestLabelMessage->place(-x=>180,-y=>140);
61
62   #Button Enter
63   $EnterButton=$top->Button(-text=>'Enter',-
     command=>sub{&ShowMessage});
64   $EnterButton->place(-x=>440,-y=>260,-width=>50);
65
66   #Button to exit
67   $exitbutton=$top->Button(-text=>'Exit',-command=>sub{exit});
68   $exitbutton->place(-x=>500,-y=>260,-width=>50);
69   ########################################
70
71   #Message about the autor
```

```
72   $mensaje=$top->Label(-text=>'This software has been made by Dorian
     Oria');
73   $mensaje->place(-x=>2,-y=>235);
74
75   $email=$top->Label(-text=>'e-mail: dorian_oria@yahoo.com');
76   $email->place(-x=>63,-y=>250);
77
78
79   MainLoop;
80
81   #End of the construction of main window
82   ##############################################
83
84   sub check_geo {
85   $onoffg="";
86   $onoffb=0;
87   $TestListbox->configure(-state=>'normal');
88   $message="You have pressed the\n Geophone option";
89
90   }
91
92   sub impbox {
93   $onoffg=0;
94   $onoffb="";
95   $TestListbox->configure(-state=>'disabled');
96   $message="You have pressed the\n Box option";
97   }
98
99   sub ShowMessage {
100  $SelectedTestMessage1="You have selected the following tests:\n";
101  $SelectedTestMessage2="";
102  @NSelectedTest=$TestListbox->curselection;
103  $length=@NSelectedTest;
104  for ($i=0;$i<$length;$i++) {
105    $SelectedTest[$i]=$TestListbox->get($NSelectedTest[$i]);
106    $SelectedTestMessage2=$SelectedTestMessage2."$SelectedTest[$i]\n";
107  }
108  $SelectedTestMessage=$SelectedTestMessage1.$SelectedTestMessage2;
109  }
```

The window shown in figure 7.13 comes up after running this script.

Such as the last widgets, because this is based on the previous one, we will discuss only the changes. As you can see, the script is smaller. In fact, practically in the definition of the Checkbuttons we invested 24 lines, comparing with 5 defining the Listbox.

The construction of the Listbox starts in line 27:

$TestListbox=$top->Listbox(-selectmode =>'multiple',-height=>4,-bg=>'darkgreen',

-fg=>'yellow');

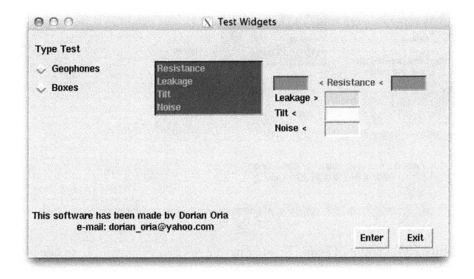

Figure 7.13. Output of Script 7.7.

An interesting property with Listboxes is the option **-selectedmode**. In this case we assign the option 'multiple', but it can be single, browse and extended. This last one works in a similar way to the option 'multiple'. The difference is that, in order to be able to select more than one option, it is necessary to use the key Control (Ctrl from keyboard) or Shift. The options single and browse (default option) have a similar behavior. Only for illustration we have changed the background and the foreground color of the widget. The foreground affects the color of the font before every option is selected.

When the script is run, the Listbox is disabled. It is necessary to add the options (line 28), before activating this property (line 29). Something that you must not

Advanced programming in Perl for Beginners.

forget is that, in order for the widget to be visible in the window, it must be inserted (line 30). Remember that you can use the **pack** option, but I mentioned earlier I do not like this option because it makes the position of the widget very difficult to handle, at least for me. Instead, I prefer to use **place**.

To enable the use of the Listbox, in execution time you must select the option 'Geophones'. The application will look as shown in Figure 7.14.

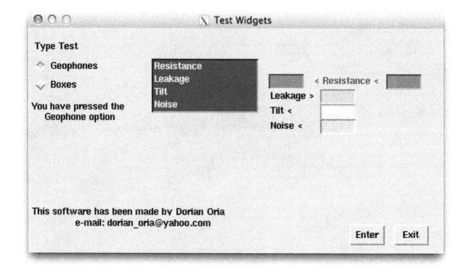

Figure 7.14. Output of Script 7.7, after having selected the option 'Geophones'.

In line 59 we have added an additional label, to indicate the tests that have been selected. The message that will show the content of this label is named $SelectedTestMessage.

Because the widget Listbox does not have the option -command, we have added an additional Button in line 63. After having selected the tests, press this button and the message $SelectedTestMessage is built (Figure 7.15). This happens in the subroutine **ShowMessage** (line 99), which is invoked from the button 'Enter' in line 63.

In this subroutine we have used two additional variables before to build $SelectedTestMessage. These variables are $SelectedTestMessage1 and $SelectedTestMessage2 (lines 100 and 101). Because $SelectedTestMessage2 depends on the selected tests, it is initialized empty ("").

In line 102 we are using the method **curselection** that returns a list containing the numerical indexes of all of the elements in the Listbox that are currently selected. This list can be stored into an array, in this case called @NselectedTest.

In line 103, the instruction

$length=@NSelectedTest;

gets the size of the array. This will allow controlling the next 'for' structure of control. In this structure finally the variable $SelectedTestMessage2 will be constructed.

Finally, in line 108 the definitive message $SelectedTestMessage is constructed, using the concatenation operator (.). In this case, the final message is the concatenation between $SelectedTestMessage1 and $SelectedTestMessage2.

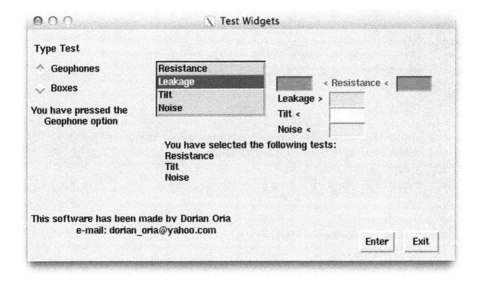

Figure 7.15. Output of Script 7.7, after having selected several tests from the List box.

7.7.1 Tied Interface (Listbox).

This widget can also be tied to a scalar or array variable, with different behavior depending on the variable type. The following code is based on the previous one.

```
1   use Tk;
2   use Tk::Radiobutton;
3   use Tk::Listbox;
4
5   #This variables make that no radiobutton is selected
6   $onoffg=0;
7   $onoffb=0;
8
9   #Construction of the main window
10  my $top = new MainWindow(-title=>'Test Widgets');
11  $top->configure(-width=>570);
12  $top->configure(-height=>300);
13  $top->resizable(0,0);
14
15  $labelTypeTest=$top->Label(-text=>'Type Test');
16  $labelTypeTest->place(-x=>6,-y=>15);
17
18  #Radiobuttons
19  $geo=$top->Radiobutton(-command=>sub{&check_geo},-
    selectcolor=>'lightgreen',-text=>'Geophones',-variable=>\$onoffg);#,-
    value=>0);
20  $geo->place(-x=>6,-y=>40);
21
22  $box=$top->Radiobutton(-command=>sub{&impbox},-
    selectcolor=>'lightgreen',-text=>'Boxes',-variable=>\$onoffb);
23  $box->place(-x=>6,-y=>65);
24  ##########################################
25
26  #Listbox
27  $TestListbox=$top->Listbox(-selectmode =>'multiple',-height=>4,-
    bg=>'darkgreen',-fg=>'yellow');
28  $TestListbox->insert('end','Resistance',"Leakage","Tilt","Noise");
29  tie @Array,"Tk::Listbox",$TestListbox;
30  @Array=sort(@Array);
31  $TestListbox->configure(-state=>'disabled');
32  $TestListbox->place(-x=>170,-y=>40);
33
34  ##########################################
35
36  #Text boxes with cut values for geophones
37  $res_text=$top->Label(-text=>'< Resistance <',-
    foreground=>'darkgreen');
```

```perl
38  $res_text->place(-x=>390,-y=>60);
39  $lim_inf = $top->Entry(-width => '6', -relief => 'sunken',-
    background=>'red');
40  $lim_inf->place(-x => 330,-y=>60);
41  $lim_sup=$top->Entry(-width => '6', -relief => 'sunken',-
    background=>'red');
42  $lim_sup->place(-x => 490,-y=>60);
43  $leak_tetxt=$top->Label(-text=>'Leakage >');
44  $leak_tetxt->place(-x=>330,-y=>80);
45  $lim_leak= $top->Entry(-width => '6', -relief => 'sunken',-
    background=>'lightgreen');
46  $lim_leak->place(-x => 400,-y=>80);
47  $tilt_text=$top->Label(-text=>'Tilt <');
48  $tilt_text->place(-x=>330,-y=>100);
49  $lim_tilt= $top->Entry(-width => '6', -relief => 'sunken',-
    background=>'yellow');
50  $lim_tilt->place(-x => 400,-y=>100);
51  $noise_text=$top->Label(-text=>'Noise <');
52  $noise_text->place(-x=>330,-y=>120);
53  $lim_noise= $top->Entry(-width => '6', -relief => 'sunken',-
    background=>'lightblue');
54  $lim_noise->place(-x => 400,-y=>120);
55
56  #Label to show a message
57  $LabelMessage=$top->Label(-textvariable=>\$message);
58  $LabelMessage->place(-x=>2,-y=>95);
59
60  #Label to show the selected test
61  $SelectedTestLabelMessage=$top->Label(-
    textvariable=>\$SelectedTestMessage,-justify=>'left');
62  $SelectedTestLabelMessage->place(-x=>180,-y=>140);
63
64  #Button Enter
65  $EnterButton=$top->Button(-text=>'Enter',-
    command=>sub{&ShowMessage});
66  $EnterButton->place(-x=>440,-y=>260,-width=>50);
67
68  #Button to exit
69  $exitbutton=$top->Button(-text=>'Exit',-command=>sub{exit});
70  $exitbutton->place(-x=>500,-y=>260,-width=>50);
71  ###############################################
72
73  #Message about the autor
```

```
74   $mensaje=$top->Label(-text=>'This software has been made by Dorian
     Oria');
75   $mensaje->place(-x=>2,-y=>235);
76
77   $email=$top->Label(-text=>'e-mail: dorian_oria@yahoo.com');
78   $email->place(-x=>63,-y=>250);
79
80   MainLoop;
81
82   #End of the construction of main window
83   ###############################################
84
85   sub check_geo {
86   $onoffg="";
87   $onoffb=0;
88   $TestListbox->configure(-state=>'normal');
89   $message="You have pressed the\n Geophone option";
90   }
91
92   sub impbox {
93   $onoffg=0;
94   $onoffb="";
95   $TestListbox->configure(-state=>'disabled');
96   $message="You have pressed the\n Box option";
97   }
98
99   sub ShowMessage {
100  $SelectedTestMessage1="You have selected the following tests:\n";
101  $SelectedTestMessage2="";
102  @NSelectedTest=$TestListbox->curselection;
103  $length=@NSelectedTest;
104  for ($i=0;$i<$length;$i++) {
105  $SelectedTest[$i]=$Array[$NSelectedTest[$i]];
106  $SelectedTestMessage2=$SelectedTestMessage2."$SelectedTest[$i]\n";
107  }
108  $SelectedTestMessage=$SelectedTestMessage1.$SelectedTestMessage2;
109  }
```

We have added the lines 29 and 30. In line 29, we have tied the array @Array to the Listbox defined by $TestListbox. This means that the content of the Listbox will be the content of @Array. But, in addition, changes in @Array will affect the content of the Listbox. In our example, we have sorted @Array in line 30. The instruction, such as it was written, sorts an array in ASCII (alphabetical) order. To sort an array in reverse ASCII (Alphabetical) order, use the following instruction:

sort {$b cmp $a} (@Array);

After running the script, the following window comes up:

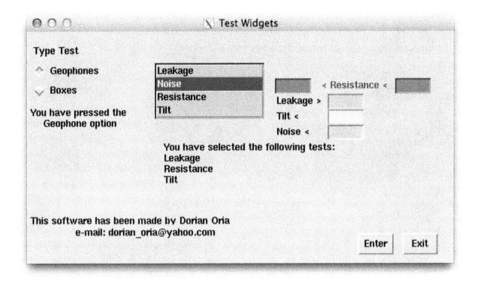

Figure 7.16. Output of Script 7.8, after having selected 3 tests.

Compare with Figure 7.15. The list in Figure 7.16 is sorted alphabetically.

In Script 7.7, we have written in line 105 the instruction

$SelectedTest[$i]=$TestListbox->get($NSelectedTest[$i]);

to build an array with the values contained into the Listbox. Now, we are using the instruction (line 105)

$SelectedTest[$i]=$Array[$NSelectedTest[$i]];

to do the same. As you can see, the difference is that we already have an array associated to the Listbox (@Array).

Advanced programming in Perl for Beginners.

7.8 Text.

Unlike the Entry widget, with this widget we can handle information with more than one line. In addition, the Entry widget is used more to handle variables and Text widget is used fundamentally to work with more information, such as messages, text files content, etc. I like this widget, because, in addition, it comes with a pre-built menu that can be invoked with the right button of the mouse. The following code is a modification of the previous one. We have added a Text widget, where we will show information of a geophone test file.

Script 7.9

```
1    use Tk;
2    use Tk::Radiobutton;
3    use Tk::Listbox;
4    use Tk::Text;
5
6    #This variables make that no radiobutton is selected
7    $onoffg=0;
8    $onoffb=0;
9    $vacio="";
10
11   #Construction of the main window
12   my $top = new MainWindow(-title=>'Test Widgtes');
13   $top->configure(-width=>550);
14   $top->configure(-height=>600);
15   #$top->resizable(0,0);
16
17   $labelTypeTest=$top->Label(-text=>'Type Test');
18   $labelTypeTest->place(-x=>6,-y=>15);
19
20   #Radiobuttons
21   $geo=$top->Radiobutton(-command=>sub{&check_geo},-
     selectcolor=>'lightgreen',-text=>'Geophones',-variable=>\$onoffg);#,-
     value=>0);
22   $geo->place(-x=>6,-y=>40);
23
24   $box=$top->Radiobutton(-command=>sub{&impbox},-
     selectcolor=>'lightgreen',-text=>'Boxes',-variable=>\$onoffb);
25   $box->place(-x=>6,-y=>65);
26   ##################################################
27
28   #Listbox
```

```
29  %options=ReturnType=>"element";
30  $TestListbox=$top->Listbox(-selectmode =>'multiple',-height=>4,-
    bg=>'darkgreen',-fg=>'yellow');
31  $TestListbox->insert('end','Resistance',"Leakage","Tilt","Noise");
32  tie @Array,"Tk::Listbox",$TestListbox;
33  @Array=sort(@Array);
34  $TestListbox->configure(-state=>'disabled');
35  $TestListbox->place(-x=>170,-y=>40);
36
37  ###############################################
38
39  #Text boxes with cut values for geophones
40  $res_text=$top->Label(-text=>'< Resistance <',-
    foreground=>'darkgreen');
41  $res_text->place(-x=>390,-y=>60);
42  $lim_inf = $top->Entry(-width => '6', -relief => 'sunken',-
    background=>'red');
43  $lim_inf->place(-x => 330,-y=>60);
44  $lim_sup=$top->Entry(-width => '6', -relief => 'sunken',-
    background=>'red');
45  $lim_sup->place(-x => 490,-y=>60);
46  $leak_tetxt=$top->Label(-text=>'Leakage >');
47  $leak_tetxt->place(-x=>330,-y=>80);
48  $lim_leak= $top->Entry(-width => '6', -relief => 'sunken',-
    background=>'lightgreen');
49  $lim_leak->place(-x => 400,-y=>80);
50  $tilt_text=$top->Label(-text=>'Tilt <');
51  $tilt_text->place(-x=>330,-y=>100);
52  $lim_tilt= $top->Entry(-width => '6', -relief => 'sunken',-
    background=>'yellow');
53  $lim_tilt->place(-x => 400,-y=>100);
54  $noise_text=$top->Label(-text=>'Noise <');
55  $noise_text->place(-x=>330,-y=>120);
56  $lim_noise= $top->Entry(-width => '6', -relief => 'sunken',-
    background=>'lightblue');
57  $lim_noise->place(-x => 400,-y=>120);
58
59  #Label to show a message
60  $LabelMessage=$top->Label(-textvariable=>\$message);
61  $LabelMessage->place(-x=>2,-y=>95);
62
63  #Label to show the selected test
64  $SelectedTestLabelMessage=$top->Label(-
```

```perl
        textvariable=>\$SelectedTestMessage,-justify=>'left');
65    $SelectedTestLabelMessage->place(-x=>180,-y=>140);
66
67    #Text widget
68    $ShowText=$top->Text(-bg=>'lightyellow');
69    $ShowText->place(-x=>2,-y=>220);
70
71    #Button Open
72    $OpenButton=$top->Button(-text=>'Open',-
        command=>sub{&OpenFile});
73    $OpenButton->place(-x=>380,-y=>570,-width=>50);
74
75    #Button Enter
76    $EnterButton=$top->Button(-text=>'Enter',-
        command=>sub{&ShowMessage});
77    $EnterButton->place(-x=>440,-y=>570,-width=>50);
78
79    #Button to exit
80    $exitbutton=$top->Button(-text=>'Exit',-command=>sub{exit});
81    $exitbutton->place(-x=>500,-y=>570,-width=>50);
82    ##############################################
83
84    #Message about the autor
85    $mensaje=$top->Label(-text=>'This software has been made by Dorian
        Oria');
86    $mensaje->place(-x=>2,-y=>185);
87
88    $email=$top->Label(-text=>'e-mail: dorian_oria@yahoo.com');
89    $email->place(-x=>63,-y=>200);
90
91
92    MainLoop;
93
94    #End of the construction of main window
95    ##############################################
96
97    sub check_geo {
98    $onoffg="";
99    $onoffb=0;
100   $TestListbox->configure(-state=>'normal');
101   $message="You have pressed the\n Geophone option";
102   }
103
```

```
104   sub impbox {
105   $onoffg=0;
106   $onoffb="";
107   $TestListbox->configure(-state=>'disabled');
108   $message="You have pressed the\n Box option";
109   }
110
111   sub ShowMessage {
112   $SelectedTestMessage1="You have selected the following tests:\n";
113   $SelectedTestMessage2="";
114   @NSelectedTest=$TestListbox->curselection;
115   $length=@NSelectedTest;
116   for ($i=0;$i<$length;$i++) {
117    $SelectedTest[$i]=$Array[$NSelectedTest[$i]];
118    $SelectedTestMessage2=$SelectedTestMessage2."$SelectedTest[$i]\n";
119   }
120   $SelectedTestMessage=$SelectedTestMessage1.$SelectedTestMessage2;
121   }
122
123   sub OpenFile {
124   my @types =
125      ( ["Test files",  ['*.geo','*.txt']],
126        ["All files",  '*.*']);
127    $resumen = $top->getOpenFile(-filetypes => \@types,-title =>"Test
      Widgets",
128    -defaultextension=>'geo');
129    $iresumen=$resumen ne $vacio;
130    if ($iresumen==1) {$TestFile=$resumen}
131    if ($iresumen!=1) {$TestFile="";}
132    $top->configure(-title=>'Test Radiobutton '.$TestFile);
133    open (IN,$TestFile);
134    $Line=<IN>;
135    while($Line) {
136     $ShowText->Insert($Line);
137     $Line=<IN>;
138    }
139    close IN;
140   }
```

Figure 7.17 shows the window that comes up after running this script.

In line 9 we have added the variable $vacio="". We will use this variable later in the script when comparing strings to know if a file has been opened or not.

Advanced programming in Perl for Beginners.

The construction of the Text widget has been made in lines 68 and 69. We have added the 'Open' button, which allows opening a geophone test file and to show its contents into the Text widget. This button was added in lines 72 and 73. After pressing this button, the window shown in Figure 7.18 comes up:

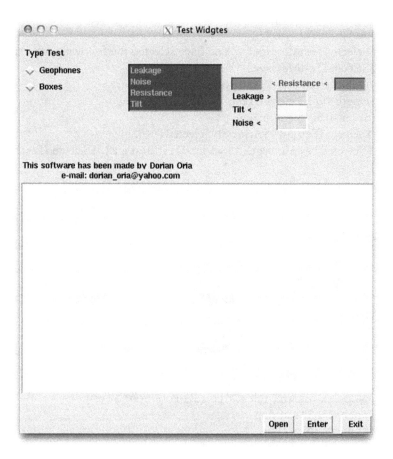

Figure 7.17. Output of Script 7.9.

This is possible because of the code in the subroutine **OpenFile**. To show this window (Figure 7.18), we have used the widget **getOpenFile**. The kind of files the program can read by default are with '.geo' or '.txt' extensions. This is defined using the variable @types in line 124. We have used the reserved word **my**, that means @types is only valid in the context of the subroutine. You can identify another variable with this name, but only out of the subroutine.

After coming up, the widget getOpenFile gives the name of the file selected (including its complete path) as a result. In line 127, we have defined the variable $resumen. In the properties of the widget, we have defined that the type of files established in the array @types, that the default extension is '.geo' and the title of the window.

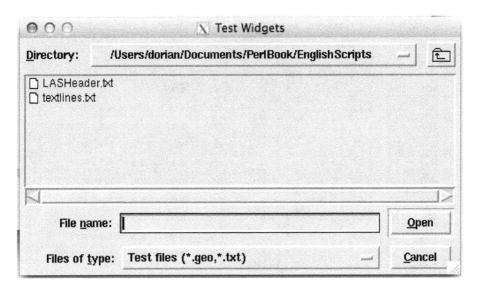

Figure 7.18. Window asking for a file to open.

One possible option is that the user does not open a file, and instead cancels the operation. Trying to anticipate this, we have added line 129. In this line, the value of $result is compared against $vacio, using the special operator "ne" (if not). This operator is used when is desired to compare two strings. If $result is empty ($result is " "), the variable $iresult takes a value other than 1. Otherwise, if the variable $result is not empty, the variable $iresult takes the value of 1. Depending on the values of $iresult, the variable $TestFile will take the value of $result or empty.

In line 132, we have added the value of the variable $TestFile to the title of the MainWindow (Figure 7.19).

Between lines 133 and 139 a geophone test file is opened, read it and its contents shown in the Text widget (Figure 7.19).

Advanced programming in Perl for Beginners.

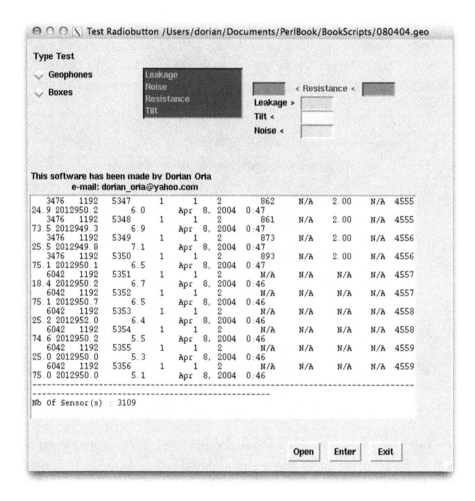

Figure 7.19. Application after opening a geophone test file.

In line 136, the lines read are inserted into the Text widget using the method 'Insert'.

The menu that can be seen in the Text widget in Figure 7.20 appears after pressing the right button of the mouse over the text widget.

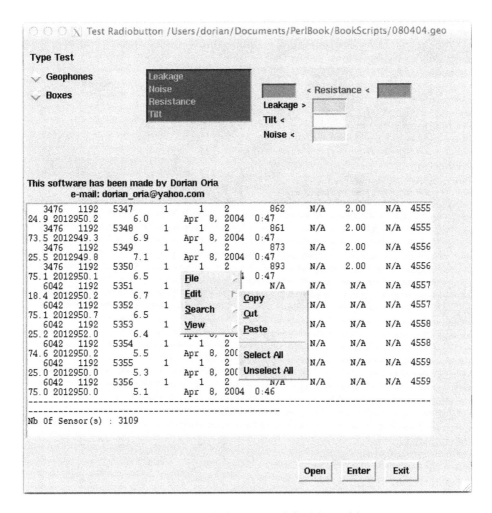

Figure 7.20. Built-in menu of the Text widget.

By default, the wrap mode to see text into the widget is 'Character' (Figure 7.21). If you select the option 'None', the text will be shown in a better way (Figure 7.22). This widget works almost like a text editor. It has some enhancements. For example, you can know what line you are in, go to the line you want, copy, paste, cut, select all, etc. Something interesting with Perl is that you must assure the Caps Lock is not activated, in order to use Ctrl+c (not C), Ctrl+x (not X) and Ctrl+v(not V). Additionally, you can use the keys Home, End, the combination Ctrl+Home, Ctrl+End, Delete, Page Up and Page Dn.

Advanced programming in Perl for Beginners.

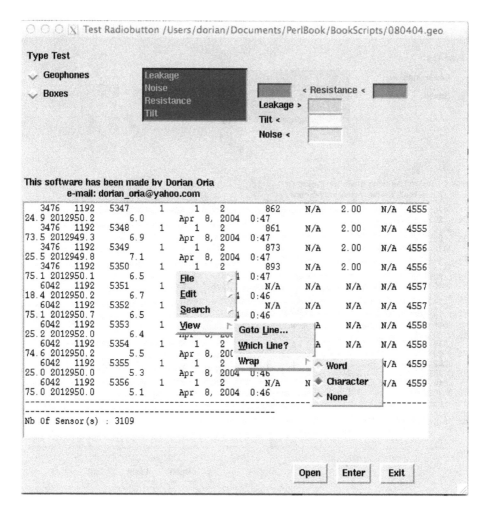

Figure 7.21. Using the built-in menu of the Text widget to change the option wrap.

If you want the text file to look like Figure 7.22, you can add the option

-wrap=>none into the script in line 68:

$ShowText=$top->Text(-bg=>'lightyellow',-wrap=>none);

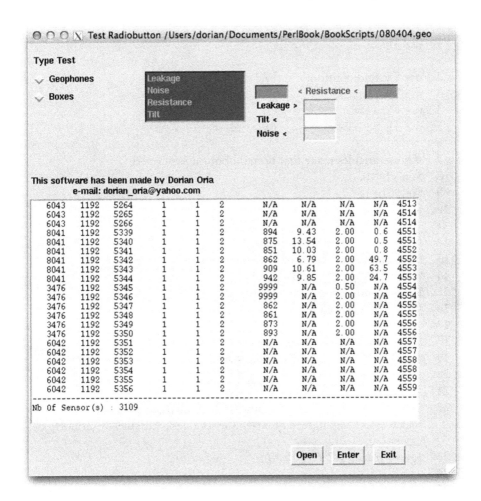

Figure 7.22. Text into the widget after using the option -wrap=>none.

7.9 Scroll bars.

This is a great moment to introduce you to the use of scrollbars. These are usually used with Listbox, Text, and Mainwindow and allow navigating into the widget, to deploy more information that can normally be contained in the widget. For example, in Figure 7.22, the text file cannot be seen completely, because the width of the widget is not enough. But, imagine that, for design reasons, we cannot make this widget any wider. We can solve this using scrollbars. The following script is based on the previous one.

```
1   use Tk;

2   use Tk::Radiobutton;
3   use Tk::Listbox;
4   use Tk::Text;
5   use Tk::Scrollbar;
6
7   #This variables make that no radiobutton is selected
8   $onoffg=0;
9   $onoffb=0;
10  $vacio="";
11
12  #Construction of the main window
13  my $top = new MainWindow(-title=>'Test Widgets');
14  $top->configure(-width=>550);
15  $top->configure(-height=>600);
16  #$top->resizable(0,0);
17
18  $labelTypeTest=$top->Label(-text=>'Type Test');
19  $labelTypeTest->place(-x=>6,-y=>15);
20
21  #Radiobuttons
22  $geo=$top->Radiobutton(-command=>sub{&check_geo},-
    selectcolor=>'lightgreen',-text=>'Geophones',-variable=>\$onoffg);#,-
    value=>0);
23  $geo->place(-x=>6,-y=>40);
24
25  $box=$top->Radiobutton(-command=>sub{&impbox},-
    selectcolor=>'lightgreen',-text=>'Boxes',-variable=>\$onoffb);
26  $box->place(-x=>6,-y=>65);
27  #############################################
28
29  #Listbox
30  %options=ReturnType=>"element";
31  $TestListbox=$top->Listbox(-selectmode =>'multiple',-height=>4,-
    bg=>'darkgreen',-fg=>'yellow');
32  $TestListbox->insert('end','Resistance',"Leakage","Tilt","Noise");
33  tie @Array,"Tk::Listbox",$TestListbox;
34  @Array=sort(@Array);
35  $TestListbox->configure(-state=>'disabled');
36  $TestListbox->place(-x=>170,-y=>40);
37
```

```perl
38
39   ##################################
40
41   #Text boxes with cut values for geophones
42   $res_text=$top->Label(-text=>'< Resistance <',-
     foreground=>'darkgreen');
43   $res_text->place(-x=>390,-y=>60);
44   $lim_inf = $top->Entry(-width => '6', -relief => 'sunken',-
     background=>'red');
45   $lim_inf->place(-x => 330,-y=>60);
46   $lim_sup=$top->Entry(-width => '6', -relief => 'sunken',-
     background=>'red');
47   $lim_sup->place(-x => 490,-y=>60);
48   $leak_tetxt=$top->Label(-text=>'Leakage >');
49   $leak_tetxt->place(-x=>330,-y=>80);
50   $lim_leak= $top->Entry(-width => '6', -relief => 'sunken',-
     background=>'lightgreen');
51   $lim_leak->place(-x => 400,-y=>80);
52   $tilt_text=$top->Label(-text=>'Tilt <');
53   $tilt_text->place(-x=>330,-y=>100);
54   $lim_tilt= $top->Entry(-width => '6', -relief => 'sunken',-
     background=>'yellow');
55   $lim_tilt->place(-x => 400,-y=>100);
56   $noise_text=$top->Label(-text=>'Noise <');
57   $noise_text->place(-x=>330,-y=>120);
58   $lim_noise= $top->Entry(-width => '6', -relief => 'sunken',-
     background=>'lightblue');
59   $lim_noise->place(-x => 400,-y=>120);
60
61   #Label to show a message
62   $LabelMessage=$top->Label(-textvariable=>\$message);
63   $LabelMessage->place(-x=>2,-y=>95);
64
65   #Label to show the selected test
66   $SelectedTestLabelMessage=$top->Label(-
     textvariable=>\$SelectedTestMessage,-justify=>'left');
67   $SelectedTestLabelMessage->place(-x=>180,-y=>140);
68
69   #Text widget
70   $ShowText=$top->Scrolled('Text',-bg=>'lightyellow',-width=>77, -
     scrollbars=>osoe,-wrap=>none);
71   $ShowText->place(-x=>2,-y=>220);
72
```

```perl
73   #Button Open
74   $OpenButton=$top->Button(-text=>'Open',-
     command=>sub{&OpenFile});
75   $OpenButton->place(-x=>380,-y=>570,-width=>50);
76
77   #Button Enter
78   $EnterButton=$top->Button(-text=>'Enter',-
     command=>sub{&ShowMessage});
79   $EnterButton->place(-x=>440,-y=>570,-width=>50);
80
81   #Button to exit
82   $exitbutton=$top->Button(-text=>'Exit',-command=>sub{exit});
83   $exitbutton->place(-x=>500,-y=>570,-width=>50);
84   ##########################################
85
86   #Message about the autor
87   $mensaje=$top->Label(-text=>'This software has been made by Dorian
     Oria');
88   $mensaje->place(-x=>2,-y=>185);
89
90   $email=$top->Label(-text=>'e-mail: dorian_oria@yahoo.com');
91   $email->place(-x=>63,-y=>200);
92
93   MainLoop;
94
95   #End of the construction of main window
96   ##########################################
97
98   sub check_geo {
99   $onoffg="";
100  $onoffb=0;
101  $TestListbox->configure(-state=>'normal');
102  $message="You have pressed the\n Geophone option";
103
104  }
105
106  sub impbox {
107  $onoffg=0;
108  $onoffb="";
109  $TestListbox->configure(-state=>'disabled');
110  $message="You have pressed the\n Box option";
111  }
112
```

```
113   sub ShowMessage {
114   $SelectedTestMessage1="You have selected the following tests:\n";
115   $SelectedTestMessage2="";
116   @NSelectedTest=$TestListbox->curselection;
117   $length=@NSelectedTest;
118   for ($i=0;$i<$length;$i++) {
119    $SelectedTest[$i]=$Array[$NSelectedTest[$i]];
120    $SelectedTestMessage2=$SelectedTestMessage2."$SelectedTest[$i]\n";
121   }
122   $SelectedTestMessage=$SelectedTestMessage1.$SelectedTestMessage2;
123   }
124
125   sub OpenFile {
126   my @types =
127      ( ["Test files",  ['*.geo','*.txt']],
128        ["All files",   '*.*']);
129     $resumen = $top->getOpenFile(-filetypes => \@types,-title =>"Test
      Widgets",
130      -defaultextension=>'geo');
131     $iresumen=$resumen ne $vacio;
132     if ($iresumen==1) {$TestFile=$resumen}
133     if ($iresumen!=1) {$TestFile="";}
134     $top->configure(-title=>'Test Radiobutton '.$TestFile);
135     open (IN,$TestFile);
136     $Line=<IN>;
137     while($Line) {
138      $ShowText->Insert($Line);
139      $Line=<IN>;
140     }
141     close IN;
142   }
```

Once this script is executed, we will be able to see the same window shown in Figure 7.17.

Usually the scrollbars do not appear until it is necessary. Later we will see why this happens.

Just like we did in the previous one, load a geophone test file (included with this book). The window will look as shown in the next figure.

Advanced programming in Perl for Beginners.

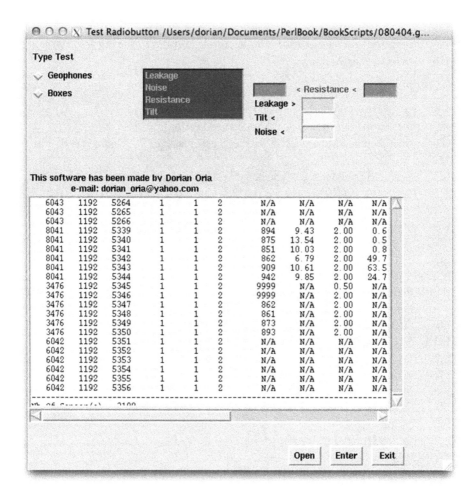

Figure 7.23. Text widget showing scrollbars.

The scrollbars will allow the user to go to the end or the beginning of the file.

Unlike the previous script, we have added line 5. This instruction invokes the use of the module necessary to use scrollbars.

In the previous one, we built the Text widget with the following instruction (line 68):

$ShowText=$top->**Text**(-bg=>'lightyellow');

In this new script, we have made a couple of changes (now in line 70):

$ShowText=$top->**Scrolled**('Text',-bg=>'lightyellow',-width=>77, - scrollbars=>osoe,-wrap=>none);

The first difference is the use of the word 'Scrolled', instead of 'Text'. Now, immediately after the first parenthesis, the word 'Text' appears. This is the name of the widget we want to 'scroll'. After that, we state some properties of the Text widget (-bg, -width, -wrap) and the position of the scrollbars. In this case, we have indicated -scrollbars=>osoe. The allowed values are: w (west), n (north), e (east), s (south) or a combination of them (for example: wn, se, s, n, etc). In our case, the letter 'o' before the permitted values indicates to Perl to show scrollbars only if it is necessary. If we do not use the letter 'o', then the scrollbars will appear immediately once the script is executed. Do the test as homework

(i.e. -scrollbars=>se).

7.10 Scale.

This widget allows creating a 'slider' widget, representing a numeric value with the Scale method. You can associate the behavior of another widget with Scale. For example, the next script, based on the previous one, put the cursor in the line specified by the Scale widget.

Script 7.11

```
1    use Tk;
2    use Tk::Radiobutton;
3    use Tk::Listbox;
4    use Tk::Text;
5    use Tk::Scrollbar;
6    use Tk::Scale;
7
8    #This variables make that no radiobutton is selected
9    $onoffg=0;
10   $onoffb=0;
11   $vacio="";
12
13   #Construction of the main window
14   my $top = new MainWindow(-title=>'Test Widgets');
15   $top->configure(-width=>550);
16   $top->configure(-height=>650);
17   $top->resizable(0,0);
18
```

```perl
19  $labelTypeTest=$top->Label(-text=>'Type Test');
20  $labelTypeTest->place(-x=>6,-y=>15);
21
22  #Radiobuttons
23  $geo=$top->Radiobutton(-command=>sub{&check_geo},-
    selectcolor=>'lightgreen',-text=>'Geophones',-variable=>\$onoffg);#,-
    value=>0);
24  $geo->place(-x=>6,-y=>40);
25
26  $box=$top->Radiobutton(-command=>sub{&impbox},-
    selectcolor=>'lightgreen',-text=>'Boxes',-variable=>\$onoffb);
27  $box->place(-x=>6,-y=>65);
28  ##########################################
29
30  #Listbox
31  %options=ReturnType=>"element";
32  $TestListbox=$top->Listbox(-selectmode =>'multiple',-height=>4,-
    bg=>'darkgreen',-fg=>'yellow');
33  $TestListbox->insert('end','Resistance',"Leakage","Tilt","Noise");
34  tie @Array,"Tk::Listbox",$TestListbox;
35  @Array=sort(@Array);
36  $TestListbox->configure(-state=>'disabled');
37  $TestListbox->place(-x=>170,-y=>40);
38
39  ##########################################
40
41  #Text boxes with cut values for geophones
42  $res_text=$top->Label(-text=>'< Resistance <',-
    foreground=>'darkgreen');
43  $res_text->place(-x=>390,-y=>60);
44  $lim_inf = $top->Entry(-width => '6', -relief => 'sunken',-
    background=>'red');
45  $lim_inf->place(-x => 330,-y=>60);
46  $lim_sup=$top->Entry(-width => '6', -relief => 'sunken',-
    background=>'red');
47  $lim_sup->place(-x => 490,-y=>60);
48  $leak_tetxt=$top->Label(-text=>'Leakage >');
49  $leak_tetxt->place(-x=>330,-y=>80);
50  $lim_leak= $top->Entry(-width => '6', -relief => 'sunken',-
    background=>'lightgreen');
51  $lim_leak->place(-x => 400,-y=>80);
52  $tilt_text=$top->Label(-text=>'Tilt <');
53  $tilt_text->place(-x=>330,-y=>100);
```

```
54  $lim_tilt= $top->Entry(-width => '6', -relief => 'sunken',-
    background=>'yellow');
55  $lim_tilt->place(-x => 400,-y=>100);
56  $noise_text=$top->Label(-text=>'Noise <');
57  $noise_text->place(-x=>330,-y=>120);
58  $lim_noise= $top->Entry(-width => '6', -relief => 'sunken',-
    background=>'lightblue');
59  $lim_noise->place(-x => 400,-y=>120);
60
61  #Label to show a message
62  $LabelMessage=$top->Label(-textvariable=>\$message);
63  $LabelMessage->place(-x=>2,-y=>95);
64
65  #Label to show the selected test
66  $SelectedTestLabelMessage=$top->Label(-
    textvariable=>\$SelectedTestMessage,-justify=>'left');
67  $SelectedTestLabelMessage->place(-x=>180,-y=>140);
68
69  #Text widget
70  $ShowText=$top->Scrolled('Text',-bg=>'lightyellow',-width=>77, -
    scrollbars=>osoe,-wrap=>none);
71  $ShowText->place(-x=>2,-y=>220);
72
73  #Button Open
74  $OpenButton=$top->Button(-text=>'Open',-
    command=>sub{&OpenFile});
75  $OpenButton->place(-x=>380,-y=>570,-width=>50);
76
77  #Button Enter
78  $EnterButton=$top->Button(-text=>'Enter',-
    command=>sub{&ShowMessage});
79  $EnterButton->place(-x=>440,-y=>570,-width=>50);
80
81  #Button to exit
82  $exitbutton=$top->Button(-text=>'Exit',-command=>sub{exit});
83  $exitbutton->place(-x=>500,-y=>570,-width=>50);
84  ##############################################
85
86  #Message about the autor
87  $mensaje=$top->Label(-text=>'This software has been made by Dorian
    Oria');
88  $mensaje->place(-x=>2,-y=>185);
89
```

```
90   $email=$top->Label(-text=>'e-mail: dorian_oria@yahoo.com');
91   $email->place(-x=>63,-y=>200);
92
93   MainLoop;
94
95   #End of the construction of main window
96   ###############################################
97
98   sub check_geo {
99   $onoffg="";
100  $onoffb=0;
101  $TestListbox->configure(-state=>'normal');
102  $message="You have pressed the\n Geophone option";
103
104  }
105
106  sub impbox {
107  $onoffg=0;
108  $onoffb="";
109  $TestListbox->configure(-state=>'disabled');
110  $message="You have pressed the\n Box option";
111  }
112
113  sub ShowMessage {
114  $SelectedTestMessage1="You have selected the following tests:\n";
115  $SelectedTestMessage2="";
116  @NSelectedTest=$TestListbox->curselection;
117  $length=@NSelectedTest;
118  for ($i=0;$i<$length;$i++) {
119   $SelectedTest[$i]=$Array[$NSelectedTest[$i]];
120   $SelectedTestMessage2=$SelectedTestMessage2."$SelectedTest[$i]\n";
121  }
122  $SelectedTestMessage=$SelectedTestMessage1.$SelectedTestMessage2;
123  }
124
125  sub OpenFile {
126  my @types =
127     ( ["Test files",  ['*.geo','*.txt']],
128       ["All files",   '*.*']);
129   $resumen = $top->getOpenFile(-filetypes => \@types,-title =>"Test
     Widgets",
130    -defaultextension=>'geo');
131   $iresumen=$resumen ne $vacio;
```

```
132    if ($iresumen==1) {$TestFile=$resumen}
133    if ($iresumen!=1) {$TestFile="";}
134    $top->configure(-title=>'Test Radiobutton '.$TestFile);
135    $lines=0;
136    open (IN,$TestFile);
137    $Line=<IN>;
138    while($Line) {
139     $lines++;
140     $ShowText->Insert($Line);
141     $Line=<IN>;
142    }
143    close IN;
144    #Scale Widget
145    $ScaleValue=1;
146    $ticks=int($lines/4);
147    $ScaleButton=$top->Scale(-orient=>'horizontal',-length=>350,-
       from=>1,-to=>$lines,-tickinterval=>$ticks,-command=>\&SelectLine,-
       showvalue=>1,-variable=>$ScaleValue);
148     $ScaleButton->place(-x=>2,-y=>570);
149    }
150
151    sub SelectLine {
152     $ShowText->SetCursor("$ScaleValue.0");
153    }
```

We have added line 6 to invoke the module responsible for this widget. Something interesting in this script is that the new widget is built during execution, after opening the geophone test file. The construction of this widget starts on line 145. We have added the variable $ScaleValue=1. This variable is associated to the widget with the property -variable (line 147). It is necessary to initialize this variable. The widget is built on line 147. Some properties used here: orientation (in our case we chose 'horizontal', the smallest and biggest value that the widget can represent (it is the same range of course for $ScaleValue and is delimited for the properties **from** and **to**), the interval between ticks (whose value is defined using the variable $ticks on line 146), the expected behaviour every time the user clicks on the widget (-command=>sub{SelectLine}).

The subroutine SelectLine only has one instruction. When the user presses the Scale widget, the cursor will be located on the line whose number will be the same as the value of $ScaleValue (this happens in the Text widget).

Advanced programming in Perl for Beginners.

After executing the script and having opened the file, you will see the window as shown in figure 7.24.

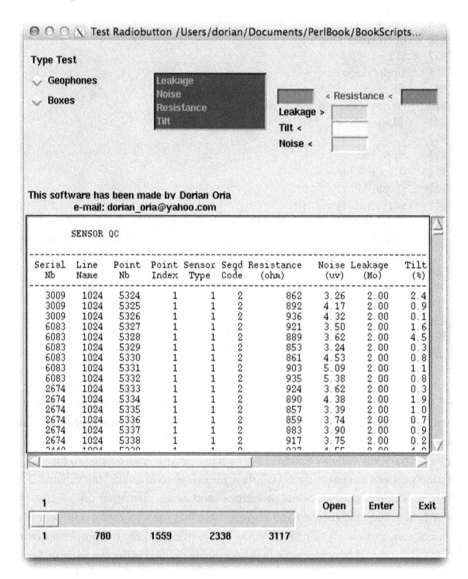

Figure 7.24 Output of Script 7.11, after having opened a geophone test file.

In this case, one perceptible difference is that we are seeing the file from the beginning. This is because we assign $ScaleValue=1 as the initial value. Then, in the subroutine SelectLine, there is an instruction that locates the cursor in the value given by $ScaleValue, in this case, in position 1.0. This means in, Perl/Tk notation, line 1, character 0.

Once the file is displayed, you can see the Scale widget. Click on the Text Widget and you will see the cursor blinking.

7.11 Menubutton.

So far, we have been using buttons in our Main Window. Usually, the programs have two or more options to access their functions: tool bars or menus. With this widget, we will add menus to our program.

Script 7.12

```
1   use Tk;
2   use Tk::Radiobutton;
3   use Tk::Listbox;
4   use Tk::Text;
5   use Tk::Scrollbar;
6   use Tk::Scale;
7   use Tk::Menubutton;
8
9   #This variables make that no radiobutton is selected
10  $onoffg=0;
11  $onoffb=0;
12  $vacio="";
13
14  #Construction of the main window
15  my $top = new MainWindow(-title=>'Test Widgets');
16  $top->configure(-width=>550);
17  $top->configure(-height=>650);
18  $top->resizable(0,0);
19
20  $labelTypeTest=$top->Label(-text=>'Type Test');
21  $labelTypeTest->place(-x=>6,-y=>30);
22
23  #Radiobuttons
24  $geo=$top->Radiobutton(-command=>sub{&check_geo},-
    selectcolor=>'lightgreen',-text=>'Geophones',-variable=>\$onoffg);#,-
    value=>0);
25  $geo->place(-x=>6,-y=>50);
26
27  $box=$top->Radiobutton(-command=>sub{&impbox},-
```

```
     selectcolor=>'lightgreen',-text=>'Boxes',-variable=>\$onoffb);
28   $box->place(-x=>6,-y=>75);
29   ################################################
30
31   #Menu button
32   $Menu=$top->Menubutton(-text=>"Options",-tearoff => 0,-
     menuitems=>[['command'=>"Enter","-
     command"=>\&ShowMessage,"-
     underline"=>1],['command'=>"Open","-command"=>\&OpenFile,"-
     underline"=>0],['command'=>"Exit","-command"=>sub{exit},"-
     underline"=>2]]);
33   $Menu->place(-x=>0,-y=>0);
34
35   #Listbox
36   %options=ReturnType=>"element";
37   $TestListbox=$top->Listbox(-selectmode =>'multiple',-height=>4,-
     bg=>'darkgreen',-fg=>'yellow');
38   $TestListbox->insert('end','Resistance',"Leakage","Tilt","Noise");
39   tie @Array,"Tk::Listbox",$TestListbox;
40   @Array=sort(@Array);
41   $TestListbox->configure(-state=>'disabled');
42   $TestListbox->place(-x=>170,-y=>40);
43
44   ################################################
45
46   #Text boxes with cut values for geophones
47   $res_text=$top->Label(-text=>'< Resistance <',-
     foreground=>'darkgreen');
48   $res_text->place(-x=>390,-y=>60);
49   $lim_inf = $top->Entry(-width => '6', -relief => 'sunken',-
     background=>'red');
50   $lim_inf->place(-x => 330,-y=>60);
51   $lim_sup=$top->Entry(-width => '6', -relief => 'sunken',-
     background=>'red');
52   $lim_sup->place(-x => 490,-y=>60);
53   $leak_tetxt=$top->Label(-text=>'Leakage >');
54   $leak_tetxt->place(-x=>330,-y=>80);
55   $lim_leak= $top->Entry(-width => '6', -relief => 'sunken',-
     background=>'lightgreen');
56   $lim_leak->place(-x => 400,-y=>80);
57   $tilt_text=$top->Label(-text=>'Tilt <');
58   $tilt_text->place(-x=>330,-y=>100);
59   $lim_tilt= $top->Entry(-width => '6', -relief => 'sunken',-
```

```
60    background=>'yellow');
      $lim_tilt->place(-x => 400,-y=>100);
61    $noise_text=$top->Label(-text=>'Noise <');
62    $noise_text->place(-x=>330,-y=>120);
63    $lim_noise= $top->Entry(-width => '6', -relief => 'sunken',-
      background=>'lightblue');
64    $lim_noise->place(-x => 400,-y=>120);
65
66    #Label to show a message
67    $LabelMessage=$top->Label(-textvariable=>\$message);
68    $LabelMessage->place(-x=>2,-y=>95);
69
70    #Label to show the selected test
71    $SelectedTestLabelMessage=$top->Label(-
      textvariable=>\$SelectedTestMessage,-justify=>'left');
72    $SelectedTestLabelMessage->place(-x=>180,-y=>140);
73
74    #Text widget
75    $ShowText=$top->Scrolled('Text',-bg=>'lightyellow',-width=>77, -
      scrollbars=>osoe,-wrap=>none);
76    $ShowText->place(-x=>2,-y=>220);
77
78
79    #Button Open
80    $OpenButton=$top->Button(-text=>'Open',-
      command=>sub{&OpenFile});
81    $OpenButton->place(-x=>380,-y=>570,-width=>50);
82
83    #Button Enter
84    $EnterButton=$top->Button(-text=>'Enter',-
      command=>sub{&ShowMessage});
85    $EnterButton->place(-x=>440,-y=>570,-width=>50);
86
87    #Button to exit
88    $exitbutton=$top->Button(-text=>'Exit',-command=>sub{exit});
89    $exitbutton->place(-x=>500,-y=>570,-width=>50);
90    ################################################
91
92    #Message about the autor
93    $mensaje=$top->Label(-text=>'This software has been made by Dorian
      Oria');
94    $mensaje->place(-x=>2,-y=>185);
95
```

```
96    $email=$top->Label(-text=>'e-mail: dorian_oria@yahoo.com');
97    $email->place(-x=>63,-y=>200);
98
99
100   MainLoop;
101
102   #End of the construction of main window
103   ##########################################
104
105   sub check_geo {
106   $onoffg="";
107   $onoffb=0;
108   $TestListbox->configure(-state=>'normal');
109   $message="You have pressed the\n Geophone option";
110
111   }
112
113   sub impbox {
114   $onoffg=0;
115   $onoffb="";
116   $TestListbox->configure(-state=>'disabled');
117   $message="You have pressed the\n Box option";
118   }
119
120   sub ShowMessage {
121   $SelectedTestMessage1="You have selected the following tests:\n";
122   $SelectedTestMessage2="";
123   @NSelectedTest=$TestListbox->curselection;
124   $length=@NSelectedTest;
125   for ($i=0;$i<$length;$i++) {
126    $SelectedTest[$i]=$Array[$NSelectedTest[$i]];
127    $SelectedTestMessage2=$SelectedTestMessage2."$SelectedTest[$i]\n";
128   }
129   $SelectedTestMessage=$SelectedTestMessage1.$SelectedTestMessage2;
130   }
131
132   sub OpenFile {
133   my @types =
134        ( ["Test files",  ['*.geo','*.txt']],
135         ["All files",   '*.*']);
136    $resumen = $top->getOpenFile(-filetypes => \@types,-title =>"Test
      Widgets",
137    -defaultextension=>'geo');
```

```
138    $iresumen=$resumen ne $vacio;
139    if ($iresumen==1) {$TestFile=$resumen}
140    if ($iresumen!=1) {$TestFile="";}
141    $top->configure(-title=>'Test Radiobutton '.$TestFile);
142    $lines=0;
143    open (IN,$TestFile);
144    $Line=<IN>;
145  # $ShowText->selectAll;
146    while($Line) {
147     $lines++;
148     $ShowText->Insert($Line);
149     $Line=<IN>;
150    }
151    close IN;
152    #Scale Widget
153    $ScaleValue=1;
154    $ticks=int($lines/4);
155    $ScaleButton=$top->Scale(-orient=>'horizontal',-length=>350,-
       from=>1,-to=>$lines,
156            -tickinterval=>$ticks,-command=>\&SelectLine, -
       showvalue=>1,
157            -variable=>\$ScaleValue);
158     $ScaleButton->place(-x=>2,-y=>570);
159    }
160
161    sub SelectLine {
162     $ShowText->SetCursor("$ScaleValue.0");
163    }
```

This script is based on the previous one. We have added line 7 to invoke the module of Menubutton. This was added in lines 32 and 33. To ease the comprehension, we added the same functions of the buttons labelled 'Open', 'Enter' and 'Exit' to the Menubutton options. So, if you choose 'Open' in the menu (Figure 7.25), the program will perform the same task as the button 'Open'.

7.12 Optionmenu.

This widget is a compact option to Radiobuttons. If we have many options, then we may not have enough space in our window to deploy them (or esthetically it would look ugly). So, Optionmenu will occupy a portion of the space equivalent to a Button, while offering any number of options. Imagine for example, the case

Advanced programming in Perl for Beginners.

where the birth month is asked for. Imagine using twelve Radiobuttons. Instead, a more elegant way is only using one Optionmenu widget for all months. As an example, we will change the Radiobuttons in our previous script to an Optionmenu widget, as illustrated in the script 7.13.

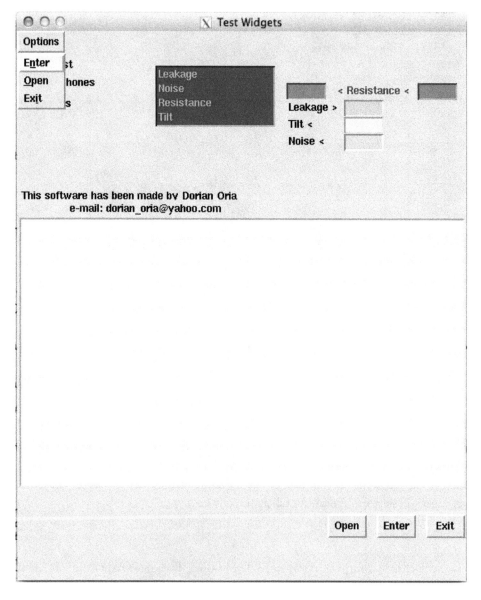

Figure 7.25. Output of Script 7.12.

```
1   use Tk;
2   use Tk::Listbox;
3   use Tk::Text;
4   use Tk::Scrollbar;
5   use Tk::Scale;
6   use Tk::Menubutton;
7   use Tk::Optionmenu;
8
9   $vacio="";
10
11  #Construction of the main window
12  my $top = new MainWindow(-title=>'Test Widgets');
13  $top->configure(-width=>550);
14  $top->configure(-height=>650);
15  $top->resizable(0,0);
16
17  $labelTypeTest=$top->Label(-text=>'Type Test');
18  $labelTypeTest->place(-x=>6,-y=>40);
19
20  #OptionMenu
21  $OptionMenu=$top->Optionmenu(-command=>sub{&TypeTest},-
    variable=>\$option,-
    options=>[[TypeTest=>1],[Geophones=>2],[Boxes=>3]]);
22  $OptionMenu->place(-x=>6,-y=>60);
23  ################################################
24
25  #Menu button
26  $Menu=$top->Menubutton(-text=>"Options",-tearoff => 0,-
    menuitems=>[['command'=>"Enter","-
    command"=>\&ShowMessage,"-
    underline"=>1],['command'=>"Open","-command"=>\&OpenFile,"-
    underline"=>0],['command'=>"Exit","-command"=>sub{exit},"-
    underline"=>2]]);
27  $Menu->place(-x=>0,-y=>0);
28
29  #Listbox
30  %options=ReturnType=>"element";
31  $TestListbox=$top->Listbox(-selectmode =>'multiple',-height=>4,-
    bg=>'darkgreen',-fg=>'yellow');
32  $TestListbox->insert('end','Resistance',"Leakage","Tilt","Noise");
33  tie @Array,"Tk::Listbox",$TestListbox;
34  @Array=sort(@Array);
```

```perl
35  $TestListbox->configure(-state=>'disabled');
36  $TestListbox->place(-x=>170,-y=>40);
37
38  ###############################################
39
40  #Text boxes with cut values for geophones
41  $res_text=$top->Label(-text=>'< Resistance <',-
    foreground=>'darkgreen');
42  $res_text->place(-x=>390,-y=>60);
43  $lim_inf = $top->Entry(-width => '6', -relief => 'sunken',-
    background=>'red');
44  $lim_inf->place(-x => 330,-y=>60);
45  $lim_sup=$top->Entry(-width => '6', -relief => 'sunken',-
    background=>'red');
46  $lim_sup->place(-x => 490,-y=>60);
47  $leak_tetxt=$top->Label(-text=>'Leakage >');
48  $leak_tetxt->place(-x=>330,-y=>80);
49  $lim_leak= $top->Entry(-width => '6', -relief => 'sunken',-
    background=>'lightgreen');
50  $lim_leak->place(-x => 400,-y=>80);
51  $tilt_text=$top->Label(-text=>'Tilt <');
52  $tilt_text->place(-x=>330,-y=>100);
53  $lim_tilt= $top->Entry(-width => '6', -relief => 'sunken',-
    background=>'yellow');
54  $lim_tilt->place(-x => 400,-y=>100);
55  $noise_text=$top->Label(-text=>'Noise <');
56  $noise_text->place(-x=>330,-y=>120);
57  $lim_noise= $top->Entry(-width => '6', -relief => 'sunken',-
    background=>'lightblue');
58  $lim_noise->place(-x => 400,-y=>120);
59
60  #Label to show a message
61  $LabelMessage=$top->Label(-textvariable=>\$message);
62  $LabelMessage->place(-x=>2,-y=>95);
63
64  #Label to show the selected test
65  $SelectedTestLabelMessage=$top->Label(-
    textvariable=>\$SelectedTestMessage,-justify=>'left');
66  $SelectedTestLabelMessage->place(-x=>180,-y=>140);
67
68  #Text widget
69  $ShowText=$top->Scrolled('Text',-bg=>'lightyellow',-width=>77, -
    scrollbars=>osoe,-wrap=>none);
```

```
70  $ShowText->place(-x=>2,-y=>220);
71
72
73  #Button Open
74  $OpenButton=$top->Button(-text=>'Open',-
    command=>sub{&OpenFile});
75  $OpenButton->place(-x=>380,-y=>570,-width=>50);
76
77  #Button Enter
78  $EnterButton=$top->Button(-text=>'Enter',-
    command=>sub{&ShowMessage});
79  $EnterButton->place(-x=>440,-y=>570,-width=>50);
80
81  #Button to exit
82  $exitbutton=$top->Button(-text=>'Exit',-command=>sub{exit});
83  $exitbutton->place(-x=>500,-y=>570,-width=>50);
84  ##############################################
85
86  #Message about the autor
87  $mensaje=$top->Label(-text=>'This software has been made by Dorian
    Oria');
88  $mensaje->place(-x=>2,-y=>185);
89
90  $email=$top->Label(-text=>'e-mail: dorian_oria@yahoo.com');
91  $email->place(-x=>63,-y=>200);
92
93  MainLoop;
94
95  #End of the construction of main window
96  ##############################################
97
98  sub check_geo {
99  $TestListbox->configure(-state=>'normal');
100 $message="You have pressed the\n Geophone option";
101 }
102
103 sub impbox {
104 $TestListbox->configure(-state=>'disabled');
105 $message="You have pressed the\n Box option";
106 }
107
108 sub ShowMessage {
109 $SelectedTestMessage1="You have selected the following tests:\n";
```

```perl
110    $SelectedTestMessage2="";
111    @NSelectedTest=$TestListbox->curselection;
112    $length=@NSelectedTest;
113    for ($i=0;$i<$length;$i++) {
114     $SelectedTest[$i]=$Array[$NSelectedTest[$i]];
115     $SelectedTestMessage2=$SelectedTestMessage2."$SelectedTest[$i]\n";
116    }
117    $SelectedTestMessage=$SelectedTestMessage1.$SelectedTestMessage2;
118    }
119
120    sub OpenFile {
121    my @types =
122       ( ["Test files",  ['*.geo','*.txt']],
123         ["All files",   '*.*']);
124     $resumen = $top->getOpenFile(-filetypes => \@types,-title =>"Test
       Widgets",
125     -defaultextension=>'geo');
126     $iresumen=$resumen ne $vacio;
127     if ($iresumen==1) {$TestFile=$resumen}
128     if ($iresumen!=1) {$TestFile="";}
129     $top->configure(-title=>'Test Radiobutton '.$TestFile);
130     $lines=0;
131     open (IN,$TestFile);
132     $Line=<IN>;
133     while($Line) {
134      $lines++;
135      $ShowText->Insert($Line);
136      $Line=<IN>;
137     }
138     close IN;
139     #Scale Widget
140     $ScaleValue=1;
141     $ticks=int($lines/4);
142     $ScaleButton=$top->Scale(-orient=>'horizontal',-length=>350,-
       from=>1,-to=>$lines,
143             -tickinterval=>$ticks,-command=>\&SelectLine, -
       showvalue=>1,
144             -variable=>\$ScaleValue);
145     $ScaleButton->place(-x=>2,-y=>570);
146    }
147
148    sub SelectLine {
149     $ShowText->SetCursor("$ScaleValue.0");
```

```
150  }
151
152  sub TypeTest {
153  if ($option==2) {
154   &check_geo;
155  }
156  if ($option==3) {
157   &impbox;
158  }
159  }
```

The Optionmenu was added on lines 21 and 22. We have tried to mimic the same behaviour as Radiobuttons. In this case, the possible options are 'Geophones' and 'Boxes'. Notice that every option in the widget has a number associated. The first one is really a message, to avoid the option 'Geophones' appearing immediately once the script is executed. The variable $option will retrieve the value of the selected option, so it is possible to use it as a condition to do a task. To avoid big changes, we added the subroutine **TypeTest** (line 152). Depending on the value of $option, the subroutine check_geo or impbox will be executed. Because we eliminate the Radiobuttons in this script, we eliminated the variables that controlled their behaviours ($onoffg and $onoffb). After you run it, you will see the window shown in Figure 7.26. The application will show a similar behaviour to the previous one, when we used Radiobuttons.

7.13 Labframe.

This widget allows creating a frame for enclosing other widgets. There is another one called Frame, but I like LabFrame because in addition it also allows using a label for the widget. Usually a Frame is used to enclose widgets that are related and helps to improve the design and appearance of the application. For example, gender and type of test (Radiobuttons), soccer teams and option tests (Checkbuttons), etc. The following script is based on the previous one, but we will go back to Radiobuttons and we will enclose them into a LabFrame.

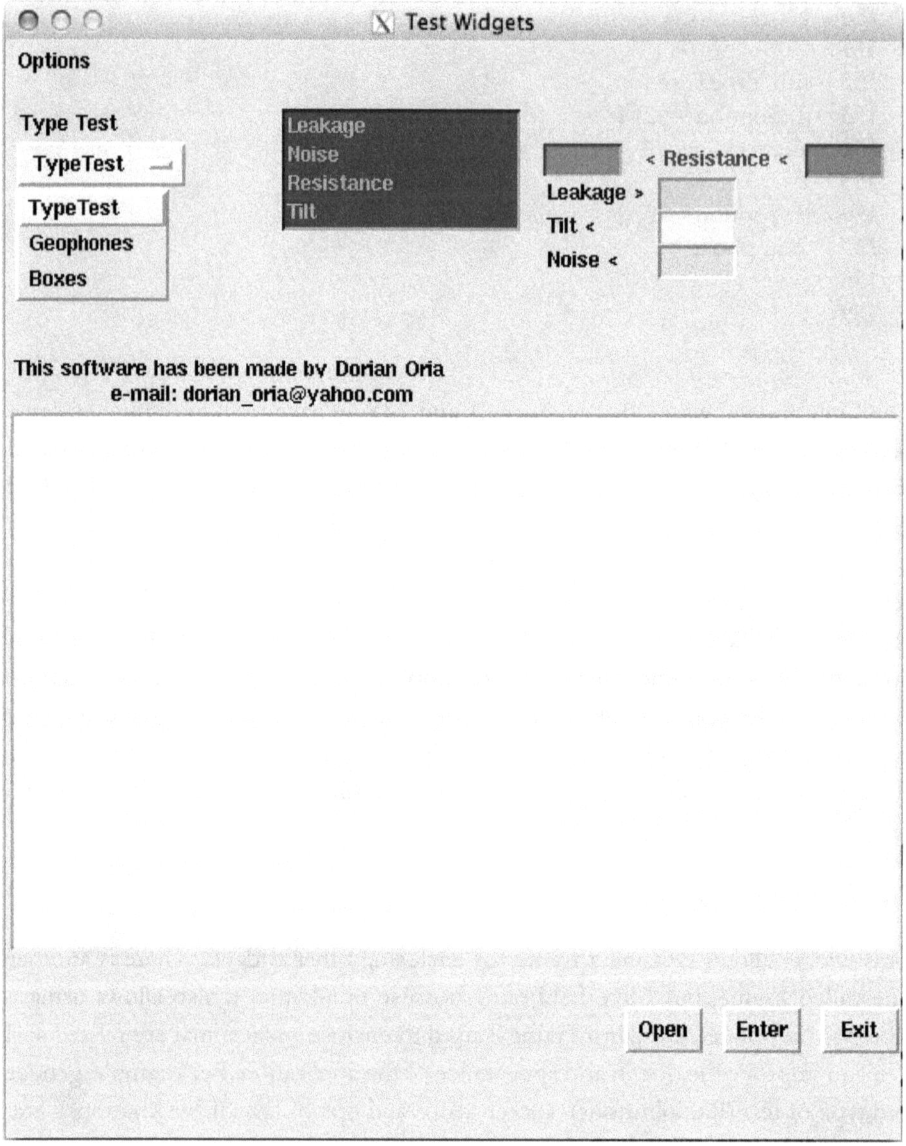

Figure 7.26. Output of Script 7.13.

Script 7.14

```
use Tk;
use Tk::Radiobutton;
use Tk::Listbox;
use Tk::Text;
```

```perl
5   use Tk::Scrollbar;
6   use Tk::Scale;
7   use Tk::Menubutton;
8   use Tk::LabFrame;
9
10  #This variables make that no radiobutton is selected
11  $onoffg=0;
12  $onoffb=0;
13  $vacio="";
14
15  #Construction of the main window
16  my $top = new MainWindow(-title=>'Test RadioButton');
17  $top->configure(-width=>550);
18  $top->configure(-height=>650);
19  $top->resizable(0,0);
20
21  #LabFrame
22  $Frame=$top->LabFrame(-label=>"Type Test",-
    labelside=>"acrosstop",-width=>90,-height=>40);
23  $Frame->place(-x=>6,-y=>20);
24
25  #Radiobuttons
26  $geo=$Frame->Radiobutton(-command=>sub{&check_geo},-
    selectcolor=>'lightgreen',-text=>'Geophones',-variable=>\$onoffg);#,-
    value=>0);
27  $geo->place(-x=>0,-y=>0);
28
29  $box=$Frame->Radiobutton(-command=>sub{&impbox},-
    selectcolor=>'lightgreen',-text=>'Boxes',-variable=>\$onoffb);
30  $box->place(-x=>0,-y=>20);
31  ##############################################
32
33  #Menu button
34  $Menu=$top->Menubutton(-text=>"Options",-tearoff => 0,-
    menuitems=>[['command'=>"Enter","-
    command"=>\&ShowMessage,"-
    underline"=>1],['command'=>"Open","-command"=>\&OpenFile,"-
    underline"=>0],['command'=>"Exit","-command"=>sub{exit},"-
    underline"=>2]]);
35  $Menu->place(-x=>0,-y=>0);
36
37  #Listbox
38  %options=ReturnType=>"element";
```

```
39   $TestListbox=$top->Listbox(-selectmode =>'multiple',-height=>4,-
     bg=>'darkgreen',-fg=>'yellow');
40   $TestListbox->insert('end','Resistance',"Leakage","Tilt","Noise");
41   tie @Array,"Tk::Listbox",$TestListbox;
42   @Array=sort(@Array);
43   $TestListbox->configure(-state=>'disabled');
44   $TestListbox->place(-x=>120,-y=>40);
45
46   ################################################
47
48   #Text boxes with cut values for geophones
49   $res_text=$top->Label(-text=>'< Resistance <',-
     foreground=>'darkgreen');
50   $res_text->place(-x=>390,-y=>60);
51   $lim_inf = $top->Entry(-width => '6', -relief => 'sunken',-
     background=>'red');
52   $lim_inf->place(-x => 330,-y=>60);
53   $lim_sup=$top->Entry(-width => '6', -relief => 'sunken',-
     background=>'red');
54   $lim_sup->place(-x => 490,-y=>60);
55   $leak_tetxt=$top->Label(-text=>'Leakage >');
56   $leak_tetxt->place(-x=>330,-y=>80);
57   $lim_leak= $top->Entry(-width => '6', -relief => 'sunken',-
     background=>'lightgreen');
58   $lim_leak->place(-x => 400,-y=>80);
59   $tilt_text=$top->Label(-text=>'Tilt <');
60   $tilt_text->place(-x=>330,-y=>100);
61   $lim_tilt= $top->Entry(-width => '6', -relief => 'sunken',-
     background=>'yellow');
62   $lim_tilt->place(-x => 400,-y=>100);
63   $noise_text=$top->Label(-text=>'Noise <');
64   $noise_text->place(-x=>330,-y=>120);
65   $lim_noise= $top->Entry(-width => '6', -relief => 'sunken',-
     background=>'lightblue');
66   $lim_noise->place(-x => 400,-y=>120);
67
68   #Label to show a message
69   $LabelMessage=$top->Label(-textvariable=>\$message);
70   $LabelMessage->place(-x=>2,-y=>95);
71
72   #Label to show the selected test
73   $SelectedTestLabelMessage=$top->Label(-
     textvariable=>\$SelectedTestMessage,-justify=>'left');
```

```
74    $SelectedTestLabelMessage->place(-x=>180,-y=>140);
75
76    #Text widget
77    $ShowText=$top->Scrolled('Text',-bg=>'lightyellow',-width=>77, -
      scrollbars=>osoe,-wrap=>none);
78    $ShowText->place(-x=>2,-y=>220);
79
80    #Button Open
81    $OpenButton=$top->Button(-text=>'Open',-
      command=>sub{&OpenFile});
82    $OpenButton->place(-x=>380,-y=>570,-width=>50);
83
84    #Button Enter
85    $EnterButton=$top->Button(-text=>'Enter',-
      command=>sub{&ShowMessage});
86    $EnterButton->place(-x=>440,-y=>570,-width=>50);
87
88    #Button to exit
89    $exitbutton=$top->Button(-text=>'Exit',-command=>sub{exit});
90    $exitbutton->place(-x=>500,-y=>570,-width=>50);
91    ##############################################
92
93    #Message about the autor
94    $mensaje=$top->Label(-text=>'This software has been made by Dorian
      Oria');
95    $mensaje->place(-x=>2,-y=>185);
96
97    $email=$top->Label(-text=>'e-mail: dorian_oria@yahoo.com');
98    $email->place(-x=>63,-y=>200);
99
100   MainLoop;
101
102   #End of the construction of main window
103   ##############################################
104
105   sub check_geo {
106   $onoffg="";
107   $onoffb=0;
108   $TestListbox->configure(-state=>'normal');
109   $message="You have pressed the\n Geophone option";
110   }
111
112   sub impbox {
```

```
113    $onoffg=0;
114    $onoffb="";
115    $TestListbox->configure(-state=>'disabled');
116    $message="You have pressed the\n Box option";
117    }
118
119    sub ShowMessage {
120    $SelectedTestMessage1="You have selected the following tests:\n";
121    $SelectedTestMessage2="";
122    @NSelectedTest=$TestListbox->curselection;
123    $length=@NSelectedTest;
124    for ($i=0;$i<$length;$i++) {
125     $SelectedTest[$i]=$Array[$NSelectedTest[$i]];
126     $SelectedTestMessage2=$SelectedTestMessage2."$SelectedTest[$i]\n";
127    }
128    $SelectedTestMessage=$SelectedTestMessage1.$SelectedTestMessage2;
129    }
130
131    sub OpenFile {
132    my @types =
133       ( ["Test files",  ['*.geo','*.txt']],
134        ["All files",  '*.*']);
135     $resumen = $top->getOpenFile(-filetypes => \@types,-title =>"Test
       Radiobutton",
136     -defaultextension=>'geo');
137     $iresumen=$resumen ne $vacio;
138     if ($iresumen==1) {$TestFile=$resumen}
139     if ($iresumen!=1) {$TestFile="";}
140     $top->configure(-title=>'Test Radiobutton '.$TestFile);
141     $lines=0;
142     open (IN,$TestFile);
143     $Line=<IN>;
144     while($Line) {
145     $lines++;
146     $ShowText->Insert($Line);
147     $Line=<IN>;
148     }
149     close IN;
150     #Scale Widget
151     $ScaleValue=1;
152     $ticks=int($lines/4);
153     $ScaleButton=$top->Scale(-orient=>'horizontal',-length=>350,-
       from=>1,-to=>$lines,
```

```
154           -tickinterval=>$ticks,-command=>\&SelectLine, -
      showvalue=>1,
155          -variable=>\$ScaleValue);
156    $ScaleButton->place(-x=>2,-y=>570);
157  }
158
159  sub SelectLine {
160    $ShowText->SetCursor("$ScaleValue.0");
161  }
```

In line 8 the invocation to the module that controls the LabFrame was added. The widget has been defined on lines 22 and 23. LabFrame is not simply a decorative rectangle to improve the appearance of the application. Something interesting about them is that the widgets you want to put into them, can be 'tied' to them, so, if you have to move the widgets, only move the LabFrame, because the widgets inside are referred to it. The definition of the Radiobuttons is almost the same as the previous examples, but the difference is that now they are inside the LabFrame $Frame (defined on line 22). In Script 7.11 we defined the Radiobuttons belonging to $top. Now, on lines 26 and 29, we tied them to $Frame. So, the positions given by -x and -y are related to this widget, not to $top (the MainWindow).

Try to change the position of $Frame, without changing anything else and check out the results.

Figure 7.27 shows the output after running this script.

Now, we are ready to develop our own applications. In the next chapters, I will show you some practical examples, related to geosciences.

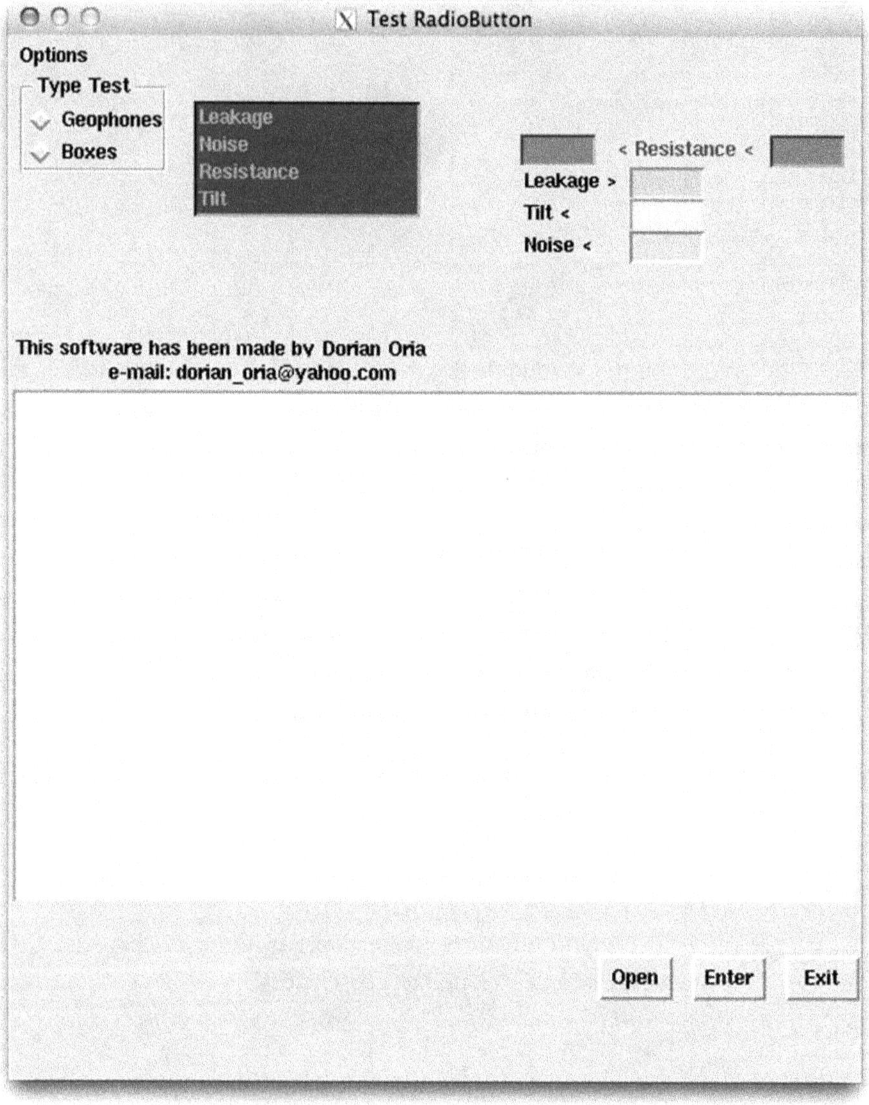

Advanced programming in Perl for Beginners.

Figure 7.27. Output of Script 7.14.

Chapter 8.

Well logs.

8.1 Introduction.

In the following, we will see different applications developed in Perl to help the processing of information generated in different fields of geosciences. The majority of the programs shown here were developed towards information management: quality control, load data into databases, etc., but the sky is the limit. I hope they serve to give you ideas about the immense possibilities of Perl.

8.2 LAS files.

Log ASCII Standard (LAS) was designed in 1990 by the Canadian Well Logging Society for local Canadian markets to standardize the binary format used to digitize well logs. The simplicity and flexibility of the LAS ASCII-type encoding quickly led to its worldwide acceptance and use.

The next lines (enclosed) show an example of this kind of format and some values of several well logs.

```
~Version Information Section
VERS.      2.0                    : CWLS LOG ASCII Standard
WRAP.      NO                     : One line per depth step
~Well Information Section
STRT.M     1625.0413                  : Start Depth
STOP.M     2074.9260                  : Stop Depth
STEP.M     0.1524                 : Step
NULL.      -999.0000              : Null Value
COMP.      COMPANY                     : Company
WELL.      WELL-879                   : Well
FLD .      FIELD                  : Field
LOC .      X=652584.28               : Location
LOC1.      Y=2239145.94              : Location 1
CTRY.      COUNTRY                    : Country
STAT.      STATE                  : State
CNTY.      COUNTY                     : County
UWI .                            : UWI Number
API .                            : API Number
SECT.      --                    : Section
TOWN.      --                      : Township
RNGE.      --                    : Range
PDAT.      NT                      : Perm Datum
EPD .      189.0                 : Elevation
LMF .      MR                      : Log Measured From
DMF .      MR                      : Drill Measured From
APD .      5.5                   : Above Perm Datum
```

Advanced programming in Perl for Beginners.

```
EKB .      194.9                    : Elev-Kelly Bushing.
EDF .      194.5                    : Elev-Drill Floor
EGL .      189.0                    : Elev-Ground Level
SRVC.      SC, Inc.                  : Service Company
DATE.       8 Jun 2005 @ 8:41         : Date
~Parameter Information Section
RUN .      1                        : Run #
DATE.      5-JUN-2004                 : Date log was run
TDD .      2177                     : Depth - Driller
TDL .      2177                     : Depth - Logger
BLI .      2175                     : Bottom Log Interval
TLI .      800.5                    : Top Log Interval
CBD .      7.625 @ 799               : Casing - Driller
CBL .      800.5                    : Casing - Logger
BS  .      6.75                     : Bit Size
DFT .      VERSADRILL                 : Type of Fluid In Hole
DFD .      1.48                     : Drilling Fluid Density
DFV .      55                       : Drilling Fluid Viscosity
DFPH.      --                       : Drilling Fluid pH
DFL .      4.0                      : Drilling Fluid Loss
MSS .      --                      : Source of Sample
RMS .      --                      : Mud Resitivity
MST .      --                      : Rm Temperature
RMFS.      --                       : Mud Filtrate Resistivity
MFST.      --                       : Rmf Temperature
RMCS.      --                       : Mud Cake Resitivity
MCST.      --                       : Rmc Temperature
MFSS.      --                       : Source of Rmf
MCSS.      --                       : Source of Rmc
RMBH.      --                        : Rm at BHT
BHT .      --                       : Bottom Hole Temperature
MRT .      87 C                   : Max Recorded Temperature
RUN .      2                        : Run #
DATE.                                : Date log was run
TDD .                                : Depth - Driller
TDL .                                : Depth - Logger
BLI .                               : Bottom Log Interval
TLI .                               : Top Log Interval
CBD .                                : Casing - Driller
CBL .                               : Casing - Logger
BS  .                              : Bit Size
DFT .                                : Type of Fluid In Hole
DFD .                                : Drilling Fluid Density
DFV .                                : Drilling Fluid Viscosity
DFPH.                                : Drilling Fluid pH
DFL .                               : Drilling Fluid Loss
MSS .                               : Source of Sample
```

```
RMS .                          : Mud Resitivity
MST .                          : Rm Temperature
RMFS.                           : Mud Filtrate Resistivity
MFST.                           : Rmf Temperature
RMCS.                          : Mud Cake Resitivity
MCST.                          : Rmc Temperature
MFSS.                          : Source of Rmf
MCSS.                          : Source of Rmc
RMBH.                           : Rm at BHT
BHT .                          : Bottom Hole Temperature
MRT .                          : Max Recorded Temperature
RUN .        3                  : Run #
DATE.                           : Date log was run
TDD .                          : Depth - Driller
TDL .                          : Depth - Logger
BLI .                         : Bottom Log Interval
TLI .                         : Top Log Interval
CBD .                          : Casing - Driller
CBL .                          : Casing - Logger
BS  .                        : Bit Size
DFT .                           : Type of Fluid In Hole
DFD .                          : Drilling Fluid Density
DFV .                          : Drilling Fluid Viscosity
DFPH.                           : Drilling Fluid pH
DFL .                          : Drilling Fluid Loss
MSS .                          : Source of Sample
RMS .                          : Mud Resitivity
MST .                          : Rm Temperature
RMFS.                           : Mud Filtrate Resistivity
MFST.                          : Rmf Temperature
RMCS.                           : Mud Cake Resitivity
MCST.                           : Rmc Temperature
MFSS.                          : Source of Rmf
MCSS.                          : Source of Rmc
RMBH.                           : Rm at BHT
BHT .                          : Bottom Hole Temperature
MRT .                          : Max Recorded Temperature
~Curve Information Section
DEPTH.M                           : 1
SMALL.                          : 2
SW.DEC                          : 3
SWBAV.                          : 4
T.DEGF                          : 5
TEXGM.                           : 6
VCLAY.DEC                         : 7
W.                        : 8
~ASCII Log Data Section
```

1625.0413	0.5572	1.0000	0.5097	165.8427	1.2194	0.5097	2.0000
1625.1936	0.5188	1.0000	0.4492	165.8490	1.2713	0.4492	2.0000
1625.3461	0.5009	1.0000	0.4714	165.8553	1.2705	0.4714	2.0000
1625.4984	0.5164	1.0000	0.4478	165.8616	1.3031	0.4478	2.0000
1625.6509	0.5149	1.0000	0.5086	165.8679	1.2836	0.5086	2.0000
1625.8032	0.5566	1.0000	0.5554	165.8742	1.2813	0.5554	2.0000
1625.9556	0.5677	1.0000	0.5801	165.8805	1.2821	0.5801	2.0000
1626.1080	0.5762	1.0000	0.5962	165.8868	1.2929	0.5962	2.0000
1626.2604	0.5767	1.0000	0.6059	165.8931	1.3056	0.6059	2.0000
1626.4128	0.5975	1.0000	0.6389	165.8994	1.2749	0.6389	2.0000
1626.5652	0.5396	1.0000	0.5360	165.9057	1.2880	0.5360	2.0000
1626.7177	0.5314	1.0000	0.5225	165.9120	1.2611	0.5225	2.0000
1626.8700	0.5598	1.0000	0.5769	165.9184	1.2530	0.5769	2.000
1627.0225	0.4970	1.0000	0.4716	165.9247	1.3039	0.4716	1.9595

Now, imagine the following problem. We have a lot of LAS files. We need to make an inventory of them extracting, from every file, information about: client, well name, location (not only coordinates, but also country, state and county), well logs contain into every file, date when logs were run, top and base of the logs, etc.

Some ideas to deal with the problem are:

- It will be necessary to read several files, so, we could use a 'for-next' control structure.
- We have to open every file and read them, in order to look for the required information.
- Look into every file for words or expressions that allows identifying where the data is.
- It is necessary to assume that all the files have the same structure.

The following script reads several LAS files that are listed in a text file. Extract from every file the well name, top and base of every log according to information in the header and the top and base according with the real data (it reads the whole file), the name of every log into the file. All this information is written in a text file. In addition, the name of every LAS file and the name of every well are written in the same file, according to the name of it.

Script 8.1

```
1$ListaRegistros='/Users/dorian/Documents/PerlBook/LAS/archivosLAS.txt';
2$datos_registros='/Users/dorian/Documents/PerlBook/LAS/datos.txt';
```

```
3$reg_sin_formato='/Users/dorian/Documents/PerlBook/LAS/sin_formato
 .txt';
4$i=0;
5open (IN,$ListaRegistros);
6$lineaLista=<IN>;
7while ($lineaLista) {
8 chomp $lineaLista;
9 $registros[$i]=$lineaLista;
10 $i++;
11 $lineaLista=<IN>;
12}
13close IN;
14open (OUT,'>'.$datos_registros);
15print OUT
 "WellName\tTop\tBase\tRealTop\tRealBase\tLogs\tFileName\tWellName
 AccordingFileName\n";
16open (SIN,'>',$reg_sin_formato);
17for ($j=0;$j<$i;$j++) {
18 $r=0;
19 $s=0; $c=0;
20 open (REG,$registros[$j]);
21 $Record=$registros[$j];
22 @record=split(/uw/i,$registros[$j]);
23 $lineaReg=<REG>;
24 while ($lineaReg) {
25 chomp $lineaReg;
26 if ($lineaReg =~ m/STRT/) {
27  @array=split (" ",$lineaReg);
28  $cima=$array[1];
29 }
30 @array=();
31 if ($lineaReg =~ m/STOP/) {
32  @array=split (" ",$lineaReg);
33  $base=$array[1];
34 }
35 @array=();
36 if ($lineaReg =~ m/WELL/) {
37  @array=split (":",$lineaReg);
38  @subarray=split("[.]",$array[0]);
39  $wellName=$subarray[1];
40  if ($Record =~ m/$wellName/i) {
41   $record[0]=$wellName;
42  }
```

```perl
43 }
44 @array=();
45 if ($lineaReg =~ m/DEPT/) {
46  $aux=1;
47 }
48 if ($aux==1 && $r>1 && $lineaReg =~ m/[~]/i) {
49  $aux=0;
50 }
51 if ($aux==1) {
52  $r++;
53  if ($r>1) {
54   @array=split ("[.]",$lineaReg);
55   $curvas[$c]=$array[0];
56   $c++;
57  }
58 }
59 if ($aux==0 && $lineaReg =~ m/~A/i) {
60  $aux2=1;
61 }
62 if ($aux2==1) {
63  $s++;
64  @array2=split(" ",$lineaReg);
65  if ($s==2) {
66   $length=@array2-1;
67   $length2=@curvas;
68   if ($length==$length2) {
69    $tiene_formato=1;
70   }
71   if ($length!=$length2) {
72    $tiene_formato=0;
73   }
74   $cimaReal=$array2[0];
75  }
76 }
77 if ($aux2==1 && $s>2) {
78  @array2=split(" ",$lineaReg);
79  $length=@array2-1;
80  $length2=@curvas;
81  if ($length==$length2) {
82   $baseReal=$array2[0];
83  }
84 }
85 $lineaReg=<REG>;
```

```
 86 }
 87 close REG;
 88 if ($tiene_formato==0) {
 89   print SIN "$wellName\t$Record\n";
 90 }
 91 if ($tiene_formato==1) {
 92   for ($a=0;$a<$c;$a++) {
 93     print OUT
     "$wellName\t$cima\t$base\t$cimaReal\t$baseReal\t$curvas[$a]\t$registros[
     $j]\t$record[0]\n";
 94   }
 95 }
 96 $aux2=0;
 97 @curvas=();
 98}
 99close SIN;
100close OUT;
```

Before the execution of the script, it is necessary to create a text file with a list of the LAS files you want to check. You can name this file with any name. In our case, we called the file **archivosLAS.txt** and it looks as shown in the next figure:

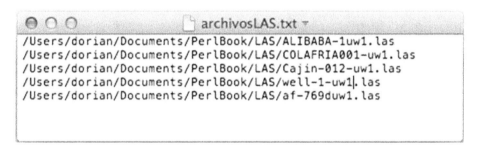

Figure 8.1. Text file with a list of LAS files to be processed.

This file can be done using any of the following instructions, depending on the operative system:

Table 8.1 Instructions to create a file with the list of LAS files.

Operative System	Instruction
Windows (from command prompt)	dir /b/s *.las > archivosLAS.txt
OSX, Linux, Unix	find $PWD –name '*.las' >

Advanced programming in Perl for Beginners.

	archivosLAS.txt
	ls –d $PWD/*.las > archivosLAS.txt

Notice that, for every file, the complete path is included. This is not necessary if the script is executed in the same path where the LAS files are.

In line 1 the variable $ListaRegistros and the complete path where the file archivosLAS.txt is stored, are declared.

It will give, as results, a couple of text files. The first of them, **datos.txt**, which will contain the results of it, organized in columns. The second one, **sin_formato.txt**, will contain those files that contain information from every log, but not in column format. Figure 8.2 shows a file, where, for every depth, the information of the logs looks like packages. Instead, Figure 8.3 shows for, every depth, the information of every log in the same line. So, the information is in column format.

The files that do not have the column format will have to be processed in order to give them the appropriate format.

```
  ● ○ ○                              well-1.las ▾
~A Log Data Section
   1600.0476
       0.1115       0.1115       0.0000       0.0000       0.1050      95.8473
       0.0000       0.0000       0.0000      70.6650      70.2926       6.8409
      -0.0072       0.0000       0.0000       0.0000       0.2891       0.5274
       0.0000       0.2891       0.1210       0.0016       0.1195       0.2142
       0.3201       2.4768       0.9330       0.9112       0.4726       0.9646
       0.5274       1.9942
   1600.2001
       0.1134       0.1134       0.0000       0.0000       0.1032      96.3686
       0.0000       0.0000       0.0000      70.1957      69.7593       6.8255
      -0.0077       0.0000       0.0000       0.0000       0.2972       0.5199
       0.0000       0.2972       0.1192       0.0010       0.1193       0.2188
       0.3239       2.4798       0.9507       0.9241       0.4801       0.9743
       0.5199       1.9942
   1600.3524
       0.1135       0.1135       0.0000       0.0000       0.1058      95.9909
       0.0000       0.0000       0.0000      67.9166      67.3656       6.7947
      -0.0071       0.0000       0.0000       0.0000       0.2940       0.5292
       0.0000       0.2940       0.1217       0.0016       0.1213       0.2175
       0.3211       2.4755       0.9357       0.8703       0.4708       0.9660
       0.5292       1.9961
   1600.5049
       0.1134       0.1134       0.0000       0.0000       0.1069      96.5299
       0.0000       0.0000       0.0000      65.1793      64.6814       6.8024
      -0.0061       0.0000       0.0000       0.0000       0.2920       0.5377
       0.0000       0.2920       0.1228       0.0022       0.1224       0.2165
       0.3250       2.4737       0.9264       0.8157       0.4623       0.9604
       0.5377       1.9991
```

Figure 8.2. Log file showing information organized as packages.

```
⊝⊝⊝                              well_2.las — Modificado
~A Log Data Section
  1510.00    0.1167    0.0915    2.4840   -16.8610   -1.9794    1.0000    0.7746   145.7289    0.5290
  1510.25    0.1006    0.0756    2.5110   -16.9380   -2.0484    1.0000    0.7743   145.7388    0.5254
  1510.50    0.1000    0.0751    2.5120   -16.9070   -2.0094    1.0000    0.8471   145.7487    0.5221
  1510.75    0.0827    0.0579    2.5410   -16.8430   -1.9374    1.0000    0.8348   145.7586    0.5218
  1511.00    0.1036    0.0787    2.5060   -16.7330   -1.8194    1.0000    0.7936   145.7686    0.5220
  1511.25    0.1119    0.0870    2.4920   -16.5600   -1.6384    1.0000    0.7809   145.7785    0.5231
  1511.50    0.1107    0.0856    2.4940   -16.3640   -1.4344    1.0000    0.7632   145.7884    0.5271
  1511.75    0.1125    0.0872    2.4910   -16.3520   -1.4144    1.0000    0.7655   145.7983    0.5305
  1512.00    0.1238    0.0985    2.4720   -16.6460   -1.7004    1.0000    0.8222   145.8082    0.5318
  1512.25    0.1381    0.1034    2.4450   -17.0910   -2.1374    0.9983    0.8639   145.8181    0.5298
  1512.50    0.1360    0.1038    2.4490   -17.1250   -2.1634    0.9970    0.7896   145.8280    0.5284
  1512.75    0.1267    0.1017    2.4670   -16.6120   -1.6424    1.0000    0.7561   145.8380    0.5266
  1513.00    0.1346    0.1038    2.4520   -16.3210   -1.3434    0.9967    0.7832   145.8479    0.5281
  1513.25    0.1323    0.1034    2.4570   -16.5810   -1.5954    0.9983    0.8526   145.8578    0.5300
  1513.50    0.1137    0.0883    2.4890   -16.9220   -1.9284    1.0000    0.7439   145.8677    0.5322
  1513.75    0.0851    0.0597    2.5370   -17.1090   -2.1074    1.0000    0.6645   145.8776    0.5345
  1514.00    0.0839    0.0583    2.5390   -17.0850   -2.0754    1.0000    0.6421   145.8875    0.5378
  1514.25    0.0976    0.0718    2.5160   -16.8610   -1.8434    1.0000    0.7053   145.8974    0.5431
  1514.50    0.0994    0.0733    2.5130   -16.5720   -1.5464    1.0000    0.7498   145.9074    0.5479
  1514.75    0.0982    0.0720    2.5150   -16.1700   -1.1364    1.0000    0.6988   145.9173    0.5514
  1515.00    0.0833    0.0570    2.5400   -15.7750   -0.7334    1.0000    0.7187   145.9272    0.5539
```

Figure 8.3. Log file showing information organized as columns.

The variable $i is a counter used to count the lines in the file archivosLAS.txt. The final value of $i gives us the quantity of LAS files to be processed.

The file archivosLAS.txt is read between lines 5 and 13. The name of every file is stored in the array @registros (remember that, even though explicitly you will not see the expression @registros in the script, every element of it is referred by $registros[index]). This array is built in line 9.

On line 14 the output file is opened, which will contain the results of the script (datos.txt). Remember, you must use the character '>' to indicate to Perl that the file is opened in writing mode.

Because all the data will be stored in columns, we added a header for every column in line 15. Notice that after every column title there is a combination of the characters '\t'. They tell Perl to add a tab after every column title.

On line 16 we open the file that will contain the name of those files with log information with a format different to column format.

Line 17 starts the structure 'for-next', that will control the process to open every LAS file indicated in the file archivosLAS.txt (stored in the array @registros).

The structure starts in $j=0 (because arrays in Perl are 0-indexed) and runs until $j<$i, where $i is the number of records in @registros. Another way to get the number of records is with the instruction $length=@registros. The variable $length really can take any name, but in the way that the instruction is built (scalar=array), it means 'assign the length of array @registros to $length.'

Advanced programming in Perl for Beginners.

Looking at the example of the LAS file shown at the beginning of this chapter, we can see that the name of the well is in the same line where the word 'WELL' is located. The top of the measurements is in the same line as the word 'STRT'. The base is in the same line as the word 'STOP'. The available logs in every file can be located after the word 'DEPTH' and before a character "~". We will use these words and characters as string patterns to finally find the information we need.

The LAS files are opened on line 20. On line 21 we assign the value of every element of the array @registros to the variable $Record.

One of the values we need to recover is the name of the well according to the name of file. To do this, we use the instruction:

@record=split(/uw/i,$registros[$j]);

The instruction **split** takes the expression used as splitter and the string we want to split as parameters. The result is an array, which is stored in @record. In this case, we saw that all the files have in common the string 'uw'. So, we used it as splitter. According to Figure 8.1, the name of the well will be the first element of the array, it means $record[0].

The reading process of every LAS file actually starts on line 24 with the structure 'while'.

Between lines 26 and 29, there is an 'if' control structure that allows finding the string with the pattern 'STRT'. If the pattern is found, the line is split and its values stored in the array @array. On line 28 we use the variable $cima to store the value of the top, that will be stored in $array[1].

Because we are using @array as temporal variable and later in other structures, it is preferable to empty the array. This is done on line 30.

Between lines 31 and 34 there is another 'if' control structure that allows finding the string with the pattern 'STOP'. If the pattern is found, the line is split and its values stored in the array @array. On line 33 we use the variable $base to store the value of the base, that will be in $array[1].

@array is empty on line 35 once again. Between lines 36 and 43, we have the 'if' structure to find the pattern 'WELL'. Once the pattern is found, we split the line and store the results in @array. But, because in this case we are using ':' as splitter, the final result is still not the well name. In this case, again, we split the variable that contains the pattern ($array[0]), but using the character '.' as a splitter. Finally, the name of the well will be in $subarray[1] and stored in the variable $wellname.

If $Record (or $registros[index]) contains the pattern $wellname, then $record receives the value of $wellname. This is a way to check that both the name of the well according to the name file and the name of the well according to information in the file are the same.

Between lines 45 and 47, there is an 'if' structure to find the pattern 'DEPTH'. This structure is interesting in one aspect. When the pattern is found, $aux takes the value 1. Remember we are using this pattern to identify the point where the types of logs are. According to our LAS file model, the name of the first log is in the next line. The last one will be before the next character '~'. The searching of this character is made in the next "if" structure (between lines 48 and 50). Because along the file there are several characters '~', the 'if' sentence has several conditions: $r (initialize in line 18) must be greater than 1 ($r counts the lines below the pattern 'DEPTH'). The condition $r>1 guarantees that the program will consider the existence of, at least, one log.

The next 'if' structure (between lines 51 and 58) allows getting the names of every log into the file. The 'if' structure inside guarantees that the names of the logs will be read in the next line (below the pattern 'DEPTH'). Because all the names of the logs have a period '.' immediately after, we use this character as a splitter. The values are stored in @array and the name of the log will be $array[0]. Because this variable is temporal, the definitive value is stored in the array @curvas. $c is used to increase the size of the array.

Between lines 59 and 61 there is an 'if' structure that will allow finding the pattern that indicates where the data of every log starts. In this case, we have used the pattern '~A'. When this pattern is found, $aux2 takes the value 1. This variable works as a flag as well.

The first column of data corresponds to depth. So, the first value we find will correspond to the real top of the measurements. Because the values start in the next line after the pattern, we use the variable $s (initialize on line 19) to help us to identify when we reach this line.

To know if the data is in column format, we read the first line of data and split it

Advanced programming in Perl for Beginners.

using one space (' ') Perl really takes this value as one or more spaces. The resulting array is stored in @array2. We calculate the length and assign to the variable $length. Because @array2 includes the value of depth, we do $length=@array2-1. In the next line (line 67) we calculate the length of the array @curvas ($length2). If $length has the same value of $length2, then the file has the data in column format. Otherwise, the name of the file is written into the file whose path is $reg_sin_formato (line 89).

The value of the top will be $array2[0], stored in $cimaReal (line 74).

To know what the base of the measurements is, we consider that, after reading the first line of data (if data is in column format) any depth after it can be the base. However, because this value will be overwritten until the end of the reading process, the final read value would be the real base of the measurements (line 82).

In the case that, into the file, there is data in column format, all the variables found are written in $datos_registros (line 93). Remember that, when we are working with files, really we use an alias. For example, for the file in the path $datos_registros, the alias is 'OUT', so on the line 93 when we are indicating to write data (print) in OUT, actually we are telling the script to write in $datos_registros.

Finally, do not forget to close the files (lines 99 and 100).

Figure 8.4 shows an example of a list of files that does not comply with the column format and Figure 8.5 shows an example of a file with data extracted from LAS files.

Figure 8.4. List of files with no column format.

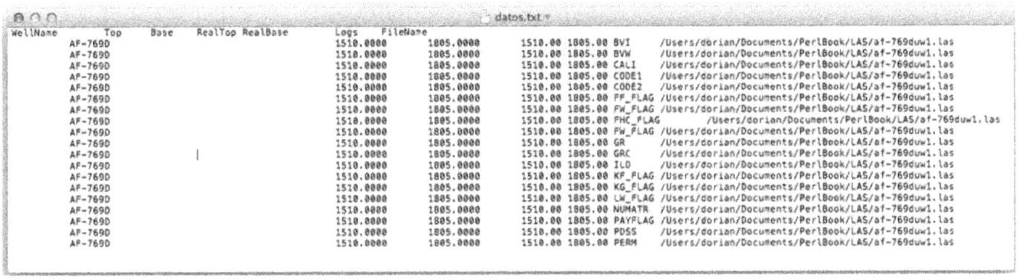


```
WellName        Top     Base    RealTop RealBase        Logs    FileName
        AF-769D                                 1510.0000       1805.0000       1510.00 1805.00 BVI     /Users/dorian/Documents/PerlBook/LAS/af-769duw1.las
        AF-769D                                 1510.0000       1805.0000       1510.00 1805.00 BVW     /Users/dorian/Documents/PerlBook/LAS/af-769duw1.las
        AF-769D                                 1510.0000       1805.0000       1510.00 1805.00 CALI    /Users/dorian/Documents/PerlBook/LAS/af-769duw1.las
        AF-769D                                 1510.0000       1805.0000       1510.00 1805.00 CODE1   /Users/dorian/Documents/PerlBook/LAS/af-769duw1.las
        AF-769D                                 1510.0000       1805.0000       1510.00 1805.00 CODE2   /Users/dorian/Documents/PerlBook/LAS/af-769duw1.las
        AF-769D                                 1510.0000       1805.0000       1510.00 1805.00 FF_FLAG /Users/dorian/Documents/PerlBook/LAS/af-769duw1.las
        AF-769D                                 1510.0000       1805.0000       1510.00 1805.00 FW_FLAG /Users/dorian/Documents/PerlBook/LAS/af-769duw1.las
        AF-769D                                 1510.0000       1805.0000       1510.00 1805.00 FHC_FLAG        /Users/dorian/Documents/PerlBook/LAS/af-769duw1.las
        AF-769D                                 1510.0000       1805.0000       1510.00 1805.00 FW_FLAG /Users/dorian/Documents/PerlBook/LAS/af-769duw1.las
        AF-769D                                 1510.0000       1805.0000       1510.00 1805.00 GR      /Users/dorian/Documents/PerlBook/LAS/af-769duw1.las
        AF-769D                                 1510.0000       1805.0000       1510.00 1805.00 GRC     /Users/dorian/Documents/PerlBook/LAS/af-769duw1.las
        AF-769D                                 1510.0000       1805.0000       1510.00 1805.00 ILD     /Users/dorian/Documents/PerlBook/LAS/af-769duw1.las
        AF-769D                                 1510.0000       1805.0000       1510.00 1805.00 KF_FLAG /Users/dorian/Documents/PerlBook/LAS/af-769duw1.las
        AF-769D                                 1510.0000       1805.0000       1510.00 1805.00 KG_FLAG /Users/dorian/Documents/PerlBook/LAS/af-769duw1.las
        AF-769D                                 1510.0000       1805.0000       1510.00 1805.00 LW_FLAG /Users/dorian/Documents/PerlBook/LAS/af-769duw1.las
        AF-769D                                 1510.0000       1805.0000       1510.00 1805.00 NUMATR  /Users/dorian/Documents/PerlBook/LAS/af-769duw1.las
        AF-769D                                 1510.0000       1805.0000       1510.00 1805.00 PAYFLAG /Users/dorian/Documents/PerlBook/LAS/af-769duw1.las
        AF-769D                                 1510.0000       1805.0000       1510.00 1805.00 PDSS    /Users/dorian/Documents/PerlBook/LAS/af-769duw1.las
        AF-769D                                 1510.0000       1805.0000       1510.00 1805.00 PERM    /Users/dorian/Documents/PerlBook/LAS/af-769duw1.las
```

Figure 8.5 Data extracted from LAS files.

Chapter 9.

Velocity model files.

9.1 Introduction.

Usually, Openworks™, Charisma™, Petrel™ and other interpretation platforms have their own requirements for formats of every kind of geological or geophysical data, in particular for velocity information. For example, the output velocity model file of the processing software Omega™InVa™ looks like Figure 9.1.

```
# NOMBRE DEL ESTUDIO: ESTUDIO_DE_PRUEBA
# COMPANIA DE PROCESO: WESTERNGECO
# RESPONSABLES DEL PROYECTO: DORIAN ORIA SAN MARTIN
# FECHA DE PROCESO: ENERO 2005
# TIPO DE PROCESO LIGADO AL CPO. DE VELS: PRE-STACK
TIME MIGRATION
# TIPO DE VELOCIDAD: RMS
# CAMPO ORIGINAL DE VELOCIDADES
# TIPO DE ESTUDIO: MARINO STREAMER
# DATUM = 0
# TIPO DE SOFTWARE DE PROCESAMIENTO: OMEGA, INVA
# RANGO DE INLINE: 2880-1896 RANGO DE XLINE: 524-1052
# MUESTREO ESPACIAL DE LAS FUNCIONES DE VELOCIDAD:
INLINE: EVERY 40 (1km), XLINE: EVERY 80 (1km)
# MUESTREO TEMPORAL DE LAS FUNCIONES DE VELOCIDAD:
PICADO ORIGINAL
# TAMANO DEL BIN FINAL: 1 x 1km
# DATUM_LEVEL = PROMEDIO DEL NIVEL DEL MAR
# datum CDP    Coord_X Coord_Y    tiempo  Velocidad Inline   Xline
   0 221866820 820993.00 2161948.00    0   1500   1896   860
                    869   1506
                    1124  1552
                    1437  1644
```

Figure 9.1. Velocity model file for Omega™InVa™.

GeoFrame™ needs the information as shown in Figure 9.2.

```
1896 860 820993.00 2161948.00 0 1500
1896 860 820993.00 2161948.00 869 1506
1896 860 820993.00 2161948.00 1124 1552
1896 860 820993.00 2161948.00 1437 1644
1896 860 820993.00 2161948.00 1750 1759
1896 860 820993.00 2161948.00 1982 1852
```

Advanced programming in Perl for Beginners.

```
1896 860 820993.00 2161948.00 2193 1936
1896 860 820993.00 2161948.00 2433 2032
1896 860 820993.00 2161948.00 2543 2072
1896 860 820993.00 2161948.00 2843 2209
```

Figure 9.2. Velocity model file for Geoframe™.

The first column is the Inline, the second one is the Xline, the third one is the X-Coordinate, the fourth one Y-Coordinate the fifth one is the time and the last one is the velocity.

Script 9.1 converts the information from Omega™ to GeoFrame™ format.

Script 9.1

```perl
 1 $InputFile='G:\disk1\velocity\OmegaVelocity.txt';
 2 $OutputFile='G:\disk1\velocity\GeoFrameVelocity.txt';
 3 $firstLine=16;
 4 open (IN,$InputFile);
 5 open (OUT,'>'.$OutputFile);
 6 $lineas=0;
 7 $linea=<IN>;
 8 while ($linea) {
 9  $lineas++;
10  if ($lineas>=$firstLine) {
11   chomp $linea;
12   @valores=split(" ",$linea);
13   $length=@valores;
14   if ($length==8) {
15    $IL=$valores[6];
16    $XL=$valores[7];
17    $x=$valores[2];
18    $y=$valores[3];
19    print OUT "$IL $XL $x $y $valores[4] $valores[5]\n";
20   }
21   if ($length<8) {
22    print OUT "$IL $XL $x $y $valores[0] $valores[1]\n";
23   }
24  }
25  $linea=<IN>;
26 }
27 close IN;
28 close OUT;
```

On the first line we assign the full path of the file to $InputFile with the Omega™ format. The output file will be the file **GeoFramaVelocity.txt**. The full path was assigned to the variable $OutputFile.

We will use the variable $firstLine as a flag that indicates the last line of the header. The data will start on the next line (line 17 according our previous example, Figure 9.1)

On line 4 we open the input file in reading mode. On line 5 we open the output file in writing mode.

The process of reading the input file starts on line 8 with the sentence **while**. The data will be from line 17 of the input file. This is the reason for the instruction on line 10. Once this condition is satisfied, we create the array @valores, using space (' ') as splitter. The variable $length will contain the length of the array. We will use the value of this variable to know when we have another velocity curve (another CDP). In our case, when $length is 8, it means we are starting a new velocity curve. We get the values of every variable we need and we write them so many times before we find another array with length equal to 8.

The following output file comes from other processing software:

```
# Nombre del estudio: PRE-STACK TIME MIGRATION Y
PROFUNDIDAD DE DIAMANTE
# DORIAN 3D
# Clave : JDSJDSHKS
# Compania de proceso: XXXX
# Responsable de proceso : DORIAN ORIA SAN MARTIN
# Fecha de proceso: Mayo 2006
# Tipo de proceso ligado a las velocidades: PRE-STACK TIME
MIGRATION
# Tipo de velocidad : MIGRATION VELOCITY VRMS
# Tipo de estudio : LAND
#
# Tipo de software de procesamiento : Geovecteur 2.1
# Rango de INLINE 1200,1211-3491,3550 y XLINE 11,267-1697,1750
# Muestreo espacial Inline cada 10  Xline cada 10
# Muestreo temporal cada 48 ms
# Tamaño del bin sin interporal 25 x 25
# LANDMARK VELOCITY FUNCTION
# 21/04/06
```

Advanced programming in Perl for Beginners.

```
# FUNCTION_TYPE = TVrms
# LINEAR_UNITS = METERS
#LINE 1200
    200.0 796411.8 2013675.0   8.00  1383.00
                    56.00  1383.00
                   104.00  1397.00
                   152.00  1481.00
                   200.00  1577.00
                   248.00  1738.00
                   296.00  1884.00
                   344.00  1955.00
                   392.00  2019.00
                   440.00  2047.00
                   488.00  2068.00
                   536.00  2058.00
```

Figure 9.3. Velocity model file.

The following script converts this format in GeoFrame™ format:

Script 9.2

```
1  $fileInput='D:\dorian\SEGY\VEL-MIG-LANDMARK.txt';
2  $fileOutput='D:\dorian\SEGY\VEL-MIG-SCOTTMCKAY.txt';
3  $firstline=20;
4  #################################################
5  $l=0;
6  $numeral='#';
7  open (OUT,'>'.$fileOutput);
8  open (IN,$fileInput);
9  $lineaIN=<IN>;
10 while ($lineaIN) {
11   $l++;
12   if ($l>=$firstline) {
13     @array=split(' ',$lineaIN);
14     $lenght=@array;
15     $firstChar=substr($array[0],0,1);
16     $EsNumeral=$firstChar eq $numeral;
17     if ($EsNumeral==1) {
18       $Inline=$array[1];
19     }
20     if ($lenght==5) {
21       $Xline=$array[0];
22       $XCoord=$array[1];
```

```
23   $YCoord=$array[2];
24   $time=$array[3];
25   $attribute=$array[4];
26   print OUT
     "$Inline\t$Xline\t$XCoord\t$YCoord\t$time\t$attribute\n";
27   }
28   if ($lenght==2 && $EsNumeral!=1) {
29     print OUT
       "$Inline\t$Xline\t$XCoord\t$YCoord\t$array[0]\t$array[1]\n";
30   }
31 }
32 $lineaIN=<IN>;
33 }
34 close IN;
35 close OUT;
```

The difference between this script and the previous one is the criteria to be used to identify the beginning and the end of a velocity function. According to the example shown in Figure 9.3, the first velocity function starts on line 20. But, in Omega™ format, all the information was in the same line. In this case, the name of the line is on a line before the line of the data. Something we can notice is that the line starts with the character '#'. We use this character as pattern, but we use a different methodology. In this case because the character is always the first one of the string, we split the line and the array resulting is stored in @array. For the first function, $arrays[0] is #LINE. We get the character '#' from this string using the function **substr** (line 15). On line 16 we do the comparison between strings (remember that Perl treats numbers and strings differently) $firstChar (line 15) and the character '#' stored in the variable $numeral. In this case we are using **eq** ('equal') to compare both strings. The result of comparison is stored in $EsNumeral (line 16). If this variable takes the value 1 (true, both strings are the same), then the value of the inline is $array[1] (line 18) and the data of the velocity function will start in the next line (when the length of @array is 5, line 20).

To generate stacked data in Focus™, it needs the velocity files to be sorted by CDP in ascending order. In seismic marine data acquisition usually the processing on board (for QC purposes) is done for every single sequence. Because it is necessary to produce brute stacks, in the way a velocity model was generated. But, in some cases, it is necessary to make a stack with the information of all the sequences together. Under these circumstances, it is necessary to have only one velocity model in only one file, but we have several coming from every single sequence. The

Advanced programming in Perl for Beginners.

problem consists in making only one file, with all the CDP's sorted. The following script takes velocity laws coming from different Focus™ file jobs and puts them together in one file. An example of how these jobs look is shown in Figure 9.4:

Script 9.3

```perl
1  $firstChar='*';
2  $stringHANDVEL='HANDVEL';
3  $files='G:\Vel-All\files.txt';
4  $output='G:\Vel-All\velUnSort.txt';
5  open (FILES,$files);
6  open (OUT,'>'.$output);
7  $linea=<FILES>;
8  while ($linea) {
9    $l=0;
10   $primeraLinea=1000;
11   chomp $linea;
12   open (IN,$linea);
13   $LINEA=<IN>;
14   while ($LINEA) {
15     chomp $LINEA;
16     $firstCharLine=substr($LINEA,0,1);
17     $resultado=$firstCharLine eq $firstChar;
18     $cadena=substr($LINEA,0,7);
19     $resultado2=$cadena eq $stringHANDVEL;
20     $l++;
21     if ($resultado2==1) {
22       $primeraLinea=$l;
23     }
24     if ($l>=$primeraLinea && $resultado!=1) {
25       print OUT "$LINEA\n";
26     }
27     $LINEA=<IN>;
28   }
29   close IN;
30   $linea=<FILES>;
31 }
32 close FILES;
33 close OUT;
```

The velocity job files end with the expression *END. We could use this string as a pattern for matching, indicating the end of the file. However, we will use the character "*" as a string pattern to make the exercise more interesting.

```
113_009_l1213p1_velan - WordPad
File  Edit  View  Insert  Format  Help

*JOB      NPRC3D  3D
*CALL     DSIN
LABEL     113_L1213p1_SHOT_PREPRO
FILEID    0000400600a00bc1.000000.00000962
ORDER     CDP       OFFSET
REARR3D   INLINE
GROUP     1210    1220    10      7344    17012   300     21
*CALL     FILTER
BAND
                  2       4       40      60
*CALL     AGC     500
*CALL     VELDEF  CDP                     V1213P1
HANDVEL   6526105
12        1626    392     1688    1104    1867    2232    2122
3092      2414    3632    2615    4944    3299    7000    4100
HANDVEL   6526405
12        1626    392     1688    1104    1867    2232    2122
3092      2414    3632    2615    4944    3299    7000    4100
HANDVEL   6526705
12        1626    392     1688    1104    1867    2232    2122
3092      2414    3632    2615    4944    3299    7000    4100
HANDVEL   6527005
12        1626    392     1688    1104    1867    2232    2122
3092      2414    3632    2615    4944    3299    7000    4100

For Help, press F1
```

Figure 9.4. Velocity job file (Focus™).

The first line contains the variable that will be used as a pattern.

As you can notice, every velocity law starts with the string 'HANDVEL'. This will be used as a pattern as well and is assigned to the variable $stringHANDVEL on the second line.

On the third line there is a variable that contains the complete path to the file that contains the list of files with the velocity laws. This file looks as shown in Figure 9.5.

The fourth line contains the name of the output file.

On the fifth line, the file shown in Figure 9.5 is opened, in read-only mode.

On the sixth line, the file that will contain the results after running the script is opened.

Advanced programming in Perl for Beginners.

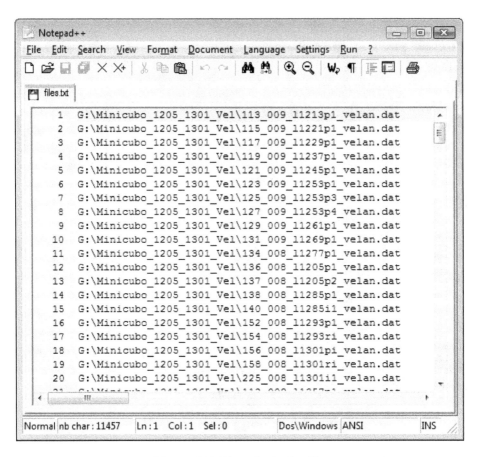

Figure 9.5. List of velocity files.

Important!

If you are working on Windows, you can use a command prompt window (cmd) to make this file. Use the following instruction:

dir /b/s *.dat > files.txt

If you are working on Linux or Unix, you can write this in the shell:

find /data3/PROJECT/Vel1 /data3/PROJECT/Vel2 –name "*.dat" – print > files.txt

---

The file with the list of velocity files is read from line 7.

The variable $l on line 9 is a counter of the number of the lines into the velocity files.

On line 10 the variable $primeraLinea is initialized and we assigned a big value to it. This is intended to guarantee that the condition declared on the line 21 be complied with (this is the first condition that must be complied). Once this condition is satisfied, the variable $primeraLinea takes the value of the number of the first line where the expression 'HANDVEL' is found.

From line 12 every velocity file indicated in the file $files (line 3) is opened.

The result of this script will be a file with all the velocity laws, but still without being CDP sorted. An example of this file is shown in Figure 9.6.

```
velUnSort.txt ▾
12      1498    460     1644    1024    1838    1652    2031
2436    2318    3192    2664    3520    2812    4148    3081
4620    3274    5216    3495    5700    3665    7000    4105
HANDVEL 23813420
12      1498    580     1668    1056    1833    1968    2158
2436    2318    2856    2502    3404    2761    3996    3016
4620    3274    5216    3495    5616    3627    7000    4105
HANDVEL 1
12      1498    1024    1851    2436    2229    3192    2680
3996    3220    7000    4105
HANDVEL 21406399
12      1498    492     1652    1024    1851    2180    2168
2684    2373    3168    2591    3672    2801    4620    3172
7000    4105
HANDVEL 21406699
12      1498    492     1652    1024    1851    1792    2054
2180    2168    2684    2373    3000    2513    3596    2740
4040    2906    4760    3194    7000    4105
HANDVEL 1
12      1498    1024    1851    2436    2229    3192    2680
3996    3220    7000    4105
HANDVEL 22273450
12      1498    528     1674    1200    1901    2440    2268
3136    2648    3740    2906    4668    3259    5684    3626
7000    4105
HANDVEL 22273750
12      1498    528     1674    1056    1853    1700    2041
2792    2430    3552    2809    4192    3067    4912    3351
5464    3552    6028    3761    7000    4105
HANDVEL 22274050
12      1498    528     1674    1024    1842    1852    2098
2412    2307    2748    2425    3436    2753    4116    3006
5112    3390    6028    3761    7000    4105
HANDVEL 22274350
12      1498    528     1674    1024    1842    1852    2098
2412    2307    2748    2425    3192    2637    3996    2962
5004    3347    5540    3578    7000    4105
HANDVEL 22274650
12      1498    284     1574    668     1722    1180    1906
```

Figure 9.6. Output of Script 9.3.

Advanced programming in Perl for Beginners.

Now, we have to sort the information shown in Figure 9.6, so that the processing software can use it. To do that, we can use Script 9.4.

```
1  $sourceLetter="HANDVEL";
2
3  $files='G:\Vel-All\velUnSort.txt';
4  $output='G:\Vel-All\Vel-All.txt';
5  $i=0;
6  $l=0;
7  $string="";
8  open (FILES,$files);
9  open (OUT,'>'.$output);
10 print OUT "*CALL  VELDEF cdp        VMC3TST1\n";
11 $linea=<FILES>;
12 while ($linea) {
13  $HandvelWord=substr($linea,0,7);
14
15  @array2=split(" ",$linea);
16  $resultado=$HandvelWord eq $sourceLetter;
17
18  $Linea[$l]=$linea;
19  if ($resultado==1)
20  {
21   chomp $linea;
22   @array=split(" ",$linea);
23   $CDP[$i]=$array[1];
24   $i++;
25  }
26  if ($resultado!=1 && $l>1)
27  {
28   $string=$string.$linea;
29  }
30  if ($resultado==1 && $i>1)
31  {
32   $cdp{$CDP[$i-2]}=$string;
33   $string="";
34  }
35  $l++;
36  $linea=<FILES>;
37 }
38 $cdp{$CDP[$i-1]}=$Linea[$l-2].$Linea[$l-1];
39 @Linea=();
```

```
40 close FILES;
41 $j=0;
42 @CDPSort=sort{$a <=> $b} (@CDP);
43 foreach $item (@CDPSort) {
44  $CDPDebug{$CDPSort[$j]}=1;
45  $j++;
46 }
47 @Keys=keys(%CDPDebug);
48 @KeysSort=sort{$a <=> $b} (@Keys);
49 $j=0;
50 foreach $item (@KeysSort) {
51  print OUT "HANDVEL $KeysSort[$j]\n$cdp{$KeysSort[$j]}";
52  $j++;
53 }
54 close OUT;
```

The input file for this script is the file shown in Figure 9.6.

The variable $files on line 3 contains the complete path of the file with the velocity laws CDP unsorted.

On line 4 the variable that contains the complete path of the output file is defined. Remember that this file will have the CDP information sorted, such as is needed by the processing software Focus™.

On line 8, the file with the unsorted information is opened in reading mode and on line 9 the output file (in writing mode), which will contain the sorted information, is opened.

The output file will need the header information that is written on line 10.

Every velocity function begins with the word 'HANDVEL'. This is because we will use it as pattern to know when the script finds a velocity function. On line 1 we have defined a variable that contains that pattern.

On line 13, while we are reading the file, we are saving the first seven characters of every line in the variable $HandvelWord. When this string of characters is the same as HANDVEL, we can say that we have found a velocity function.

Between lines 19 and 25, there is an *if* structure that allows determining the number of CDP.

Advanced programming in Perl for Beginners.

We are interested in that the output file has the same format as shown in Figure 9.6, with CDP sorted. So, we are interested in copying the velocity functions as they are in the original file (Figure 9.6). This string is built between lines 26 and 37.

Notice that, on line 32, we are building a *hash*, where the *keys* are the CDP numbers.

The rest of the script is for sorting the *keys*. Once they are sorted, the velocity functions for every CDP can be written in the output file (line 51)

It is important to emphasize that the time and velocity information for every CDP are pairs sorted. For example, let's see Figure 9.6. Let's take as an example the CDP 22274350 (HANDVEL 22274350). The velocity function for this CDP would be as shown in Table 9.1.

Table 9.1. Velocity function.

CDP 22274350	
Time (ms)	**Velocity (m/s)**
12	1498
528	1674
1024	1842
1852	2098
2412	2307
2748	2425
3192	2637
3996	2962
5004	3347
5540	3578
7000	4105

Figure 9.7 shows how the final file looks, once the velocity functions have been CDP sorted.

```
Vel-All.txt
*CALL    VELDEF   cdp                        VMC3TST1
HANDVEL  1
12       1498     1044     1807     2416     2177     4364     2682
6932     3766
HANDVEL  6
12       1626     392      1688     1104     1867     2232     2122
3092     2414     3632     2615     4944     3299     7000     4100
HANDVEL  7
12       1626     392      1688     1100     1861     2260     2150
3112     2551     3688     2774     4956     3198     7000     4100
HANDVEL  1560466
24       1500     1676     2141     2420     2421     3132     2689
3836     2945     5016     3371     6896     4012
HANDVEL  1560766
24       1500     1084     1914     1676     2141     2420     2421
3132     2689     3836     2945     5016     3371     6896     4012
HANDVEL  1561066
24       1500     528      1686     1084     1914     1676     2153
2420     2421     3132     2689     3836     2945     5016     3371
6896     4012
HANDVEL  1561366
24       1500     528      1686     1084     1914     1676     2153
2420     2421     3132     2689     3836     2945     5016     3371
6896     4012
HANDVEL  1561666
24       1500     528      1686     1100     1896     1668     2129
2452     2403     3180     2677     3836     2945     5016     3371
6896     4012
HANDVEL  1561966
24       1500     1100     1896     1668     2129     2452     2403
```

Figure 9.7. Output of Script 9.4.

Chapter 10.

SEG-Y files.

10.1 SEG-Y files.

The SEG Y format is used in the geophysics world to represent seismic information. It has been developed by Society of Geophysics Engineers (SEG). It is possible to use this format to handle the seismic information in its different stages of the processing: shot gathers (raw data), CDP gathers or stacks.

The SEG Y format consists of three parts: a text header (usually known as EBCDIC header), a binary header and the body of a trace. In addition, it has its own header (trace header). Figure 10.1 schematically shows the structure of a SEG Y file. Figure 10.2 shows how the information appears in every trace. For more information, please visit http://seg.org/publications/tech-stand/

EBCDIC	BINARY	TH Trace 1	Data Trace 1	TH Trace 2	Data Trace 2	
3200 bytes	400 bytes	240 bytes	N bytes	240 bytes	N bytes	• • •

Figure 10.1. SEG-Y file structure.

Below we will study every part of a SEG-Y file carefully.

10.1.1 Text Header (EBCDIC).

The first part or text header (EBCDIC) has 3200 bytes of extension. The text header usually contains information about what is represented by the SEG Y file. For example the name of the survey, area, processing applied to the data, short description of the processing sequence, the location of important information as fold of every trace (post stack data), shot point, CDP, coordinates and others. Figure 10.3 is an example of text header, extracted from a file with stacked information. It is common that text header format varies, depending on software or standards.

Advanced programming in Perl for Beginners.

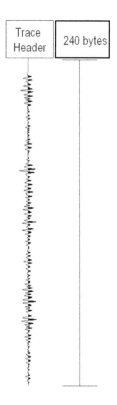

Figure 10.2. Trace structure (trace header + data).

As we mentioned above, the text header is usually known as EBCDIC, because it is the format used to pack this information into the file. Additional details can be found at http://en.wikipedia.org/wiki/EBCDIC .

The following script takes a SEG Y file as input from the command line, gets the first 3200 bytes from it and converts them from EBCDIC format to ASCII. The output is a text file with the ASCII (text) information.

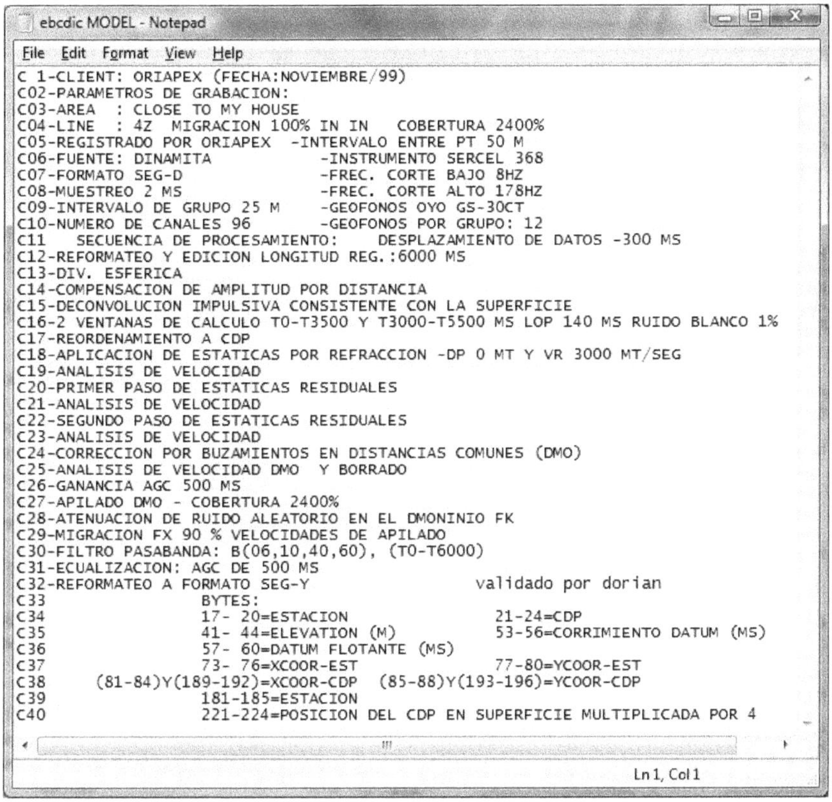

Figure 10.3. Example of text header (EBCDIC).

Script 10.1

```
1  use Encode;
2  open (IN,$ARGV[0]);
3  binmode(IN);
4  open (EBCDIC,'>ebcdic.txt');
5  read (IN,$buf,3200);
6  $string = decode("cp37", $buf);
7  for ($a=0;$a<40;$a++) {
8   $pos=$a*80;
9   $linea=substr($string,$pos,80);
10  print "$linea\n";
11  print EBCDIC "$linea\n";
12 }
13 close EBCDIC;
14 close IN;
```

Advanced programming in Perl for Beginners.

On the first line, the reserved word **use** tells the Perl interpreter that it includes the module as a part of the script. In this case, the necessary module is **Encode**.

On the second line, the special variable $ARGV[0] takes the value of a string that indicates the complete path of the SEG Y file to be opened. Remember that this variable will take as its value the complete path of the SEG-Y file to be read and it is introduced from the command prompt (or shell window).

Figure 10.4 shows the way the script must be run.

Figure 10.4. Running Script 10.1.

On the third line, the instruction **binmode**() is telling to the Perl interpreter to open the file in binary mode (the way that SEG Y files are always opened).

On line 4, the file that will contain the EBCDIC information is opened. The character '>' indicates that the file is opened in writing mode.

On line 5, the first 3200 bytes of the SEG Y file are read and assigned to the variable $buf.

On line 6, the variable $string will contain a chain of characters (3200) converted from EBCDIC to ASCII format. This is done using the instruction **decode**, with the option 'cp37'. According to the SEGY format the characters are together inside text header, one after the other. Because **decode** gives back a string of characters without format, we need a routine that gives us the appropriate format to read it properly. From line 7 to 12, the control structure **for-next** extracts every 80 characters from the text header, to make every line of the header appear as shown in Figure 10.3.

On line 13 the file EBCDIC is closed. While the file is open, the script will not write the file properly.

On line 14 the input file is closed.

10.1.2   Binary header.

This part of a SEG Y file comes after the EBCDIC and occupies the range of bytes from 3201 to 3600 (400 bytes in length). The binary header contains information that is mandatory to be able to read the SEG Y file. Even though the standard contains several variables that are mandatory, the most important ones are the number of samples per data trace (bytes 3221-3222) and the data sample format code (bytes 3225-3226). This information is required for every application to be able to read the file. If something is wrong in these values, the file will look corrupt.

Another variable that is very important is the sample interval (bytes 3217-3218). This value must be in microseconds. This information is necessary in order to create the scale whaen it is time to display it. However, this is not a critical value to read the data.

The following Perl script reads some variables of the binary header.

Script 10.2

```
 1  open (IN,$ARGV[0]);
 2  binmode(IN);
 3  read (IN,$buf,3600);
 4  $LineNumberString=substr($buf,3204,4);
 5  $LineNumber=unpack("N",$LineNumberString);
 6  $srString = substr ($buf,3216,2) ;
 7  $sr=unpack("n",$srString);
 8  $nsamplesString=substr ($buf,3220,2) ;
 9  $nsamples=unpack("n",$nsamplesString);
10  $codeString=substr($buf,3224,2) ;
11  $code=unpack("n",$codeString);
12  $TraceSortingCodeString=substr($buf,3228,2);
13  $TraceSortingCode=unpack("n",$TraceSortingCodeString);
14  if ($code==1) {
15   $mensajeFormato="32 bits Floating Point";
16  }
17  if ($code==2) {
18   $mensajeFormato="32 bits Fixed Point";
19  }
20  if ($code==3) {
21   $mensajeFormato="16 bits Fixed Point";
22  }
23  if ($code==4) {
24   $mensajeFormato="32 bits Fixed Point with Gain Values";
```

```
25 }
26 if ($code==5) {
27   $mensajeFormato="32 bits IEEE Floating Point";
28 }
29 if ($code==8){
30   $mensajeFormato="8 bits";
31 }
32 print "The number of the line is $LineNumber\n";
33 print "Sample Rate is $sr microseconds\n";
34 print "Sample Rate is ".($sr/1000)." in milliseconds\n";
35 print "Number of samples per trace is $nsamples\n";
36 print "Assuming trace data starts at 0 s, the length of data is ".(($nsamples-
   1)*$sr/1e6)." seconds\n";
37 print "Data sample format code $code, so the format of data is
   $mensajeFormato\n";
38 print "Trace sorting code is $TraceSortingCode\n";
39 close IN
```

This script must be run in the same way shown in Figure 10.4.

The output will look like as shown in Figure 10.5.

```
⊖ ○ ○              📁 EnglishScripts — bash — 81×9
MacBook-Air-de-Dorian:EnglishScripts dorian$ perl Script10-2.pl Archivo.SEGY
The number of the line is 3
Sample Rate is 4000 microseconds
Sample Rate is 4 in milliseconds
Number of samples per trace is 1501
Assuming trace data starts at 0 s, the length of data is 6 seconds
Data sample format code 1, so the format of data is 32 bits Floating Point
Trace sorting code is 1
MacBook-Air-de-Dorian:EnglishScripts dorian$ ▊
```

Figure 10.5. Output of Script 10.2.

The SEG Y file is opened with the instructions of the two first lines.

On third line, the first 3600 bytes of the SEG Y file, are read and stored under the variable $buf. $buf is a string of bytes.

On line four, with the instruction **substr** the bytes 3205 to 3208 from the variable $buf are extracted and stored in the variable $LineNumberString.

Line five contains one of the most important Perl instructions to handle SEG Y files: **unpack**. This instruction converts the binary information into something that can be read, which is ASCII format. In this case, the option 'N' converts 4-bytes strings.

Notice that, in order to read the right range of bytes, the reading must start one byte less than the range we want to read. So, according to the structure of binary header, sample rate is packed in the range of bytes 3217-3218. But, to be read, the reading must be started at byte 3216, as can be seen on line 6 of the script. Unlike $LineNumberString, $srString has a size of 2 bytes. So, to unpack this string the option 'n' (line 7) must be used.

From line 8 to 13, other variables of the binary header are read: number of samples per data trace, data sample format code and trace sorting code.

It is not possible to know the format of data directly, but it is possible to get the code and translate it according to the information shown in Table 10.1. This was programmed to help the user of the script to understand the format on lines 14 to 31.

Table 10.1. Data sample format code. Mandatory for all data.

Bytes	Description
3225-3226	1 = 4-byte IBM floating-point.
	2 = 4-byte, two's complement integer
	3 = 2-byte, two's complement integer
	4 = 4-byte fixed-point with gain (obsolete)
	5 = 4-byte IEEE floating-point
	6 = Not currently used
	7 = Not currently used
	8 = 1-byte, two's complement integer

From line 32 to 38 the values of the variables and other calculus are shown, based on these values. For example, the end time can be calculated from sample rate ($sr) and number of samples ($nsamples).

The data is packed in the binary header in the same way as the trace header. So, we will see similar instructions to unpack the information.

10.1.3 Trace Header.

Unlike the text and binary headers that are present only once in the SEG Y file structure, the trace header is repeated the same number of times as the traces in the

Advanced programming in Perl for Beginners.

file. This is because this header contains information that is unique for every trace. For example: number of the shot point, number of the CDP, coordinates, the numbers of inline and crossline (in case of 3D surveys), fold, etc.

Many programs currently work using the first version of SEG Y format (1975). This format assumed that all the traces in the file contain the same number of samples. However, the new version of the SEG Y format (not completely implemented yet) allows having traces with different number of samples and different sample rate. This is particularly useful in cases of joining more than one SEG Y file (2D or 3D). However, in case of joining SEG Y files, you must check that the data sample format code is the same. This variable is still in the domain of the binary header.

The following script shows the value of the variables SP, CDP, X-Coord y Y-Coord for the first trace of a SEG Y file.

Script 10.3

```
1  open (IN,$ARGV[0]);
2  binmode(IN);
3  read(IN,$buf,3840);
4  $spString=substr($buf,3616,4);
5  $sp=unpack("N",$spString);
6  $cdpString=substr($buf,3620,4);
7  $cdp=unpack("N",$cdpString);
8  $xString=substr($buf,3672,4);
9  $x=unpack("N",$xString);
10 $yString=substr($buf,3676,4);
11 $y=unpack("N",$yString);
12 print "The first SP is $sp\n";
13 print "The first CDP is $cdp\n";
14 print "The X-Coordinate of the first trace is $x\n";
15 print "The Y-Coordinate of the first trace is $y\n";
16 close IN
```

On the first two lines the SEG Y file is opened.

On the third line, the first 3840 bytes are read (EBCDIC=3200 + Binary=400 + Trace=240)

On the fourth line, the string that contains the number of the first shot point (SP) is extracted and stored in $spString. This is done using the instruction substr. Perl gives the same treatment to any strings; it does not matter if they are strings of

ASCII characters, or binary encoded, etc.

On the fifth line, the variable $spString is unpacked and stored in $sp.

On the sixth line, the string that contains the number of the CDP is extracted and stored in $cdpString.

On the seventh line, the variable $cdpString is unpacked and stored in $cdp.

On the eight line, the string that contains the X-Coordinate of the first trace is extracted and stored in $xString.

On the ninth line, the variable $xString is unpacked and stored in $x.

On the tenth line, the string that contains the Y-Coordinate of the first trace is extracted and stored in $yString.

On eleventh line, the variable $xyString is unpacked and stored in $y.

After running the previous script, we will see an output as shown below.

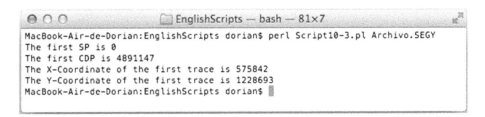

Figure 10.6. Output of Script 10.3.

10.2 Number of traces that a SEGY file contains.

The size of a SEG Y file, in bytes, can be obtained from the following equation:

$$SizeOfFile = TeHS + BinHS + nT * TrHS + nT * SDT \qquad (1)$$

Where

TeHS: text header size, it means 3200 bytes.

Advanced programming in Perl for Beginners.

BinHS: binary header size, it means 400 bytes.

nT: number of traces into the SEG Y file.

TrHS: trace header size, it means 240 bytes

SDT: size in bytes of the portion of the trace without trace header. This value can be calculated as follows:

$$SDT = nSamples * SSize \qquad (2)$$

Where

nSamples: the number of samples of every trace. This information is available in the bytes 3221-3222.

SSize: this value depends on the data sample format code (bytes 3225-3226). For example, if data sample format code is 1, then the size in bytes of every sample is 4 bytes.

The first equation can be rewritten as follows:

$$SizeOfile = 3600 + nT * (240 + nSamples * SSize) \qquad (3)$$

SizeOfFile can be obtained from the Operative System. So, the number of traces of a SEG Y file can be obtained as follows:

$$nT = \frac{SizeOfFile - 3600}{240 + nSamples * SSize}$$
(4)

The following one uses this equation to calculate the number of traces into a SEG Y file.

Script 10.4

```
1  use File::stat;
2  open (IN,$ARGV[0]);
3  binmode(IN);
4  open (LOG,'>'.$ARGV[1]);
5  $filesize=stat($ARGV[0])->size;
```

```
 6  sysseek(IN,3200,0);
 7  if (read (IN,$buf,400)){
 8   $sr=unpack("n",substr($buf,16,2));
 9   $sample=unpack("n",substr($buf,20,2));
10   $code=unpack("n",substr($buf,24,2));
11   $btr=4;
12   if ($code==8 || $code==0 || $code==6){
13    $btr=1;
14    print "Data Format: 8 bits\n";
15    print LOG "Data Format: 8 bits\n";
16   }
17   if ($code==3){
18    $btr=2;
19    print "Data Format: 16 bits\n";
20    print LOG "Data Format: 16 bits\n";
21   }
22   if ($btr==4) {
23    print "Data Format: 32 bits\n";
24    print LOG "Data Format: 32 bits\n";
25   }
26  }
27  $pertrace=($sample*$btr)+240;
28  $trazas=($filesize-3600)/$pertrace;
29  print "The SEG-Y file has $filesize bytes\n";
30  print "The Sample Rate is $sr microseconds\n";
31  print "Each trace has $sample samples\n";
32  print "So, The total number of traces is $trazas\n";
33  print
     "=============================================
     ";
34  print "  \n";
35  print LOG "The SEG-Y file has $filesize bytes\n";
36  print LOG "The Sample Rate is $sr microseconds\n";
37  print LOG "Each trace has $sample samples\n";
38  print LOG "So, The total number of traces is $trazas\n";
39  print "...Finished.\n";
```

The script must be run from the command line. The following picture shows the output of it. It needs two arguments: the first one is the input SEG Y file and the second one is an output file. This output file has the same content as the information shown in the following command prompt window.

Advanced programming in Perl for Beginners.

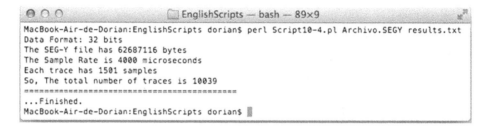

Figure 10.7. Output of Script 10.4.

On the first line the module necessary to get status info for a file is invoked. On line 2 the input file is opened (the complete path of the file is assigned to the variable $ARGV[0]). On line 3, with the instruction **binmode**, Perl understands the file must be opened in binary mode.

An output file is opened on line 4, which will contain information about the SEG Y file (stored in the file with complete path $ARGV[1]).

On line 5 we use the method size of the module File::stat to get the size in bytes of the input file ($ARGV[0]).

On line 6 we use the instruction sysseek to skip the first 3200 bytes (the size of the text header). The number 0 in the instruction sets the new position to 3200.

Between lines 7 and 26 the variables sample rate, number of samples per trace and data sample format code of the binary header are read. By default, the size for every sample is 4 bytes ($btr in line 11). The value changes to 1 if the data sample format code is 0, 6 or 8 ($code, line 10). If $code is 3, then $btr takes the value of 2.

The size of every trace, including its own header (240 bytes) is calculated on line 27 ($pertrace). This variable is the divisor in equation 4. Finally, the number of traces is calculated on line 28 ($trazas).

Between lines 29 and 34, the script shows the results in the command prompt window. The same information is written in a file between lines 35 and 39 (in our example results.txt).

10.3 Displaying seismic information in SEGY format.

The following script cannot be run if you have installed the most recent version of Perl from ActiveState. Unfortunately, Perl Tk is not a part of the new versions, but

Perl Tkx is. I say "unfortunately", because the next one can only be run with Perl Tk. An option you can test, if you have Perl from ActiveState, is installing Tk. To do this, follow the instructions given in Chapter 1.

In addition, it is necessary to install the module Tk::Zinc. To do this, you can follow the instructions given in Chapter 6.

The following is the script to display seismic information in SEGY format:

Script 10.5

```
1   use Tk;
2   use Tk::Zinc;
3   use File::stat;
4
5   $mw=MainWindow->new(-width=>1050,-height=>800);
6   $zinc=$mw->Zinc(-width => 900, -height => 700,-borderwidth => 3, -
    relief => 'sunken',-backcolor=>'white');
7   $zinc->place(-x=>0,-y=>0);
8   $boton_show=$mw->Button(-text=>'Show SEG Y',-
    command=>\&display);
9   $boton_show->place(-x=>920,-y=>40);
10  MainLoop;
11
12  sub display {
13  $i=0;
14  $file='/Users/dorian/Documents/PerlBook/EnglishScripts/Archivo.SEG
    Y';
15  $filesize = stat($file)->size;
16  ($sample,$btr,$trazas);
17  $[ = 1;
18  open (IN,$file);
19  binmode(IN);
20  read (IN,$buf,3200);
21  if (read (IN,$buf,400)){
22  $dsr = substr ($buf,17,2) ;
23  $sr = unpack ( "n" , $dsr);
24
25  $dsample = substr ($buf,21,2) ;
26  $sample = unpack ( "n" , $dsample);
27
28  $dcode= substr ($buf,25,2) ;
29  $code = unpack ( "n" , $dcode);
```

```
30
31  $btr=4;
32  if ($code==8){$btr=1;}
33  if ($code==8){$btr=1;}
34  if ($code==3){$btr=2;}
35  }
36
37  $pertrace=($sample*$btr)+240;
38  $bt=($pertrace-240)/4;
39  $trazas=($filesize-3600)/$pertrace;
40  $tr=0;
41  @array2;
42  $data;
43  $data_bytes;
44  $T;
45  while (read (IN,$buf,$pertrace)) {
46  $data_bytes=unpack("a*",$buf);
47   for ($i=0;$i<$bt;$i++) {
48    $data=substr ($data_bytes, 241+4*$i,4);
49    $[ = 0;
50    $array2[0][2*$i+1]=($i/2)+10; #time axis
51    $array2[0][2*$i]=ibm2dec($data)/1e8+30+$tr*2;
52    $[ = 1;
53   }
54   last if ($tr>600);
55   $b=$zinc->add('curve',1,$array2[0],-filled=>1,-fillrule=>'negative');
56   $tr++;
57  }
58  close IN;
59  }
60
61  sub ibm2dec {
62   my($ibm)=vec($_[$[],0,32);
63   my($sign,$mant,$t,$floatmant,$floatboth);
64   $sign=0x80000000&$ibm?-1:1;  # Determine the sign of the number.
65   $mant=0x00ffffff&$ibm;    # Mask out exponent, leaving mantissa.
66   $t=((0x7f000000&$ibm)>>22)-130; # Extract exponent, shift down, de-
    bias.
67   $floatmant=$mant/16777216.;
68   $floatboth=$sign*$floatmant*exp(($t-126.)*log(2.));
69  }
```

I will explain what is new in this script. On line 2 the necessary module to use the library Zinc is invoked.

Between lines 5 and 10 the main window of the application is built.

The subroutine display from line 12 to 59 will display the seismic data contained in the SEGY file (line 14).

From line 45, the SEGY file is read. On line 46, we use the variable $data_bytes to store the information of every trace unpacked.

From line 47 to 53 we have a loop to read the information of every sample of the seismic trace. On line 50 the time axis is built for every trace and on line 51 the array that contains the value of every sample is built. Notice that a subroutine is invoked in that line (ibm2dec). This routine (from lines 61 to 69) converts the information from binary (32 bits floating point format) to decimal format.

On line 54 we have a condition that controls the traces that will be displayed.

Finally, the graphics are done on line 55. To get more help about the module Tk::Zinc, please consult http://search.cpan.org/~zincdev/tk-zinc-3.303/Zinc.pm.

Once the script is run, you must press the button 'Show SEG Y'. After this is done, the app will look as shown in Figure 10.8.

Advanced programming in Perl for Beginners.

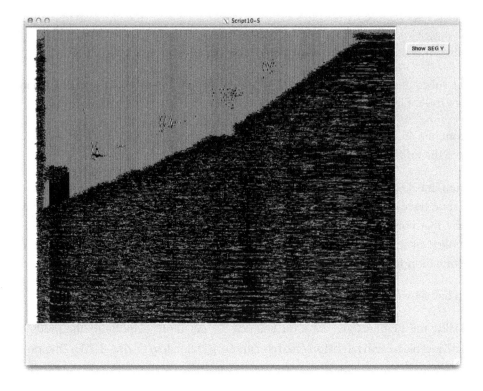

Figure 10.8. Output of Script 10.5.

Chapter 11.

Seismic Data Acquisition.

11.1 Seismic acquisition field operation.

Usually, in a seismic data acquisition survey, a lot of information is generated, with a large variety of formats. If explosives are used as sources of energy in a land survey, for example, the following are the basic stages of the operation:

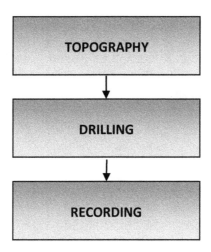

Figure 11.1. Basic stages in a seismic acquisition survey on land.

In all of these stages, a lot of information is generated. Even though all of them are important, traditionally the most important and delicate of them is the stage of recording. In this stage finally all the seismic data is recorded. It is usual that thousands of channels and cables and complex electronic devices are deployed in the field. All this equipment is very expensive and in many places it is convenient (for several reasons) to record the information as soon as possible. However, it is important, as well, that the data be recorded with the best possible quality.

In the following, we will see a script (scrip 11.1) that I programmed in 2004 to check the geophone tests and FDU equipment of Sercel 408™. This script has a lot of comments, so while you type it, you will be able to check everything you have studied in this book.

The geophone test file looks as shown in Figure 11.2. The FDU test file is shown in Figure 11.3.

080404.geo

SENSOR QC

Serial Nb	Line Name	Point Nb	Point Index	Sensor Type	Segd Code	Resistance (ohm)	Noise (uv)	Leakage (Mo)	Tilt (%)	Easting	Northing	Elevation	Latest Update
3009	1024	5324	1	1	2	862	3.26	2.00	2.4	454375.0	2004549.9	8.2	Apr 8, 2004 1:27
3009	1024	5325	1	1	2	892	4.17	2.00	0.9	454424.2	2004549.9	7.4	Apr 8, 2004 1:27
3009	1024	5326	1	1	2	936	4.32	2.00	0.1	454472.3	2004550.3	8.4	Apr 8, 2004 1:27
6083	1024	5327	1	1	2	921	3.50	2.00	1.6	454525.3	2004550.1	9.0	Apr 8, 2004 1:27
6083	1024	5328	1	1	2	889	3.62	2.00	4.5	454578.4	2004550.1	8.0	Apr 8, 2004 1:27
6083	1024	5329	1	1	2	853	3.24	2.00	0.3	454625.0	2004551.0	9.7	Apr 8, 2004 1:27
6083	1024	5330	1	1	2	861	4.53	2.00	0.8	454675.2	2004549.9	9.1	Apr 8, 2004 1:27
6083	1024	5331	1	1	2	903	5.09	2.00	1.1	454722.6	2004550.1	9.2	Apr 8, 2004 1:27
6083	1024	5332	1	1	2	935	5.38	2.00	0.8	454777.1	2004551.5	9.1	Apr 8, 2004 1:27
2674	1024	5333	1	1	2	924	3.62	2.00	0.3	454825.9	2004551.2	9.1	Apr 8, 2004 1:27

Figure 11.2. Example of geophone test file.

Boxes

Channels FDU

Serial Nb	Box Type	Ch. Nb	Line Name	Point Nb		Auto Test	Distortion (dB)	Noise (uV)	CMRR (dB)	Gain Error	Phase (us)	Crosstalk	Latest Update
2832381	FDU1	1	Aux	a4	A	ok	-112	0.46	133	0.1	2	140	Jun 29, 2003 8:44
2822453	FDU1	1	Aux	a3	A	ok	-112	0.51	134	-0.0	2	140	Jun 29, 2003 8:44
2853354	FDU1	1	Aux	a2	A	ok	-108	0.52	136	0.0	4	140	Jun 29, 2003 8:44
2851693	FDU1	1	Aux	a1	A	ok	-110	0.57	130	0.0	-1	140	Jun 29, 2003 8:44
2948343	FDU1	1	1699	5184		ok	-113	0.46	135	0.1	-2	140	Jun 29, 2003 12:41
2977834	FDU1	1	1699	5183		ok	-105	0.51	136	0.1	4	140	Jun 29, 2003 12:41
2881491	FDU1	1	1699	5182		ok	-110	0.47	133	-0.0	-5	140	Jun 29, 2003 12:41
3014084	FDU1	1	1699	5181		ok	-113	0.42	134	0.0	2	140	Jun 29, 2003 12:41
3016181	FDU1	1	1699	5180		ok	-114	0.46	139	0.1	2	140	Jun 29, 2003 12:41
2982453	FDU1	1	1699	5179		ok	-109	0.52	133	0.1	3	140	Jun 29, 2003 12:41
3152543	FDU1	1	1699	5178		ok	-111	0.52	136	0.1	3	140	Jun 29, 2003 12:41
3200783	FDU1	1	1699	5177		ok	-113	0.63	131	0.2	1	140	Jun 29, 2003 12:41
3013984	FDU1	1	1699	5176		ok	-114	0.45	136	0.1	0	140	Jun 29, 2003 12:41
3016632	FDU1	1	1699	5175		ok	-113	0.45	137	0.2	0	140	Jun 29, 2003 12:41

Figure 11.3. Example of FDU test file.

Script 11.1

```
#--------------------------------------
# Script Name: carolina.pl
# Script Version: 1.0
# Date: 03/24/04
# Author: Dorian Oria
# Description: check geophone test and boxes of SERCEL 408 recording system
#
use lib "..";
use Tk::DialogBox;
use Tk;
use Tk::Menubutton;
use Tk::Wm;
use Tk::Text;
use Tk::Scrollbar;
```

```
15  use Tk::ProgressBar;
16  use Tk::LabFrame;
17  use Tk::TextUndo;
18  use Tk::Optionmenu;
19  use Tk::Radiobutton;
20  use Tk::Widget;
21
22  ############Initializing vectors and counters ############
23
24  $onoffg=0;
25  $onoffb=0;
26
27  #Building Main Window
28  my $top = new MainWindow(-title=>'Carolina');
29  $top->configure(-width=>600);
30  $top->configure(-height=>460);
31  $top->resizable(0,0);
32  ##############################################
33
34  #Progress Bar
35  $progress=$top->ProgressBar(
36          -width=>25,
37          -from=>0,
38          -length=>400,
39          -to=>100,
40          -blocks=>100,
41          -troughcolor=>'lightgreen',
42          -gap=>2,
43          -colors=>[0,'white',20,'lightyellow',40,'yellow',60,'orange',80,'red'],
44          -variable=>\$percent_done
45          );
46
47  $progress->place(-x=>2,-y=>375);
48
    $etiqueta1=$top->Label(-textvariable=>\$aviso); #esta etiqueta esta
49  encima de la barra de progreso
```

```perl
50 $etiqueta1->place(-x=>1,-y=>355);
51
52 $etiqueta2=$top->Label(-textvariable=>\$percent);
53 $etiqueta2->place(-x=>405,-y=>375);
54
55 #End of Progress Bar
56 ##############################################
57
58 #Label indicating equipemet that is being checked
59 $checando=$top->Label(-text=>'Checking:');
60 $checando->place(-x=>4,-y=>35);
61 $aviso2=$top->Label(-textvariable=>\$equipo);
62 $aviso2->place(-x=>70,-y=>35);
63 ##############################################
64
65
66 #Frame that contains buttons to establish test parameters for geophones
   $framevalue=$top->LabFrame(-label=>'Geophone Parameters',-
67 labelside=>'acrosstop',-width=>200,-height=>115);
68 $framevalue->place(-x=>135,-y=>60);
69
70 #Text boxes with cut values for geophones
   $res_text=$framevalue->Label(-text=>'< Resistance <',-
71 foreground=>'darkgreen');
72 $res_text->place(-x=>50,-y=>2);
   $lim_inf = $framevalue->Entry(-width => '6', -relief => 'sunken',-
73 background=>'red');
74 $lim_inf->place(-x => 2,-y=>2);
   $lim_sup=$framevalue->Entry(-width => '6', -relief => 'sunken',-
75 background=>'red');
76 $lim_sup->place(-x => 142,-y=>2);
77
78 $leak_tetxt=$framevalue->Label(-text=>'Leakage >');
79 $leak_tetxt->place(-x=>2,-y=>20);
   $lim_leak= $framevalue->Entry(-width => '6', -relief => 'sunken',-
80 background=>'lightgreen');
81 $lim_leak->place(-x => 67,-y=>20);
```

```
82
83 $tilt_text=$framevalue->Label(-text=>'Tilt <');
84 $tilt_text->place(-x=>2,-y=>45);
   $lim_tilt= $framevalue->Entry(-width => '6', -relief => 'sunken',-
85 background=>'yellow');
86 $lim_tilt->place(-x => 67,-y=>45);
87
88 $noise_text=$framevalue->Label(-text=>'Noise <');
89 $noise_text->place(-x=>2,-y=>70);
   $lim_noise= $framevalue->Entry(-width => '6', -relief => 'sunken',-
90 background=>'lightblue');
91 $lim_noise->place(-x => 67,-y=>70);
92 ###############################################
93
94 #Frame that contains labesl with cut parameters for boxes SU6-R o FDU
   $frameequipo=$top->LabFrame(-label=>'Box Parameters',-
95 labelside=>'acrosstop',-width=>200,-height=>140);
96 $frameequipo->place(-x=>350,-y=>60);
97
98 $dis_text=$frameequipo->Label( -text=>'Distortion      Max');
99 $dis_text->place(-x=>2,-y=>2);
100
101 $noise_text=$frameequipo->Label( -text=>'Noise      Max');
102 $noise_text->place(-x=>2,-y=>27);
103
104 $cmr_text=$frameequipo->Label( -text=>'CMR      Min');
105 $cmr_text->place(-x=>2,-y=>47);
106
107 $x_text=$frameequipo->Label(   -text=>'X Talk      Min');
108 $x_text->place(-x=>2,-y=>67);
109
110 $gain_text=$frameequipo->Label( -text=>'Gain      Max');
111 $gain_text->place(-x=>2,-y=>87);
112
113 $phase_text=$frameequipo->Label( -text=>'Phase      Max');
114 $phase_text->place(-x=>2,-y=>107);
```

```perl
115
116 $dis_value=$frameequipo->Label(-textvariable=>\$dist);
117 $dis_value->place(-x=>65,-y=>2);
118
119 $noise_value=$frameequipo->Label(-textvariable=>\$noise);
120 $noise_value->place(-x=>65,-y=>27);
121
122 $cmr_value=$frameequipo->Label(-textvariable=>\$cmr);
123 $cmr_value->place(-x=>65,-y=>47);
124
125 $xtalk_value=$frameequipo->Label(-textvariable=>\$xtalk);
126 $xtalk_value->place(-x=>65,-y=>67);
127
128 $gain_value=$frameequipo->Label(-textvariable=>\$gain);
129 $gain_value->place(-x=>65,-y=>87);
130
131 $phase_value=$frameequipo->Label(-textvariable=>\$phase);
132 $phase_value->place(-x=>65,-y=>107);
133
134
135 #Main Menu
136 $menuframe=$top->Frame(-relief=>'ridge',-bd=>1);
137 $menuframe->place(-x=>0,-y=>0);
138 $help_menu = $menuframe->Menubutton(-text => "Help",
139         -tearoff => 0,
140         -menuitems => [
141         ["command" => "Help", -command => sub {&ayuda}],
142         "-"])->pack();
143
144 $util_menu= $menuframe->Menubutton(-text => "Geo Parameters File",
145         -tearoff => 0,
146         -menuitems => [
147         ["command" => "New" , -command => sub {&geoparnew}],
        ["command" => "Open", -command => sub
148 {&carga_geo_pam;}],
149         ["command" => "Save", -command => sub {&save}],
```

```perl
150        ["command" => "Save As", -command => sub {&saveas}],
151        "-"]
152
153      )->pack();
154
155 $box_menu= $menuframe->Menubutton(-text => "Box Parameters File",
156        -tearoff => 0,
157        -menuitems => [
158        ["command" => "FDU" , -command => sub {&FDU}],
159        ["command" => "SU6-R", -command => sub {&SU6R}],
160        "-"]
161
162      )->pack();
163 $help_menu->pack(-side=>'right');
164 $util_menu->pack(-side=>'left');
165 $box_menu->pack(-side=>'left');
166
167 ##############################################
    #Frame that contains a combobox with all the sample rates and gains,
168 depending on the equipment
169 sub FDU {
170 $equipo="FDU";
171 &etiquetas_equipo;
172 $act_fdu=1;   #indica si est· activo el equipo FDU
173 if ($act_sur==1)
174 {$combo_time_SU6->destroy;
175 $combo_gain_SU6->destroy;
176 $act_sur=0;}
177
178 $combo_time_fdu=$top->Optionmenu(-textvariable=>\$sample,
179        -options=> [["0.25 ms"],
180            ["0.50 ms"],
181            ["1.00 ms"],
182            ["2.00 ms"],
183            ["4.00 ms"]]);
184 $combo_time_fdu->place(-x=>210,-y=>30);
```

```perl
185
186 $combo_gain_fdu=$top->Optionmenu(-textvariable=>\$gain_equip,
187        -options=> [["0 dB"],
188             ["12 dB"]]);
189 $combo_gain_fdu->place(-x=>340,-y=>30);
190 return $equipo;
191 }
192
193 sub SU6R {
194 $equipo="SU6-R";
195 &etiquetas_equipo;
196 $act_sur=1;  #indicates if the SU6-R equipment is selected
197 if ($act_fdu==1)
198 {$combo_time_fdu->destroy;
199 $combo_gain_fdu->destroy;
200 $act_fdu=0;}
201
202 $combo_time_SU6=$top->Optionmenu(-textvariable=>\$sample,
203        -options=> [["1.00 ms"],
204             ["2.00 ms"],
205             ["4.00 ms"]]);
206 $combo_time_SU6->place(-x=>210,-y=>30);
207
208 $combo_gain_SU6=$top->Optionmenu(-textvariable=>\$gain_equip,
209        -options=> [["24 dB"],
210             ["36 dB"],
211             ["42 dB"],
212             ["48 dB"]]);
213 $combo_gain_SU6->place(-x=>340,-y=>30);
214 return $equipo;
215 }
216
217 ###############################################
218 #Frame that contains the buttons to choice geophone or boxes test
    $labframe=$top->LabFrame(-label=>'Test',-labelside=>'acrosstop',-
219 width=>120,-height=>55);
```

```
220 $labframe->place(-x=>2,-y=>60);
221
222 #Botones radio button para escoger cajas o geofonos
    $geo=$top->Radiobutton(-command=>sub{&check_geo},-
    selectcolor=>'lightgreen',-text=>'Geophones',-variable=>\$onoffg);#,-
223 value=>0);
224 $geo->place(-x=>6,-y=>80);
225
    $box=$top->Radiobutton(-command=>sub{&impbox},-
226 selectcolor=>'lightgreen',-text=>'Boxes',-variable=>\$onoffb);
227 $box->place(-x=>6,-y=>105);
228 ############################################
229
230 #Button to exit
231 $exitbutton=$top->Button(-text=>'Exit',-command=>sub{exit});
232 $exitbutton->place(-x=>380,-y=>420,-width=>50);
233 ############################################
234
235 #Messages about the author
    $mensaje=$top->Label(-text=>'This software has been made by Dorian
236 Oria');
237 $mensaje->place(-x=>2,-y=>405);
238
239 $email=$top->Label(-text=>'e-mail: dorian.oria@gmail.com');
240 $email->place(-x=>63,-y=>420);
241 ############################################
242
243 #Yellow window
    $topframe = $top->Frame('-relief' => 'ridge'); # contains buffer list and
244 editor
245 $topframe->place(-x=>2,-y=>230);
    $leftframe = $topframe->Frame('-relief' => 'ridge'); # this is the buffer
246 list
247 $leftframe->pack('-side','left','-fill','y',-anchor => 'nw',-expand => 1);
    $archivos = $leftframe->Scrolled(qw/TextUndo -relief sunken -height 3 -
248 bg yellow -scrollbars osoe -exportselection 1 -wrap none/);
249 $archivos->configure(-height=>7,-width=>59);
250 $archivos->pack('-side', 'top', '-expand' , 1,'-anchor' => 's','-fill','both');
```

```perl
251 $aviso="Starting...";
252 $percent=0 . "%";
253
254 &carga_automatica_geo_pam;
255
256 MainLoop;
257
258 #End of the construction of Main Window
259 ################################################
260
261 sub check_geo {
262 $mensaje_geo1="Geophone Test";
263 $mensaje_geo2="File with all geophones";
264 $mensaje_geo3="File with bad geophones";
265 $mensaje_geo4="File with resume of bad geophones";
266 $file="Geophone Test Files";
267 $ext="*.geo";
268 $l_inf_res=$lim_inf->get;
269 $l_sup_res=$lim_sup->get;
270 $l_leak=$lim_leak->get;
271 $l_tilt=$lim_tilt->get;
272 $l_noise=$lim_noise->get;
273 $ruta1=abrir($top);
    $rb=0;     #Counts the real bad elements (boxes or geophones). It means,
274 in this count is included bad elements
275         #it does not matter if they have one or more failures.
276 $b=0;
277 $j=0;
278 $i=0;
279 $n=0;
280 $k=0;
281 $noseaplicopruebares=0;
282 $noseaplicopruebaleak=0;
283 $noseaplicopruebanoise=0;
284 $noseaplicopruebatilt=0;
285 $desconectadas=0;
```

```
286 $malres=0;
287 $malleak=0;
288 $malnoise=0;
289 $maltilt=0;
290 %really_bad=();
291 @caja=();
292 @linename=();
293 @point=();
294 @resistance=();
295 @noise=();
296 @leakage=();
297 @tilt=();
298 @easting=();
299 @northing=();
300 @month=();
301 @day=();
302 @year=();
303 @hour=();
304
305 $noapli="N/A";
    $string1="Serial"; #kew word that indicates when the data is closed to
306 start in the test file
307 $string2="------"; #This string is at the end of the geophone test file
308 #########Reading of the file with geophone test ##########
309 $lf = 0;
310 open(FILE, $ruta1) or die "Can't open `$filename': $!";
311 while (sysread FILE, $buffer, 4096) {
312  $lf += ($buffer =~ tr/\n//);
313 }
    $lf=$lf-9;  #discount the lines at the begining and at the end of the file
314 without information
315 close (FILE);
316
317 ##########End of reading geophone test file ############
318
319
```

```
320  #Open the file with the results of the test for geophones
321  open(geo,$ruta1)||die ("Could not open file \n");
322
323  $linea=<geo>;
324  $aviso="Reading " . $ruta1;
325  #The searching of patterns is started here
326  while ($linea)
327  {
328  $i++;            #counts the lines into the file with data
329  if ($result1=$linea=~/$string1/)
330  {
331  $b=$i;
332  #  $r=0;
333  }
334   if ($result2=$linea=~/$string2/)
335  {
336   $k++;          #flag that indicates string2 has been found
337  }
338  if ($i-$b>2 && $k==2)
339   {
340  @array=split(" ",$linea);
     for ($a=0;$a<1;$a++) #a<10, this number indicates the quantity of
341  columns included in data test
342  {
343  $caja[$j]=$array[$a];
344  $linename[$j]=$array[$a+1];
345    $point[$j]=$array[$a+2];
346    $resistance[$j]=$array[$a+6];
347    $noise[$j]=$array[$a+7];
348    $leakage[$j]=$array[$a+8];
349    $tilt[$j]=$array[$a+9];
350    $easting[$j]=$array[$a+10];
351    $northing[$j]=$array[$a+11];
352    $month[$j]=$array[$a+13];
353    $array[$a+14]=~s/\,//; #eliminates the comma of the string day
354    $day[$j]=$array[$a+14];
```

```perl
355 $year[$j]=$array[$a+15];
356 $hour[$j]=$array[$a+16];
357 $j++;
358 }
359 }
360 $percent_done=sprintf "%.0f",($i/$lf)*100;
361 $percent=$percent_done . "%";
362 $progress->update;
363 $linea=<geo>;
364 }
365 #
366 $salida1=salvar1($top);
367 $salida2=salvar2($top);
368 $salida3=salvar3($top);
    #It is created a file with all the information extracted from geophone test
369 file
370 open (salida,'>' . $salida1); #all the elements of the test
371 open (malas,'>' . $salida2); #all the elemento of the test
372 open (real_malas,'>' . $salida3);
    print salida
    "Box\tLine\tPoint\tRes\tNoise\tLeak\tTilt\tEast\t\tNorth\t\tMonth\
373 tDay\tYear\tHour\n";
374 print malas "Box\tLine\tPoint\tValue\tTest\n";
375 $archivos->insert('end',"Resume of strings out of specifications:\n");
376 $archivos->insert('end',"Res\tLeak\tNoise\tTilt\tDiscon\n");
377 foreach (@caja)
378 {
379 $aviso="Writing Results Files...";
    $nar=$resistance[$n] eq $noapli;  #checks if there is a resistance value
380 equal to N/A
381 $nal=$leakage[$n] eq $noapli;
382 $nan=$noise[$n] eq $noapli;
383 $nat=$tilt[$n] eq $noapli;
    print salida
    "$caja[$n]\t$linename[$n]\t$point[$n]\t$resistance[$n]\t$noise[$n]\t$leak
    age[$n]\t$tilt[$n]\t$easting[$n]\t$northing[$n]\t$month[$n]\t$day[$n]\t$
384 year[$n]\t$hour[$n] \n";
```

```
385  #routine for resistance test
386  if ($resistance[$n]==9999)
387  {
388   $desconectadas++;  #counts the disconnected strings
389  }
390  if ($nar!=1)
391  {
      if ($resistance[$n]<$l_inf_res || $resistance[$n]>$l_sup_res &&
392  $resistance[$n]!=9999)
393    {
394    $aviso="Resistance";
395    $malres++;
396    $punto_pegado=$linename[$n] . $point[$n];
       $really_bad{$punto_pegado}=$really_bad{$punto_pegado} . "-" .
397  $aviso;
      print malas
398  "$caja[$n]\t$linename[$n]\t$point[$n]\t$resistance[$n]\tResistance \n";
399    }
400  }
401  Else
402  {
403   $noseaplicopruebares++;
404  }
405  #End of the resistance routine
406  #Routine for leakage test
407  if ($nal!=1)
408  {
409   if ($leakage[$n]<$l_leak && $resistance[$n]!=9999)
410    {
411    $aviso="Leakage";
412    $malleak++;
413    $punto_pegado=$linename[$n] . $point[$n];
       $really_bad{$punto_pegado}=$really_bad{$punto_pegado} . "-" .
414  $aviso;
      print malas
415  "$caja[$n]\t$linename[$n]\t$point[$n]\t$leakage[$n]\tLeakage \n";
416    }
```

```
417  }
418  Else
419  {
420  $noseaplicopruebaleak++;
421  }
422  #End of Routine for leakage test
423  #Routine for noise test
424  if ($nan!=1)
425  {
426  if ($noise[$n]>$l_noise && $resistance[$n]!=9999)
427  {
428  $aviso="Noise";
429  $malnoise++;
     print malas "$caja[$n]\t$linename[$n]\t$point[$n]\t$noise[$n]\tNoise
430  \n";
431  }
432  }
433  Else
434  {
435  $noseaplicopruebanoise++;
436  }
437  #End of Routine for noise test
438  #Routine for tilt test
439  if ($nat!=1)
440  {
441  if ($tilt[$n]>$l_tilt && $resistance[$n]!=9999 && $tilt!=100)
442  {
443  $aviso="Tilt";
444  $maltilt++;
445  $punto_pegado=$linename[$n] . $point[$n];
     $really_bad{$punto_pegado}=$really_bad{$punto_pegado} . "-" .
446  $aviso;
447  print malas "$caja[$n]\t$linename[$n]\t$point[$n]\t$tilt[$n]\tTilt \n";
448  }
449  }
450  Else
```

```perl
451  {
452  $noseaplicopruebatilt++;
453  }
454  #End of Routine for tilt test
455  $n++;
456  }
457  $length=@caja;
458
     $archivos->insert('end',
459  "$malres\t$malleak\t$malnoise\t$maltilt\t$desconectadas\n");
     $archivos->insert('end', "Resistance Test was not applied at
460  $noseaplicopruebares strings \n");
     $archivos->insert('end', "Leakage Test was not applied at
461  $noseaplicopruebaleak strings \n");
     $archivos->insert('end', "Noise Test was not applied at
462  $noseaplicopruebanoise strings \n");
     $archivos->insert('end', "Tilt Test was not applied at $noseaplicopruebatilt
463  strings \n");
464  $archivos->insert('end', "$length samples were checked\n");
465  $aviso="Ready for another test";
466  close(salida);
467  close(malas);
468  close(geo);
469  @re_bad=keys(%really_bad);
470  @re_bad_test=values(%really_bad);
471  $length=@re_bad;
     $archivos->insert('end',"There are $length strings out of
472  specifications\n");
473  print real_malas "Point\tTests\n";
474  foreach (@re_bad) {
475  print real_malas "$re_bad[$rb]\t$re_bad_test[$rb]\n";
476  $rb++;
477  }
478  close(real_malas);
479  $onoffg=0;
480  $onoffb=0;
481
```

```
482 #End of geophone test
483 }
484
485 ################Begining of the box checkin##########
486 sub impbox {
487 $mensaje_geo1="Box Test";
488 $mensaje_geo2="File with all boxes";
489 $mensaje_geo3="File with bad boxes";
490 $mensaje_geo4="File with resume of bad boxes";
491 $file="Box Test Files";
492 $ext="*.tst";
493 $ruta1=abrir($top);
494 $rb=0;
495 $b=0;
496 $j=0;
497 $i=0;
498 $n=0;
499 $k=0;
500 $maldis=0;
501 $malnoiseinst=0;
502 $malcmr=0;
503 $malgain=0;
504 $malphase=0;
505 $malxtalk=0;
506 $noseaplicopruebadis=0;
507 $noseaplicopruebanoiseinst=0;
508 $noseaplicopruebacmr=0;
509 $noseaplicopruebagain=0;
510 $noseaplicopruebaphase=0;
511 $noseaplicopruebaxtalk=0;
512 %really_bad=();
513 @caja=();
514 @linename=();
515 @point=();
516 $dist_box=();
```

```
517 $noise_box=();
518 $cmr_box=();
519 $gain_box=();
520 $phase_box=();
521 $xtalk_box=();
522 $noapli="N/A";
523 $string1="Serial";
524 $string2="------"; #This string finds the end of the file
525 ##########Reading of the file with the box tests ############
526 $lf = 0;
527 open(FILE, $ruta1) or die "Can't open `$filename': $!";
528 while (sysread FILE, $buffer, 4096) {
529   $lf += ($buffer =~ tr/\n//);
530 }
531 $lf=$lf-9;
532 close (FILE);
533
534 ######### End of Reading of the file with the box tests ########
535
536
537 #Open the file with data of the boxes
538 open(box,$ruta1)||die ("Could not open file \n");
539
540 $linea=<box>;
541 $aviso="Reading " . $ruta1;
542 #Here it starts the searching of patterns
543 while ($linea)
544 {
545   $i++;          #counts the lines into the data file
546   if ($result1=$linea=~/$string1/)
547   {
548     $b=$i;
549   }
550   if ($result2=$linea=~/$string2/)
551   {
```

```perl
552  $k++;          #flag that indicates the string2 has been found
553  }
554  if ($i-$b>2 && $k==2)
555  {
556  @array=split(" ",$linea);
557  for ($a=0;$a<1;$a++)
558  {
559  $caja[$j]=$array[$a];
560  $linename[$j]=$array[$a+2];
561    $point[$j]=$array[$a+3];
562    $dist_box[$j]=$array[$a+9];
563    $noise_box[$j]=$array[$a+10];
564    $cmr_box[$j]=$array[$a+11];
565    $gain_box[$j]=$array[$a+12];
566    $phase_box[$j]=$array[$a+13];
567    $xtalk_box[$j]=$array[$a+14];
568    $month[$j]=$array[$a+15];
569    $array[$a+16]=~s/\,//;
570    $day[$j]=$array[$a+16];
571  $year[$j]=$array[$a+17];
572  $hour[$j]=$array[$a+18];
573  $j++;
574  }
575  }
576  $percent_done=sprintf "%.0f",($i/$lf)*100;
577  $percent=$percent_done . "%";
578  $progress->update;
579  $linea=<box>;
580  }
581  #
582  $salida1=salvar1($top);
583  $salida2=salvar2($top);
584  $salida3=salvar3($top);
585  # It is created the file with the information extracted from the box test file
586  open (salida,'>' . $salida1); #all the elements of the test
```

```perl
587 open (malas,'>' . $salida2); #all the elements of the test
588 open (real_malas,'>' . $salida3);
    print salida
    "Box\tLine\tPoint\tDist\tNoise\tCMRR\tGain\tPhase\tXtalk\tMonth
589 \tDay\tYear\tHour\n";
590 print malas "Box\tLine\tPoint\tValue\tTest\n";
591 $archivos->insert('end',"Resume of boxes out of specifications:\n");
592 $archivos->insert('end',"Dist\tNoise\tCMRR\tGain\tPhase\tXtalk\n");
593 foreach (@caja)
594 {
595 $aviso="Writing Results Files...";
596 $nad=$dist_box[$n] eq $noapli; #checks for a distortion value N/A
597 $nan=$noise_box[$n] eq $noapli; #checks for a noise value N/A
598 $nac=$cmr_box[$n] eq $noapli; #checks for a cmr value N/A
599 $nag=$gain_box[$n] eq $noapli; #checks for a gain value N/A
600 $nap=$phase_box[$n] eq $noapli; #checks for a phase value N/A
601 $nax=$xtalk_box[$n] eq $noapli; #checks for a xtalk value N/A
602
    print salida
    "$caja[$n]\t$linename[$n]\t$point[$n]\t$dist_box[$n]\t$noise_box[$n]\t$
    cmr_box[$n]\t$gain_box[$n]\t$phase_box[$n]\t$xtalk_box[$n]\t$month[
603 $n]\t$day[$n]\t$year[$n]\t$hour[$n] \n";
604 #Routine for distortion test
605 if ($nad!=1)
606 {
607  if ($dist_box[$n]>$dist)
608   {
609   $aviso="Distortion";
610   $maldis++;
611   $pointdis[$maldis-1]=$linename[$n].$point[$n];
612   $punto_pegado=$linename[$n] . $point[$n];
      $really_bad{$punto_pegado}=$really_bad{$punto_pegado} . "-" .
613 $aviso;
      print malas
614 "$caja[$n]\t$linename[$n]\t$point[$n]\t$dist_box[$n]\tDistortion \n";
615   }
616  }
```

```
617  Else
618  {
619  $noseaplicopruebadis++;
620  }
621 #End of Routine for distortion test
622 #Routine for noise test
623  if ($nan!=1)
624  {
625   if ($noise_box[$n]>$noise)
626    {
627    $aviso="Noise";
628    $malnoiseinst++;
629    $pointnoiseinst[$malnoiseinst-1]=$linename[$n].$point[$n];
630    $punto_pegado=$linename[$n] . $point[$n];
       $really_bad{$punto_pegado}=$really_bad{$punto_pegado} . "-" .
631 $aviso;
       print malas
632 "$caja[$n]\t$linename[$n]\t$point[$n]\t$noise_box[$n]\tNoise \n";
633    }
634  }
635   Else
636  {
637  $noseaplicopruebanoiseinst++;
638  }
639 #End of Routine for noise test
640 #Routine for cmr test
641  if ($nac!=1)
642  {
643   if ($cmr_box[$n]<$cmr)
644    {
645    $aviso="CMRR";
646    $malcmr++;
647    $pointcmr[$malcmr-1]=$linename[$n].$point[$n];
648    $punto_pegado=$linename[$n] . $point[$n];
       $really_bad{$punto_pegado}=$really_bad{$punto_pegado} . "-" .
649 $aviso;
```

```
         print malas
650 "$caja[$n]\t$linename[$n]\t$point[$n]\t$cmr_box[$n]\tCMRR \n";
651 }
652 }
653 Else
654 {
655 $noseaplicopruebacmr++;
656 }
657 #End of Routine for cmr test
658 #Routine for gain test
659 if ($nag!=1)
660 {
661 if ($gain_box[$n]>$gain)
662 {
663 $aviso="Gain";
664 $malgain++;
665 $pointgain[$malgain-1]=$linename[$n].$point[$n];
666 $punto_pegado=$linename[$n] . $point[$n];
     $really_bad{$punto_pegado}=$really_bad{$punto_pegado} . "-" .
667 $aviso;
         print malas
668 "$caja[$n]\t$linename[$n]\t$point[$n]\t$gain_box[$n]\tGain \n";
669 }
670 }
671 Else
672 {
673 $noseaplicopruebagain++;
674 }
675 #End of Routine for gain test
676 #Routine for phase test
677 if ($nap!=1)
678 {
679 if ($phase_box[$n]>$phase)
680 {
681 $aviso="Phase";
682 $malphase++;
```

```
683    $pointphase[$malphase-1]=$linename[$n].$point[$n];
684    $punto_pegado=$linename[$n] . $point[$n];
       $really_bad{$punto_pegado}=$really_bad{$punto_pegado} . "-" .
685 $aviso;
       print malas
686 "$caja[$n]\t$linename[$n]\t$point[$n]\t$phase_box[$n]\tPhase \n";
687    }
688    }
689  Else
690    {
691  $noseaplicopruebaphase++;
692    }
693 #End of Routine for phase test
694 #Routine for xtalk test
695  if ($nax!=1)
696    {
697  if ($xtalk_box[$n]<$xtalk)
698    {
699  $aviso="Xtalk";
700  $malxtalk++;
701  $pointxtalk[$malxtalk-1]=$linename[$n].$point[$n];
702  $punto_pegado=$linename[$n] . $point[$n];
     $really_bad{$punto_pegado}=$really_bad{$punto_pegado} . "-" .
703 $aviso;
     print malas
704 "$caja[$n]\t$linename[$n]\t$point[$n]\t$xtalk_box[$n]\tXtalk \n";
705    }
706    }
707  Else
708    {
709  $noseaplicopruebaxtalk++;
710    }
711 #End of Routine for xtalk test
712  $n++;
713 }
714 $length=@caja;
715
```

```
716 $archivos->insert('end',
    "$maldis\t$malnoiseinst\t$malcmr\t$malgain\t$malphase\t$malxtalk
    \n");
717 $archivos->insert('end', "Distortion Test was not applied at
    $noseaplicopruebadis channels \n");
718 $archivos->insert('end', "Noise Test was not applied at
    $noseaplicopruebanoiseinst channels \n");
719 $archivos->insert('end', "CMRR Test was not applied at
    $noseaplicopruebacmr channels \n");
720 $archivos->insert('end', "Gain Test was not applied at
    $noseaplicopruebagain channels \n");
721 $archivos->insert('end', "Phase Test was not applied at
    $noseaplicopruebaphase channels \n");
722 $archivos->insert('end', "Xtalk Test was not applied at
    $noseaplicopruebaxtalk channels \n");
723 $archivos->insert('end', "$length channels were checked\n");
724 $aviso="Ready for another test";
725 close(salida);
726 close(malas);
727 close(box);
728 @re_bad=keys(%really_bad);
729 @re_bad_test=values(%really_bad);
730 $length=@re_bad;
731 $archivos->insert('end',"There are $length channels out of
    specifications\n");
732 print real_malas "Point\tTests\n";
733 foreach (@re_bad) {
734  print real_malas "$re_bad[$rb]\t$re_bad_test[$rb]\n";
735  $rb++;
736 }
737 close(real_malas);
738 $onoffg=0;
739 $onoffb=0;
740 }
741 #Enf of routine for box test
742
743 # General routines
744 sub abrir{ #here it is opened the file with the test results
```

```
745 my $plan;
746   my @types =
747     ( [$file, $ext],
748       ["All files", '*.*']);
749
      $plan=$top->getOpenFile(-filetypes => \@types,-title
750 =>$mensaje_geo1);
751 $archivos->insert('end',"Testing File:\n");
752 $archivos->insert('end',"$plan\n");
753   return "$plan";
754 }
755
756 #This routine loads a file with the threshold parameters fot geophone test
757 sub carga_geo_pam {
758 open (filecute,"filecute.txt");
759 $i=0;
760   my @types =
761     ( ["GeoPar Files", '*.gep'],
762       ["All Files",   '*.*' ]);
763
      $file_cute=$top->getOpenFile(-filetypes => \@types,-title
764 =>'Geophone Test Parameters');
765   print filecute "$file_cute";
766 close(filecute);
767 $archivos->insert('end',"Geophone Parameters File:\n");
768 $archivos->insert('end',"$file_cute\n");
769 open(geo_pam,$file_cute)||die ("Could not open file \n");
770
771 $linea=<geo_pam>;
772
773 #Reading of the threshold file and assigning of the values to box tests
774 while ($linea)
775 {
776   if ($i==0) {
777   @array=split(" ",$linea);
778   $li=$array[1];
```

```perl
779   $ls=$array[2];
780   }
781
782   if ($i==1) {
783    @array=split(" ",$linea);
784    $ll=$array[1];
785   }
786
787   if ($i==2) {
788    @array=split(" ",$linea);
789    $lt=$array[1];
790   }
791
792   if ($i==3) {
793    @array=split(" ",$linea);
794    $ln=$array[1];
795   }
796
797   $i++;
798
799   $linea=<geo_pam>;
800
801   }
802   &geoparnew;
803   $lim_inf->insert('0', $li);
804   $lim_sup->insert('0', $ls);
805   $lim_leak->insert('0', $ll);
806   $lim_tilt->insert('0', $lt);
807   $lim_noise->insert('0', $ln);
808   close (geo_pam);
809   }
810
811   sub geoparnew {
812
813   $lim_inf->delete(0,4);
```

```
814  $lim_sup->delete(0,4);
815  $lim_leak->delete(0,4);
816  $lim_tilt->delete(0,4);
817  $lim_noise->delete(0,4);
818  }
819
820  sub salvar1{
821  my $resumen;
822    my @types =
823      ( ["Files Text", '*.txt']);
824
825      $resumen = $top->getSaveFile(-filetypes => \@types,-title
     =>$mensaje_geo2,-defaultextension=>'txt');
826    $archivos->insert('end',"All geophones information saved as:\n");
827    $archivos->insert('end',"$resumen\n");
828    return "$resumen";
829  }
830  sub salvar2{
831  my $resumen2;
832    my @types =
833      ( ["Files Text", '*.txt']);
834
835      $resumen2 = $top->getSaveFile(-filetypes => \@types,-title
     =>$mensaje_geo3,-defaultextension=>'txt');
836  #  print "$resumen \n";
837    $archivos->insert('end',"Bad geophones information saved as:\n");
838    $archivos->insert('end',"$resumen2\n");
839    return "$resumen2";
840  }
841
842  sub salvar3{
843  my $resumen3;
844    my @types =
845      ( ["Files Text", '*.txt']);
846
847    $resumen3 = $top->getSaveFile(-filetypes => \@types,-title
```

Advanced programming in Perl for Beginners.

```
      =>$mensaje_geo4,-defaultextension=>'txt');
848 #  print "$resumen \n";
849   $archivos->insert('end',"Resume of bad geophones saved as:\n");
850   $archivos->insert('end',"$resumen3\n");
851   return "$resumen3";
852 }
853 sub saveas {
854 $l_inf_res=$lim_inf->get;
855 $l_sup_res=$lim_sup->get;
856 $l_leak=$lim_leak->get;
857 $l_tilt=$lim_tilt->get;
858 $l_noise=$lim_noise->get;
859 my $newfile;
860   my @types =
861     ( ["GeoPar Files", '*.gep']);
862
      $newfile = $top->getSaveFile(-filetypes => \@types,-title =>'Geophone
863 Parameters File',-defaultextension=>'gep');
864   $archivos->insert('end',"Geophone Parameters File:\n");
865   $archivos->insert('end',"$newfile\n");
866 open (param,'>' . $newfile);
867 print param "Res\t$l_inf_res\t$l_sup_res\n";
868 print param "Leak\t$l_leak\n";
869 print param "Tilt\t$l_tilt\n";
870 print param "Noise\t$l_noise";
871 $file_cute=$newfile;
872 close (param);
873 open (filecute,'>' . "filecute.txt");
874 print filecute "$file_cute";
875 close (filecute);
876 }
877
878
879 sub carga_automatica_geo_pam {
880 open (filecute,"filecute.txt");
881 $linea=<filecute>;
```

```
882 while ($linea) {
883 $file_cute=$linea;
884 $linea=<filecute>;
885 }
886 close(filecute);
887 open(geo_pam,$file_cute);
888 $linea=<geo_pam>;
889 $archivos->insert('end',"Last Geophone Parameters File Used:\n");
890 $archivos->insert('end',"$file_cute\n");
891 #Reading the threshold and writing of the values into the text boxes
892 while ($linea)
893 {
894  if ($i==0) {
895   @array=split(" ",$linea);
896   $li=$array[1];
897   $ls=$array[2];
898  }
899
900  if ($i==1) {
901   @array=split(" ",$linea);
902   $ll=$array[1];
903  }
904
905  if ($i==2) {
906   @array=split(" ",$linea);
907   $lt=$array[1];
908  }
909
910  if ($i==3) {
911   @array=split(" ",$linea);
912   $ln=$array[1];
913  }
914
915  $i++;
916
```

```
917  $linea=<geo_pam>;
918
919  }
920  &geoparnew;
921  $lim_inf->insert('0', $li);
922  $lim_sup->insert('0', $ls);
923  $lim_leak->insert('0', $ll);
924  $lim_tilt->insert('0', $lt);
925  $lim_noise->insert('0', $ln);
926  close (geo_pam);
927  }
928
929
930  sub save {
931  open (filec,'>' . $file_cute);
932  $l_inf_res=$lim_inf->get;
933  $l_sup_res=$lim_sup->get;
934  $l_leak=$lim_leak->get;
935  $l_tilt=$lim_tilt->get;
936  $l_noise=$lim_noise->get;
937  print filec "Res\t$l_inf_res\t$l_sup_res\n";
938  print filec "Leak\t$l_leak\n";
939  print filec "Tilt\t$l_tilt\n";
940  print filec "Noise\t$l_noise";
941  close (filec);
942  }
943
944  sub etiquetas_equipo {
945  #Button to update the configuration of SU-6R or FDU
     $up_param_box=$top->Button(-text=>'Update',-
946  command=>sub{&ok_equipo});
947  $up_param_box->place(-x=>420,-y=>30,-width=>50);
948  $etiqueta_sr=$top->Label(-text=>"Sample Rate");
949  $etiqueta_sr->place(-x=>120,-y=>35);
950  $etiqueta_gain=$top->Label(-text=>"Gain");
951  $etiqueta_gain->place(-x=>305,-y=>35);
```

```
952  return;
953  }
954
955  sub ok_equipo {
956  $cFDU="FDU" eq $equipo;
957  $cSU6="SU6-R" eq $equipo;
958  if ($cFDU==1) {
959  $csr1=0;
960  $cga1=0;
961  $csr1="0.25 ms" eq $sample;
962  $cga1="0 dB" eq $gain_equip;
963  $cga2="12 dB" eq $gain_equip;
964  $csr2="0.50 ms" eq $sample;
965  $csr3="1.00 ms" eq $sample;
966  $csr4="2.00 ms" eq $sample;
967  $csr5="4.00 ms" eq $sample;
968  $dist=-103;
969  $cmr=100;
970  $xtalk=110;
971  if ($csr1==1 && $cga1==1)
972  {
973    $gain=3;
974    $phase=30;
975    $noise=16;
976  }
977  if ($csr1==1 && $cga2==1)
978  {
979    $gain=3;
980    $phase=30;
981    $noise=4;
982  }
983
984  if ($csr2==1 && $cga1==1)
985  {
986    $gain=1.5;
```

```
987   $phase=25;
988   $noise=2;
989 }
990 if ($csr2==1 && $cga2==1)
991 {
992   $gain=1.5;
993   $phase=25;
994   $noise=0.5;
995 }
996
997 if ($csr3==1 && $cga1==1)
998 {
999   $gain=1;
1000  $phase=20;
1001  $noise=1.4;
1002 }
1003 if ($csr3==1 && $cga2==1)
1004 {
1005  $gain=1;
1006  $phase=20;
1007  $noise=0.35;
1008 }
1009
1010 if ($csr4==1 && $cga1==1)
1011 {
1012  $gain=1;
1013  $phase=20;
1014  $noise=1;
1015 }
1016 if ($csr4==1 && $cga2==1)
1017 {
1018  $gain=1;
1019  $phase=20;
1020  $noise=0.25;
1021 }
```

```
1022
1023 if ($csr5==1 && $cga1==1)
1024 {
1025   $gain=1;
1026   $phase=20;
1027   $noise=0.7;
1028 }
1029 if ($csr5==1 && $cga2==1)
1030 {
1031   $gain=1;
1032   $phase=20;
1033   $noise=0.18;
1034 }
1035 }
1036
1037 if ($cSU6==1) {
1038 $csr1="1.00 ms" eq $sample;
1039 $csr2="2.00 ms" eq $sample;
1040 $csr3="4.00 ms" eq $sample;
1041 $cga1="24 dB" eq $gain_equip;
1042 $cga2="36 dB" eq $gain_equip;
1043 $cga3="42 dB" eq $gain_equip;
1044 $cga4="48 dB" eq $gain_equip;
1045 $dist=-96;
1046 $gain=3;
1047 $phase=20;
1048 $xtalk=95;
1049 if ($csr1==1 && $cga1==1)
1050 {
1051   $cmr=83;
1052   $noise=0.73;
1053 }
1054 if ($csr1==1 && $cga2==1)
1055 {
1056   $cmr=95;
```

```
1057  $noise=0.27;
1058 }
1059 if ($csr1==1 && $cga3==1)
1060 {
1061  $cmr=101;
1062  $noise=0.22;
1063 }
1064 if ($csr1==1 && $cga4==1)
1065 {
1066  $cmr=107;
1067  $noise=0.20;
1068 }
1069
1070 if ($csr2==1 && $cga1==1)
1071 {
1072  $cmr=83;
1073  $noise=0.52;
1074 }
1075 if ($csr2==1 && $cga2==1)
1076 {
1077  $cmr=95;
1078  $noise=0.19;
1079 }
1080 if ($csr2==1 && $cga3==1)
1081 {
1082  $cmr=101;
1083  $noise=0.16;
1084 }
1085 if ($csr2==1 && $cga4==1)
1086 {
1087  $cmr=107;
1088  $noise=0.15;
1089 }
1090
1091 if ($csr3==1 && $cga1==1)
```

```
1092 {
1093   $cmr=83;
1094   $noise=0.37;
1095 }
1096 if ($csr3==1 && $cga2==1)
1097 {
1098   $cmr=95;
1099   $noise=0.14;
1100 }
1101 if ($csr3==1 && $cga3==1)
1102 {
1103   $cmr=101;
1104   $noise=0.11;
1105 }
1106 if ($csr3==1 && $cga4==1)
1107 {
1108   $cmr=107;
1109   $noise=0.10;
1110 }
1111 }
1112
1113 }
1114
1115 sub ayuda {
1116
1117 }
```

Figure 11.4 shows how the application looks.

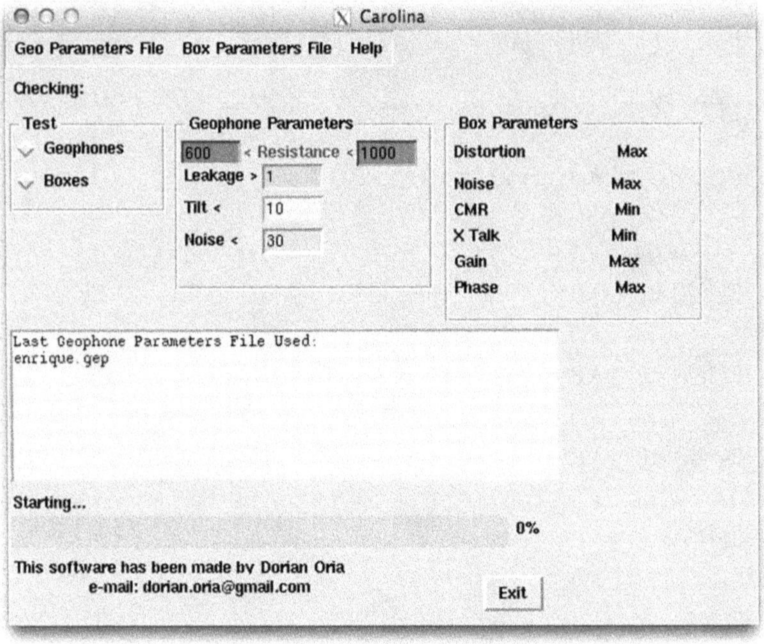

Advanced programming in Perl for Beginners.

Figure 11.4. Application designed to check the geophone and FDU tests of system Sercel™ 408 (Script 11.1).

11.2 Seismic data marine acquisition.

In this type of survey a lot of data is generated as well. Here we focus on a file that is generated with navigation information: P190.

11.2.1 P190 files.

It is a format used to handle navigation information for seismic marine surveys. For more details about P1/90 files consult the file:

http://www.seg.org/publications/tech-stand/ukooa_p1_90.pdf.

The following it is shown the first lines of a P1/90 file:

```
H0100SURVEY AREA       Four Streamer two Source 3D, Caracas 2
H0101GENERAL SURVEY DETAILS   4 CABLE, 1 VESSEL, 2 SOURCES
H0102VESSEL DETAILS       Dorian_1    1
H0103SOURCE DETAILS       G1        1 1
H0103SOURCE DETAILS       G2        1 2
H0104STREAMER DETAILS     Streamer_001    1  1 1
```

```
H0104STREAMER DETAILS     Streamer_002   1   2 2
H0104STREAMER DETAILS     Streamer_003   1   3 3
H0104STREAMER DETAILS     Streamer_004   1   4 4
H0105OTHER DETAILS     N/A
H0200SURVEY DATE       20071008
H0201TAPE DATE         TUE NOV 27 05:04:17 2007
H0202TAPE VERSION      UK00A P1/90
H0203LINE PREFIX     CII
H0300CLIENT         Carolina
H0400GEOPHYSICAL CONTRACTOR   Dorian
H0500POSITIONING CONTRACTOR   Dorian
H0600POSITIONING PROCESSING
H0700POSITIONING SYSTEM    Spectra Version 10.9.01
H0800SHOTPOINT POSITION    CENTRE OF SOURCE
H0900OFFSET SHIP SYSTEM TO SP  1  2  0.00  0.00
H0901OFFSET ANTENNA TO SYSTEM  1  2  0.00  0.00
H1000CLOCK TIME       GMT 0.000000
H1100RECEIVER GROUPS PER SHOT  1920
H1400GEODETIC DATUM AS SURVEYED WGS-84   WGS-84    6378137.000
298.2572236
H1401TRANSFORMATION TO WGS-84   0.0  0.0  0.0 0.000 0.000 0.000 0.0000000
H1500GEODETIC DATUM AS PLOTTED WGS-84   WGS-84    6378137.000 298.2572236
H1501TRANSFORMATION TO WGS-84   0.0  0.0  0.0 0.000 0.000 0.000 0.0000000
H1600DATUM SHIFTS H1400-H1500   -0.0 -0.0 -0.0-0.000-0.000-0.000-0.0000000
H1700VERTICAL DATUM     Sea Level      ECHOSOUNDER
H2600None R-/E-record depth populated from Echo1_V1
H1800PROJECTION TYPE     003 TRANSVERSE MERCATOR (NORTH)
H2000GRID UNITS       1METRES       1.000000000000
H2001HEIGHT UNITS     1METRES       1.000000000000
H2002ANGULAR UNITS     1DEGREES
H2200CENTRAL MERIDIAN    69 0 0.000W
H2301GRID ORIGIN (LAT,LONG)   0 0 0.000N 69 0 0.000W
H2302GRID ORIGIN (EAST,NORTH)  500000.00E    0.00N
H2401SCALE FACTOR      0.9996000000
H2402SCALE FACTOR (LONG)      69 0 0.000W
H2600Source Id of 0 indicates non standard gun fire
H2600Z-records contain individual source positions
H2600Line CII07E1037P1001     From Shot 1004 To Shot 1920
H2600Streamer_001 Model Line CII07E1037P1001 shots 1004 to 1920: Arc
H2600Streamer_002 Model Line CII07E1037P1001 shots 1004 to 1920: Arc
H2600Streamer_003 Model Line CII07E1037P1001 shots 1004 to 1920: Arc
H2600Streamer_004 Model Line CII07E1037P1001 shots 1004 to 1920: Arc
V07E1037P1001 1  100412 7 3.03N 704045.03W 317262.11340109.9 54.7288111545
E07E1037P1001 1 1 100412 7 2.88N 704045.08W 317260.51340105.1 54.7288111545
Z07E1037P1001 11  100412 656.91N 704046.70W 317210.51339922.1 54.7288111545
Z07E1037P1001 12  100412 657.28N 704047.97W 317172.11339933.7 54.7288111545
S07E1037P1001 12  100412 657.28N 704047.97W 317172.11339933.7 54.7288111545
C07E1037P1001 121 100412 654.19N 704046.07W 317228.91339838.4 54.7288111545
C07E1037P1001 122 100412 654.86N 704047.50W 317185.71339859.1 54.7288111545
C07E1037P1001 123 100412 655.37N 704048.95W 317142.01339875.2 54.7288111545
C07E1037P1001 124 100412 655.80N 704050.48W 317095.81339888.6 54.7288111545
T07E1037P1001 1 1 100412 338.41N 704139.40W 315579.21333832.1 54.7288111545
```

Advanced programming in Perl for Beginners.

```
T07E1037P1001  1 2 100412 340.62N 704143.57W 315453.41333900.8 54.7288111545
T07E1037P1001  1 3 100412 342.76N 704149.08W 315287.21333967.7 54.7288111545
T07E1037P1001  1 4 100412 342.83N 704152.59W 315180.91333970.6 54.7288111545
R  1 317285.81339743.0 7.1  2 317281.91339731.1 7.1  3 317278.01339719.3 7.11
R  4 317274.11339707.4 7.1  5 317270.21339695.5 7.1  6 317266.41339683.6 7.11
R  7 317262.51339671.7 7.1  8 317258.71339659.8 7.1  9 317254.81339647.9 7.11
```

Imagine for a moment we want a map to show only the coordinates of every shot point. The following script takes all the P1/90 files of a survey and extracts the coordinates for every shot point and writes them in a file. This file will contain the necessary information to make a map.

Script 11.2

```
1   $sourceLetter="S";
2   $files='E:\directory\NavigationFiles\files.txt';
3   $output='E:\directory\NavigationFiles\output-2.txt';
4   open (FILES,$files);
5   open (OUT,'>'.$output);
6   $linea=<FILES>;
7   while ($linea) {
8    chomp $linea;
9    open (IN,$linea);
10   $LINEA=<IN>;
11   while ($LINEA) {
12    $firstCharLine=substr($LINEA,0,1);
13    $resultado=$firstCharLine eq $sourceLetter;
14    if ($resultado==1)
15    {
16     $ShotName=substr($LINEA,0,13);
17     $tipo=substr($LINEA,8,1);
18     $este=substr($LINEA,47,8);
19     $norte=substr($LINEA,55,9);
20     print OUT "$ShotName\t$tipo\t$este\t$norte\n";
21    }
22    $LINEA=<IN>;
23   }
24   close IN;
25   $linea=<FILES>;
26  }
27  close FILES;
28  close OUT;
```

In the P1/90 file, the coordinates of sources are on the line that starts with the letter S (enclosed in a rectangle in the portion of the P190) So, the first line of the script is a variable that designated the character we will be looking for in the P1/90 file ($sourceLetter).

The second line is the name of the variable that contains the path to the file that contains the list of P1/90 files to be processed. This script needs the list of P1/90 files as an input to be processed. An example of this file is shown in Figure 11.5.

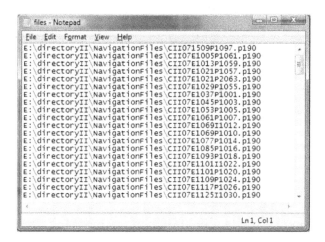

Figure 11.5. List of P190 files.

The third line is the name of the output file (including the complete path). On the fourth line the input file is opened to read it. On the fifth line the output file to write on it is opened. On the sixth line, the variable $linea takes the value of every line of the text input file. With the seventh line, the input file is read until the end of the file. On line eight, the instruction chomp eliminates the character '\n' on every line of the input file.

Because the input file contains a list of the P1/90 files to be processed, every value taken by the variable $linea is a name of a P1/90 file. On line ten, the file indicated by this variable is opened and read until line 22.

On line twelve every line of the P1/90 file is read, and the first character is extracted and stored in the variable $firstCharLine. On line thirteen we compare the variable $firstCharLine with the variable $sourceLetter (line 1). The result of this

Advanced programming in Perl for Beginners.

comparison is stored in the variable $resultado. If both variables $firstCharLine and $sourceLetter are the same, the variable $resultado takes the value of 1, which means that we found the line with the coordinates of the source. In this case lines 16 to 20 are executed. On line 20 the values are written in the output file. Figure 11.6 is an example of the output file. Such as it can be seen, the file has 4 columns (see line 20 of the script). The first one is the name of the shot. The second one indicates if the line is prime or infill (concepts that apply in seismic marine acquisition) and the third and fourth ones correspond to the coordinates east and north. When the information is displayed in a software like MapWindow GIS™, this looks as shown in Figure 11.7.

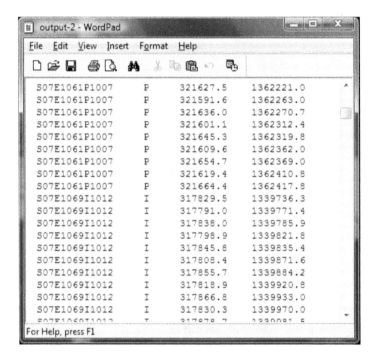

Figure 11.6. Output of Script 11.2.

Figure 11.7. Map showing shot points for a seismic marine acquisition.

The following script extracts the coordinates and depth of channel 30 in every streamer from the P1/90 file (the survey had 4 streamers and a total of 1920 channels). Because the channels are numbered from 1 to 1920, channel 30 in the streamer 1 is 30, but in streamer 2 it is 510, in streamer 3 is 990 and in streamer 4 it is 1470.

Script 11.3

```
1  $file='E:\CardonII\NavigationFiles\CII071509P1097.p190';
2  $output='E:\CardonII\NavigationFiles\CII071509P1097.channels';
3  $letraReceiver="R";
4  open (FILES,$file);
5  open (OUT,'>'.$output);
6  print OUT "Channel\tEast\tNorth\tDepth\n";
7  $linea=<FILES>;
8  while ($linea) {
9    chomp $linea;
10   $firstCharLine=substr($linea,0,1);
11   $resultado=$firstCharLine eq $letraReceiver;
12   if ($resultado==1)
13   {
```

```
14   $channel=substr($linea,53,4);
15   $eastCoord=substr($linea,58,8);
16   $northCoord=substr($linea,66,9);
17   $depth=substr($linea,76,3);
18   if ($channel==30) {
19    print OUT "C30\t$eastCoord\t$northCoord\t$depth\n";
20   }
21   if ($channel==510) {
22    print OUT "C510\t$eastCoord\t$northCoord\t$depth\n";
23   }
24   if ($channel==990) {
25    print OUT "C990\t$eastCoord\t$northCoord\t$depth\n";
26   }
27   if ($channel==1470) {
28    print OUT "C1470\t$eastCoord\t$northCoord\t$depth\n";
29   }
30   }
31   $linea=<FILES>;
32   }
33  close FILES;
34  close OUT;
```

On line 1 the variable $file contains the complete path to the input file. On the second line, the variable $output contains the path to the output file. In the P1/90, the information of the receivers (channels) is contained in every line that starts with the letter 'R'. Line 3 contains the variable that stores the value 'R'. This is the one we will look for in the P1/90 file. On line 4 we open the input file to read it. On line 5 we open the output file to write on it. On line 6 the script writes a line that contains the headers of every column of data we will extract from the P1/90 on the output file. On line 7 we assign every line of the input file to the variable $linea. On line 8 the loop that reads the file until the end starts. On line 9, the instruction **chomp** eliminates the character '\n' from the end of the line. On line 10, the first character of every line is extracted and stored in the variable $firstCharLine. On line 11 the comparison between the value of $firstCharLine and the variable $letraReceiver (line 3) is done and the result in the variable $resultado is stored. If the variable $resultado is equal to 1 (line 12) it means that the character 'R' was found and we are reading lines with information of receivers.

Line 14 contains the variable with the value of the channel. Channel 30 of every streamer (30, 510, 990 and 1470) is in the same range of characters in the

P1/90 file. It is the same situation for the rest of the information: coordinates and depth (lines 15 to 17). If the number of the channel is 30 (line 18), the script writes the name of the channel, the coordinates and depth on the output file. This operation is repeated for the other cases: channel 510 (line 21), channel 990 (line 24) and channel 1470 (line 27). Line 31 indicates to the script that the input file must be read until the end. On lines 33 and 34 the input and output files are closed.

In this one there is something interesting. From line 15 to 17 the script is extracting substrings from every line, no matter the channel of our interest (it means, channels 30, 510, 990 and 1470). Strictly speaking, an optimized version of the code should be one where these lines are included in every **if** condition, for example:

```
1  if ($channel==30) {
2    $eastCoord=substr($linea,58,8);
3    $northCoord=substr($linea,66,9);
4    $depth=substr($linea,76,3);
5    print OUT "C30\t$eastCoord\t$northCoord\t$depth\n";
6  }
```

What is the difference? In this case the code has more lines, but the process to extract the values of coordinates and depth would only happen in the case where the number of the channel is the same as the channel we are looking for. Whereas in the previous script, the extraction is done every time it reads a line. With this, even though it has more lines, the performance is better.

Chapter 12.
SEG-D files.

12.1 SEG-D files.

The SEG-D format was designed to be used in seismic data acquisition (raw data) and contains a lot of information that is not present in the SEG-Y format.

The following shows a script that allows reading several variables from a SEG-D file, such as file number, julian day, source coordinates, source elevation and other variables.

To run this one, it is necessary to install the module Math::BaseCnv (see Chapter 6 for instructions about installing modules).

Script 12.1

```
1  use File::stat;
2  use Math::BaseCnv;
3  $InputFile='00004229.segd';
4  $OutputFile='00004229.txt';
5  $suma=0;
6  $suma2=0;
7  $suma3=0;
8  &calcula_size_traza;
9  $SizeRecord=stat($InputFile)->size;
10
11 open (IN,$InputFile);
12 binmode(IN);
13 open (OUT,'>'.$OutputFile);
14 while (read (IN,$buf,$SizeRecord)) {
15 #Reading the file number
16 $GH1FN=unpack(H,substr($buf,0,1)).unpack(h,substr($buf,0,1)).unpack(H,
   substr($buf,0+1,1)).unpack(h,substr($buf,0+1,1));#las siglas significan
   General Header 1, file number
17 # End of Reading the file number
18 #Julian day
19
   $GH1JD=unpack(h,substr($buf,11,1)).unpack(H,substr($buf,12,1)).unpack(h
   ,substr($buf,12,1));
20 #End of Julian day
21 #Hour
```

```perl
22  $GH1Time=unpack(H,substr($buf,13,1)).unpack(h,substr($buf,13,1)).":".un
    pack(H,substr($buf,14,1)).unpack(h,substr($buf,14,1)).":".unpack(H,substr($
    buf,15,1)).unpack(h,substr($buf,15,1));
23  #En of hour
24  #Bytes per scan
25  $GH1BPS=unpack(H,substr($buf,19,1)).unpack(h,substr($buf,19,1)).unpack
    (H,substr($buf,20,1)).unpack(h,substr($buf,20,1)).unpack(H,substr($buf,21,1)
    ).unpack(h,substr($buf,21,1));
26  #End of Bytes per scan
27  #Record Type
28  $GH1RType=unpack("B4",substr($buf,25,1));
29  #End of record type
30  #Record length
31  $GH1RL=unpack(h,substr($buf,25,1)).unpack(H,substr($buf,26,1)).".".unpa
    ck(h,substr($buf,26,1));
32  $GH1RL=$GH1RL*1.024;
33  #End of record length
34  #SCan types per record
35  $GH1STPR=unpack(H,substr($buf,27,1)).unpack(h,substr($buf,27,1));
36  #End of SCan types per record
37  #Channels per scan type
38  $GH1CPST=unpack(H,substr($buf,28,1)).unpack(h,substr($buf,28,1));
39  #End of Channels per scan type
40  #Extended header blocks
41  $GH1ExtendedH=unpack(H,substr($buf,30,1)).unpack(h,substr($buf,30,1));
42  #End of Extended header blocks
43  #External header blocks
44  $GH1ExternalH=unpack(H,substr($buf,31,1)).unpack(h,substr($buf,31,1));
45  #End of External header blocks
46  #Begining of reading variables such as source and receivers coordinates
47  #Source East Coordinate
48  $eastSource=unpack('B64',substr($buf,1180,8));
49  $signoEastSource=substr($eastSource,0,1);
50  $exponentEastSource=substr($eastSource,1,11);
```

```
51  $exponentEastSource=cnv($exponentEastSource ,2, 10 )-1023;
52  @arrayMantissaES=split('',substr($eastSource,12,52));
53  #ciclo para variables de 64 bits (floating)
54  for ($j=0;$j<42;$j++) {
55  $suma2=$suma2+($arrayMantissaES[$j]*2**(-1*($j+1)));
56  }
57  $ES=((-1)**$signoEastSource)*($suma2+1)*(2**$exponentEastSource);
58  #End of Source East Coordinate
59  #Record length
60  $AL=unpack('B32',substr($buf,608,4));
61  $AL=cnv($AL,2,10);
62
63  #End of record length
64
65  #Sample rate
66  $SR=unpack('B32',substr($buf,612,4));
67  $SR=cnv($SR,2,10);
68
69  #End of sample rate
70
71  #Number of traces
72  $NT=unpack('B32',substr($buf,624,4));
73  $NT=cnv($NT,2,10);
74  #End of number of traces
75
76  #Number of auxiliary traces
77  $NAT=unpack('B32',substr($buf,620,4));
78  $NAT=cnv($NAT,2,10);
79  #End of Number of auxiliary traces
80
81  #Number of dead traces
82  $NDT=unpack('B32',substr($buf,628,4));
83  $NDT=cnv($NDT,2,10);
84  #End of Number of dead traces
85
```

```
86  #Number of the shot point
87  $ShotN=unpack('B32',substr($buf,644,4));
88  $ShotN=cnv($ShotN,2,10);
89  #End of Number of the shot point
90
91  #Up hole time
92  $UHT=unpack('B32',substr($buf,676,4));
93  $UHT=cnv($UHT,2,10);
94  #End of Up Hole Time
95
96  #North Source Coordinate
97  $northSource=unpack('B64',substr($buf,1188,8));
98  $signoNorthSource=substr($northSource,0,1);
99  $exponentNorthSource=substr($northSource,1,11);
100 $exponentNorthSource=cnv($exponentNorthSource ,2, 10 )-1023;
101 @arrayMantissaNS=split('',substr($northSource,12,52));
102 #ciclo para variables de 64 bits (floating)
103 for ($j=0;$j<42;$j++) {
104 $suma3=$suma3+($arrayMantissaNS[$j]*2**(-1*($j+1)));
105 }
106 $NS=((-1)**$signoNorthSource)*($suma3+1)*(2**$exponentNorthSource);
107 #End of North Source Coordinate
108
109 #Source elevation
110 $ElevSource=unpack('B32',substr($buf,1196,4));#probando esta variable
111 $signoElevSource=substr($ElevSource,0,1);
112 $exponentElevSource=substr($ElevSource,1,8);
113 $exponentElevSource=cnv($exponentElevSource ,2, 10 )-127;
114 @arrayMantissa=split('',substr($ElevSource,9,23));
115 for ($i=0;$i<23;$i++) {
116 $suma=$suma+($arrayMantissa[$i]*2**(-1*($i+1)));
117 }
118 $elevation=((-
    1)**$signoElevSource)*($suma+1)*(2**$exponentElevSource);
119 #End of Source elevation
120 $NBytes=((($AL/$SR)*1000)+1)*4;
```

```perl
121 print "File number (file): $GH1FN\n";
122 print "Julian Day: $GH1JD\n";
123 print "Hour: $GH1Time\n";
124 print "Channels per scan type: $GH1CPST\n";
125 print "Extended header blocks: $GH1ExtendedH\n";
126 print "External header blocks: $GH1ExternalH\n";
127 print "Source East Coordinate: $ES\n";
128 print " Source North Coordinate: $NS\n";
129 print "Source elevation: $elevation\n";
130 print "Record length: $AL ms\n";
131 print "Sample Rate: $SR microseconds\n";
132 print "Number of bytes per trace: $NBytes\n";
133 print "Total number of traces: $NT\n";
134 print "Number of auxiliary traces: $NAT\n";
135 print "Number of dead traces: $NDT\n";
136 print "Number of the shot point: $ShotN\n";
137 print "Up hole time (microseconds): $UHT\n";
138 }
139 close IN;
140 close OUT;
141
142 sub calcula_size_traza { #Calculation of the trace size
143 open (IN,$InputFile);
144 binmode(IN);
145 if (read (IN,$buf,3000)) {
146 ################GENERAL HEADER#############
147 #Sample rate
148 $SR=unpack('B32',substr($buf,612,4));
149 $SR=cnv($SR,2,10);
150 #Longitud del registro
151 $TiempoReg=unpack(h,substr($buf,25,1)).unpack(H,substr($buf,26,1))."."."unpack(h,substr($buf,26,1));
152 $SizeTrace=(($TiempoReg*1024)/$SR)*4+20;
153 #End of record length
154 #Channels per scan type
155 $V1=unpack(H,substr($buf,28,1)).unpack(h,substr($buf,28,1));
```

```
156  #End of Channels per scan type
157  #Extended header blocks
158  $V2=unpack(H,substr($buf,30,1)).unpack(h,substr($buf,30,1));
159  #End of Extended header blocks
160  #External header blocks
161  $V3=unpack(H,substr($buf,31,1)).unpack(h,substr($buf,31,1));
162  #Number of channels
163
     $STH1NC=unpack(H,substr($buf,72,1)).unpack(h,substr($buf,72,1)).unpack
     (H,substr($buf,73,1)).unpack(h,substr($buf,73,1));
164  #Number of cables
165
     $EXHNC=unpack(H,substr($buf,64+$V1*32+22,1)).unpack(h,substr($buf,
     64+$V1*32+22,1));
166  }
167  close IN;
168  }
```

Figure 12.1 shows the output of this script.

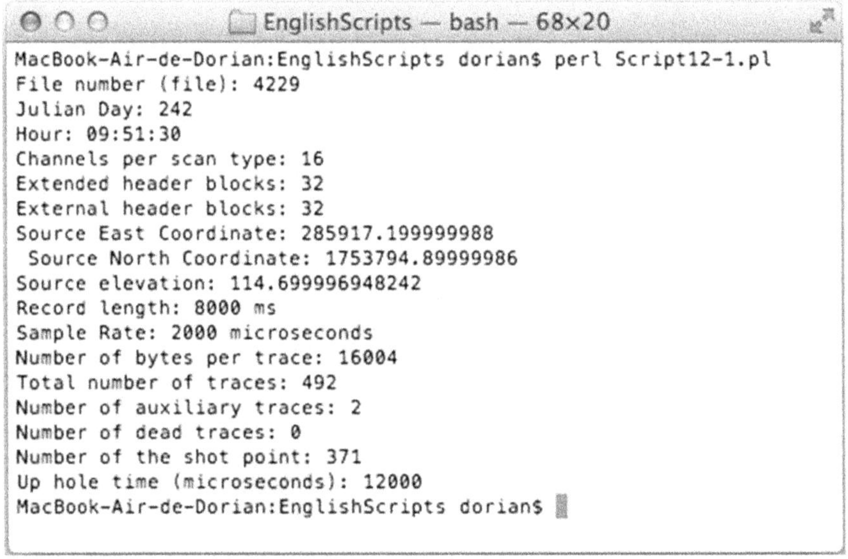

Figure 12.1. Output of Script 12.1.

References

1. Robert D. Crangle, Jr. Log ASCII Standard (LAS) files for geophysical wireline well logs and their application to geologic cross sections through the central Appalachian basin. Open File Report 2007-1142 U.S. Department of the Interior U.S. Geological Survey (http://pubs.usgs.gov/of/2007/1142/)

2. http://www.tkdocs.com

www.ingramcontent.com/pod-product-compliance
Lightning Source LLC
Chambersburg PA
CBHW060524060326
40690CB00017B/3375